THE TRUE STORY OF
MAYOR CHARLIE ROBERTSON
AND THE
YORK, PENNSYLVANIA, RACE RIOTS

MURDER
IS THE
CHARGE

WILLIAM C. COSTOPOULOS
with BRAD BUMSTED

Camino Books, Inc.
Philadelphia

Manufactured in the United States of America

1 2 3 4 5 07 06 05 04

Library of Congress Cataloging-in-Publication Data

Costopoulos, William C., 1944–
    Murder is the charge : the true story of Mayor Charlie Robertson and the
York, Pennsylvania, race riots / William C. Costopoulos ; with Brad Bumsted.
       p.   cm.
    ISBN 0-940159-88-0 (alk. paper)
    1. York (Pa.) — Race relations. 2. Riots — Pennsylvania — York — History — 20th
century. 3. African Americans — Crimes against — Pennsylvania — York —
History — 20th century. 4. Robertson, Charlie — Trials, litigation, etc. 5. Trials
(Murder) — Pennsylvania — York. 6. Mayors — Pennsylvania — York — Biography.
7. Police — Pennsylvania — York — Biography. 8. York (Pa.) — Biography.
I. Bumstead, Brad.   II. Title.

F159.Y9C67 2004
305.896073078'41 — dc22   2004001386

This book is available at a special discount on bulk purchases for promotional,
business, and educational use. For information write to:

Publisher
Camino Books, Inc.
P.O. Box 59026
Philadelphia, PA 19102

www.caminobooks.com

*Dedicated to the
people of York, Pennsylvania*

CONTENTS

PREFACE

Thirty-two years after bloody race riots left portions of the city of York, Pennsylvania, ablaze, former police officer Charles Robertson was charged with murder.

Robertson was mayor of York in 2001 when he was charged with the murder of Lillie Belle Allen for his actions as an officer in 1969.

The case from the outset was media-driven.

The prosecution was not only media-driven; it was also, in part, politically motivated.

Charles Robertson became a defendant because he was mayor.

His arrest became grist for the local and national media for almost two years, while his life hung in the balance by a thread.

In many criminal cases, especially high-profile ones, the truth often gets twisted and lost. Twisted by prosecutors, defense lawyers, witnesses, and the media; lost on the courtroom floor, where the search for truth is sacred. One purpose of this book is to lay out the truth—about Charles Robertson, his city, the events of 1969, the media, and the American criminal justice system.

In writing this book, I intend to address these issues and tell it the way I see it, without regard for political correctness or the consequences.

ACKNOWLEDGMENTS

I want to thank Brad Bumsted, who helped me write this book. His help went far beyond editorial revisions, for this book was written *with* him. Thank you, Brad, for your tireless work and insights.

I want to thank everybody in my law office who supported me through the trial in York. I would not and could not have tried this case without the help of Jayme Emig and Nick Ressetar. David Foster, Leslie Fields, George Matangos, and J. Michael Sheldon carried me and the law office from day one.

My special thanks go to Richard Oare and Rees Griffiths, my co-counsel.

I want to thank Mayor Charlie Robertson for his strength and courage throughout this exhausting ordeal.

I want to thank the York Police Department, the York Fire Department and the York Sheriff's Office for educating and supporting me throughout the proceedings.

I also want to thank my legal secretaries, Tiffany Miller and Shannon Freeman, who typed and retyped the manuscript while I stood over them at all times.

A personal thank you is in order for Ellen Wagner, Rich Oare's assistant, who got all the dirty work.

My wife, Jill, and our three daughters, Kara, Khristina, and Callista, were always there for me, even when I wasn't there for them.

PROLOGUE

The York race riots in July of 1969 were hardly unique. During the 1960s riots raged in cities across the country, from Los Angeles to Detroit to Washington, D.C. The riots were not limited to large cities.

The riots were not even unique to York. One of the first urban riots in this country occurred in York in 1803. Rioting erupted after a black woman was convicted of trying to poison two white women. It went on for three weeks. Buildings went up in flames and the militia was finally called in to settle the disturbance.[1]

What was unusual about the '69 York riots was that criminal charges would be brought 32 years later and an entire community would be torn apart again.

There were flare-ups in 1967 and 1968. By the summer of 1969, the blue-collar city was a tinderbox. At that time, York was a city of about 55,000 people of which about 10 percent was black.

During the riots, some cops overstepped their bounds. Some whites and African Americans engaged in racist acts. But there were acts of heroism as well. African Americans on one occasion acted as a "human shield" to lead a fire truck past snipers to put out fires in their York neighborhoods. Some whites helped injured African Americans. Police officers—African American and white—risked their lives on a daily basis, subjecting themselves to combat conditions to safeguard city residents.

The 1960s were confusing and complex. From Charles Manson to Woodstock, to the Vietnam War, society seemed to have been turned upside down. College campuses were exploding in violent protests. The antiwar movement grew alongside the civil rights movement. Both movements eventually turned to the very violence many of their leaders abhorred, according to Mike Young, a former Penn State University professor of public policy.

York itself was a contradiction. It had a dash of both urban and rural flavor: A tough place with a definite urban feel, York had mi-

---

[1] *Walkin' the Line* by William Ecenbarger (New York: M. Evans & Co., Inc., 2000), p. 161.

xi

crocosms of the same poverty that afflicted larger cities. Yet it was the hub of a surrounding agricultural area of dairy farms and vegetable farms, and also had a small-town character.

There were three thriving farmers' markets in York, one a few blocks from the scene of the shooting in which Charles Robertson would later be implicated. It was in many ways Middle America.

But, in 1969, York was not a quiet little Pennsylvania town. It was a combat zone.

In July, York was under martial law. A state of emergency existed from July 17 through July 29. An evening curfew was in effect from July 19. On July 22, Governor Raymond Shafer assigned units of the Pennsylvania National Guard to York. Snipers shot at firemen attempting to put out fires in black neighborhoods. Bricks were thrown through windshields of unsuspecting motorists. There were firebombs and Molotov cocktails in the hands of blacks and whites. White and African American bystanders were shot or injured. Rifle shots were fired into homes. Firefights broke out between African American combatants and the police. Army personnel carriers patrolled the streets. The York police were using two armored vehicles, "Bonny" and "Big Al."

The only York police officer to die in the line of duty was fatally shot on July 18, seated inside "Big Al" and wearing a flak jacket. Henry Schaad, 22, the son of a police officer, died August 1, 1969.

Three days after Schaad was shot, Lillie Belle Allen, a 27-year-old preacher's daughter from Aiken, South Carolina, was fatally wounded as she entered a white neighborhood on North Newberry Street at approximately 9:15 p.m.

Allen's death occurred on July 21, one night after The Eagle had landed. The nation remained glued to television sets that night in the aftermath of Neil Armstrong's first steps on the moon—and his pronouncement, "one small step for man, one giant leap for mankind." In York, whites and African Americans were showering hell on each other.

Allen was cut down in a hail of gunfire after exiting a car on North Newberry Street. She was literally blown out of her sneakers. The thunderous volley seemed to echo long afterward. By chance or unfortunate encounter, Allen and her family had driven into the territory of white gang members, the Newberry Street Boys, many of whom believed they were defending their turf in a race war. Assisted by other white gangs from across the city, the boozed-up and drug-addled shooters—armed with shotguns, rifles, and machetes—be-

lieved they represented the last line of defense for white neighborhoods against the ever-increasing violence by African Americans.

§

On March 31, 1970, federal judge William J. Nealon, in the U.S.
Middle District Court of Pennsylvania, issued his ruling in a suit alleging excesses by the York police—including illegal searches in the
'69 riots. [2] His ruling documents each alleged incident or injury, beginning on July 17. Nealon dismissed the case against the 94-man
force (that included six black officers), the mayor, and other city officials.

Nealon wrote:

> Two of the primary sites of havoc were near the intersec-
> tion of Penn and College [Avenues] and the Parkway
> Homes project. Suffice it to say that Penn and College
> were practically impassable during the nighttime hours,
> the streets were barricaded and it had literally become an
> armed camp.

> It scarcely needs stating that not every rifle shot, not every
> act of vandalism and violence and public disturbance were
> officially reported, or testified to, so that these findings
> represent only a portion of the wave of horror and panic
> that gripped the city of York during this ten-day period.
> There were references to general gunfire throughout the
> night, roving gangs with weapons, scattered attempts at
> firebombing and small children running with armed
> adults. Police vehicles were subjected to heavy fire while
> patrolling the troubled areas. Even a cursory perusal [of
> facts] points up the enormity of the problem with which
> law enforcement officials were confronted during this
> time period.

> It was, he said, "a mélange of shocking bloodletting."

> There were proven transgressions by the York Police De-
> partment during this period of violence . . . indiscriminate

---

[2] Opinion, U.S. District Judge William Nealon, No. 69–286, *Rhoda Barton and
Lewis Johnstone v. Eli Eichelberger, mayor of York, et al.*

shooting . . . racial slurs and epithets . . . police antagonism and racial taunting . . . physical manhandling and verbal insulting [of African Americans] . . . white power utterances by members of the York Police Department.

Still, Nealon wrote:

Considering that a state of emergency had been declared by the governor of Pennsylvania, and that the National Guard and state police occupied the city, and that curfews had been fixed, it is to the credit of York officials that they made every reasonable effort to comply with constitutional requirements under strenuous conditions. In no event . . . does the record exhibit an official policy authorizing unconstitutional searches.

Nealon's opinion, page after page, cites police reports: rock throwing, shots fired at passing motorists, bricks thrown at cars, firebombing of houses, police under fire while trying to help shooting victims, African Americans shot by police, whites beaten by African Americans, vandalism, officers pinned down by rifle fire in African American neighborhoods, heavy gunfire on firemen, and serious injuries of combatants and bystanders.

Nealon's ruling stated that Robertson, then a 35-year-old officer in his seventh year on the force, had shouted "white power." Many white officers had been shouting "white power." One witness testified to observing this happen 25 times.

A statement of Robertson's, after his arrest in 2001, still rings true: "You people [reporters] don't have any idea what it was like 32 years ago."

MURDER
IS THE
CHARGE

1

RIOTS

July 21, 1969
York, Pennsylvania

Sirens screamed in the distance. Spirals of smoke hovered above the south end of the city. Fear and dread lay over the city like a shroud. The smooth steel of his service revolver wasn't much comfort. His throat was already dry and his mouth tasted like cotton. He was already soaked with sweat. Another night of uncertainty and incredible tension awaited in the god-awful heat. For officers in the York police force, every call was a roll of the dice.

Officer Charlie Robertson, 35, was the assigned driver of the armored vehicle "Big Al." He was the senior guy on this detail. The makeshift personnel carrier was parked on top of a hill by Farquhar Park. The armored vehicle seemed to retain the heat of the day. At times it was unbearable. He and three police officers were waiting for their next assignment.

Charlie just shook his head because he knew what was coming.

Darkness was setting in, and that's when all hell would break loose in the city of York. It had all started four days earlier, when an African American juvenile was treated at the York Hospital for facial burns; he had informed the police that a group of white youths, known as the Girard Street Gang, or the Girarders, threw flaming liquid in his face. He later recanted his story, stating that he had burned himself while playing with lighter fluid, but the rumor of the original incident had spread throughout the city. That rumor ignited the riots, a surefire catalyst for a city festering with racial tension.

The riots started with rock throwing, then escalated to fights and random shootings. Blacks were shooting whites, whites were shooting blacks. Fires were being set everywhere, and Molotov cocktails were being thrown into closed businesses and occupied homes. Police vehicles and fire trucks were easy targets, and already four police officers had taken bullets—one fatally, on Friday night, July 18, at 11:10 p.m.

Officer Henry Schaad and three fellow officers were dispatched to the intersection of Pershing and College to assist a wounded motorcyclist. Five black males and one white male were observed at the intersection. Several rifle shots were fired at the armored vehicle, and one bullet hit Officer Schaad, ultimately taking his life. The vehicle they were riding in was "Big Al," the same armored vehicle Charlie was waiting in that night.

The bloodstains of young Schaad were still visible in the jump seat.

The 94-member York City Police Department was placed on high alert after Schaad was shot. All vacations were canceled, there were no approved leaves, and officers were put on 12-hour shifts. The shift from hell was the night shift—7:00 p.m. to 7:00 a.m.—and the younger officers, and those without families, were the first to get that assignment.

Officer James VanGreen stood outside of "Big Al," engaging in small talk with Officer Dennis McMaster and Officer Ray Markle. "Big Al" was a borrowed bank delivery car with gunports on the sides. It had metal plating but after what happened to Schaad, who could trust it? Just being in the damn thing put McMaster in a state of fear. McMaster had been sitting on the beach at Ocean City, Maryland, that very morning. He read a story in the *Baltimore Sun* about a police officer shot in York. He quickly called in to work, was told to report for duty, and made it back for the night shift. McMaster conducted his own experiment on "Big Al." Using his Smith & Wesson .357 magnum pistol with department regulation .38-caliber ammunition, he fired a round through the armored car and quickly determined it was not bulletproof. From time to time his thoughts would drift back to walking on the beach—sand under his feet, the hot sun and cool ocean breeze at his back. Then he would be jolted back to the reality of what lay ahead that night. McMaster, 25, tall, and skinny, was a chain-smoker, but nothing seemed to help his nerves. VanGreen never dreamed that he would find himself in this situation; he knew when he took the oath there would be risks, but nothing like this. Ray

Markle was the newest recruit, and wanted out. Charlie Robertson hated what was happening, but was going to see it through.

"I'm sweating from the heat," Markle said, wiping beads of sweat on his forehead with the back of his hand. Though late evening, the temperature outside was in the 90s and had been that way for days, creating a thick haze.

"You sure it's from the heat?" VanGreen asked jokingly.

Charlie laughed out loud, but all laughing and talking stopped when shots were heard in the distance. Then there were more shots, and they sounded close, real close. It was 9:20 p.m. To McMaster, it sounded like the first day of deer season.

"Let's go," Charlie said as he started up "Big Al's" engine.

The other three jumped into the armored vehicle immediately. McMaster and VanGreen unsnapped their holsters.

Charlie moved out quickly, heading down the hill toward Newberry Street. They all agreed that's where the shots were coming from. Within minutes, "Big Al" was creeping slowly onto Newberry Street, coming from the top of the hill. Charlie could see that the streetlights had been shot out, and he focused immediately on a white Cadillac, resting broadside at the railroad tracks. It had obviously been shot at because the back window was shattered, the trunk was riddled with holes, and all the tires were deflated.

VanGreen, looking out a porthole, noticed a number of white youths—who seemed to be armed—running.

Charlie Robertson was the first to get out, and VanGreen told him to be careful.

With some courage, he held his hands up in the air and yelled, "Police, police. Don't shoot."

Knowing people in the neighborhood, Robertson took off his helmet and said, "It's me, Charlie."

That seemed like a sensible thing to McMaster and he had no better idea what to do anyway. "It's me, Denny," he said.

McMaster looked into the disabled vehicle and saw four African American adults crouched below the window line, crying and terrified. He was shocked that they weren't hurt.

Lying on the street, near the driver's door, was a young African American woman bleeding profusely and about to die. Markle was told to call for an ambulance immediately.

McMaster asked if the car could be driven, and somebody inside said yes. He then asked that the car be driven to the barricades on Philadelphia Street, one block away, in the direction they came from.

The ambulance was delayed, only for seconds, at the barricades.

All four young police officers watched, incredulous, as the bloody body was put onto the gurney.

Within seconds, the radio in "Big Al" transmitted another emergency message. The officers were ordered to respond immediately to Maple and Duke, a predominantly African American area, where three fellow police officers were pinned down by rifle fire, unable to get back into their police cruiser. By the time "Big Al" arrived, the area was flooded with policemen who were waiting for the assistance of the armored car to do the extraction.

Charlie and his men received 10 to 15 rounds of rifle fire from the middle of Maple Street, but no one was hurt, and the rescue mission was a success.

There was no time to celebrate, however; around midnight four houses were reported to be on fire on West Hope Lane, located on South Penn between College Avenue and Princess. Firemen could not get there because of heavy gunfire directed at the engines and fire personnel. Approximately 75 black residents formed a line in front of the fire engines and, marching abreast, led the firemen to the scene. When the blaze was extinguished, the firemen, preparing to leave, were shot at once again from the Penn and Princess intersection.

"Big Al" was at that scene until the early morning hours.

It was a rough night for the city of York, black and white. It was a rough night for the York City Police Department and York's firemen. It was a rough night for Charlie Robertson and for VanGreen, McMaster, and Markle.

On Tuesday, July 22, 1969, at 2:05 a.m., Governor Raymond Shafer, acting on the request of York officials, declared a state of emergency. Governor Shafer called into his plush offices in Harrisburg, 22 miles from York, a lieutenant colonel of the Pennsylvania National Guard and Captain Robert Rice of the Pennsylvania State Police.

"Gentlemen," Governor Shafer began, "we have a problem in York. Go take care of it."

2

MURDER IS
THE CHARGE

Thursday, May 17, 2001
York, Pennsylvania

The cuffs were slapped on with a sharp snap, followed by a rapid series of grinding clicks. For Charles Robertson, a 29-year police veteran and mayor of York, it was the worst thing that could happen. He had spent the night before worrying about the handcuffs. Cops couldn't stand cuffs. He had cuffed many perps over the years, but the clicking had never sounded so loud as when his own wrists were cuffed that day. Robertson was transported in the back seat of an unmarked police car to a prearranged bail hearing before President Judge John Uhler of the Court of Common Pleas of York County.

It was the longest car ride Robertson had ever experienced, though it only took minutes to get to the courthouse. His life would never be the same again.

Sitting in the back seat of a police cruiser, handcuffed, was humiliating. There was no reason in the world to handcuff him, other than to embarrass him and bring indignity to his office. And who did county detective Rodney George, only three years old in 1969, think he was arresting? During the bloody York riots, Robertson was a uniformed police officer in the line of fire. This was the mayor. He had just been re-elected. He held the highest elective office in the city.

Robertson's double chin was prominent as he sat in the back of the police car, exemplifying the excess weight he was carrying. By the end of the trial—largely from stress—he would be more than 40 pounds lighter.

Wearing wire-frame glasses, Robertson was dressed in his best suit of metallic blue with a dark patterned tie, which contrasted with his crisp white shirt. On his left lapel he wore a red, campaign-style button bearing the word *York*. On his right lapel was a dime-sized white rose, the symbol of York, which called itself the "White Rose City." Robertson truly loved the city where he had been born and had grown up, where he had coached American Legion baseball for 20 years and officiated high school basketball and football for three decades. Thousands of kids grew up knowing him as a coach and simply as "Charlie." He was good-natured, affable, and gregarious, with a tough edge beneath the surface. He loved sports almost as much as his city.

All that Charles Robertson had ever dreamed of doing was serving as mayor. Now any hope of fulfilling the culmination of that dream— bringing a professional baseball team to York—was shattered.

The announcement of the mayor's arrest, charging him with the murder of Lillie Belle Allen during the 1969 race riots, brought out the media giants. They were all there: CNN, NBC, ABC, CBS, *USA Today,* the *Chicago Tribune*, the *Philadelphia Inquirer*, the *Washington Post*, the *Boston Globe*, and other national and local media representatives. Arriving early in a black Lincoln Town Car was ABC news analyst George Stephanopoulos. CNN had been lying in wait for two days. CBS was interviewing residents, waiting for live footage of the mayor's surrender. The foremost question among many of the residents was why the arrest took 32 years. Others commented that Robertson's arrest, two days after he had won the Democratic primary for his third term as mayor, was politically motivated.

The day's events began at 8:23 a.m. York Mayor Charlie Robertson arrived at District Justice Barbara Nixon's office. Overcast skies and a threatening storm seemed to reflect the mood of the city as the blue unmarked police cruiser pulled to the curb. Charlie's police commissioner, Herbert Grofcsik, escorted him through the waiting throng of frenzied media. Following closely with briefcase in hand was Richard Oare, one of Robertson's lawyers and a close friend. Robertson would not be cuffed until after his arraignment at Nixon's office, before his trip to his bail hearing at the courthouse.

The media already had the multi-page affidavit describing Robertson's role in the young black woman's death on July 21, 1969. This document contained several named witnesses who saw him at a rally of white street gangs on July 20, 1969, yelling "white power," and alleged that Charlie pumped his right fist in the air, inciting the white gangs to riot and kill. According to Fred Flickinger, who testified under oath before the grand jury, Robertson stated, "If I weren't a cop, I would be leading commando raids against niggers in the black neighborhoods." Rick Knouse, a former member of a white street gang, testified before the grand jury that Robertson gave him .30-06 ammunition and told him to "kill as many niggers as you can." Knouse further told the grand jury that he used that ammunition when he fired at Lillie Belle Allen's car. In addition, former city Police Captain Dennis McMaster told the grand jury that he witnessed Robertson providing .30-06 ammunition to Bob or Art Messersmith, two of the alleged shooters.

Camera lights flashed as television crews jockeyed for position, and the print media hungered for a comment—any comment from "Charlie" would do. Robertson was no stranger to the media, but this was on another level, and their agenda was different, and hostile. The media were not interested in city government, or bringing a minor league baseball team to York, or even the beautification of the downtown business district.

Robertson and Oare fought their way through.

"Mr. Robertson, Mr. Robertson," yelled a reporter, "did you hand out ammunition to Rick Knouse?"

"No comment," Rich Oare answered as he and the mayor and Grofcsik pushed their way through the crush of reporters.

"Mr. Robertson, did you tell Rick Knouse to kill as many blacks as he could?" yelled another reporter.

"No comment, please let us through," Oare said.

"Mr. Robertson, are you going to resign as mayor?"

"No, he's not," Oare, answered.

"Mr. Mayor, Mr. Mayor," another reporter yelled, thrusting a microphone at Charlie, "do you have any comment?"

"Thank you for calling me mayor," Robertson answered. "I'm still the mayor of the city of York."

Once Robertson finally made it into the magistrate's small hearing room, the somber process moved quickly. Nixon set a tentative preliminary hearing date for May 15, and advised him that he was now in the custody of the Pennsylvania State Police, and would remain in their custody until a common pleas judge set bail. "District justices," Nixon added, "do not have the authority to set bail in murder cases." Rodney George, the county detective, and Trooper Keith

Stone, flanking Mayor Robertson, immediately escorted him from the courtroom to a waiting police cruiser in the alley. Waiting outside the courtroom, the relentless media now had their photo opportunity; their pictures would be broadcast live throughout the country. Robertson, in custody and handcuffed, was transported in the back seat of the unmarked police car to a prearranged bail hearing before President Judge John Uhler of the Court of Common Pleas of York County.

Every small brick building, every tree bursting with the signs of spring, every alley, every small business and neighborhood that the police cruiser passed on the way to the courthouse was a familiar sight to Charlie. Robinson still had cop's eyes—icy-blue, street-smart eyes that seemed to miss very little. From long nights on patrol, he knew the city like the back of his hand. He was born in York City, attended the York public schools and graduated from York High School in 1952. After a two-year stint in the Army, Charlie joined the city police force in 1962. He served on the York City School Board for a decade. Elected mayor in 1994, and reelected in 1998, he was responsible for the beautification of that community, which included the painted murals on the buildings depicting York's historic heritage, such as one proclaiming it "Muscletown, USA." York was, after all, the home of York Barbell.

Once before Judge Uhler, in a courtroom crawling with media, defense counsel advised the court that Charles Robertson was 67 years old, born April 12, 1934; his entire life, summarized in minutes, read like a eulogy. Judge Uhler properly concluded that Mayor Charles Robertson was not a flight risk and promptly set bail at $50,000, which assured the immediate release of the Commonwealth's arrestee.

§

York County District Attorney Stanley H. Rebert had a prepared statement for the media, released the morning of Mayor Robertson's arrest. Rebert, 58, had been elected to that office in 1986, and had crushed all opponents at the polls every four years. A consummate politician and an excellent prosecutor, he anticipated the public criticism, and the accolades, his office was about to experience. Rebert always surrounded himself with loyalty and competence, or at least tried to.

Stanley Rebert was a Republican, and the chief law enforcement officer of York County.

Charles Robertson was a Democrat, and the chief executive of York City.

Rebert's first assistant, Tom Kelley, also a Republican, had been on the city council, and fought publicly with the mayor and Police Commissioner Grofcsik. Tom Kelley and Ed Paskey were assigned by Rebert to prosecute this case personally, and Rebert was sensitive to the adage that "one's political adversary should never be one's prosecutor." Accordingly, the district attorney preempted the media, declaring that justice needed to be upheld, particularly for an elected official. He stressed that a jury would determine the guilt or innocence of the mayor, and that the court of public opinion, the special interest groups, and political ballyhooing would not thwart justice.

In his written press release, and with oratorical flair, District Attorney Stan Rebert concluded with the following:

"There is no political, professional or personal issue at stake between the defendant and me, my first assistant or any other member of my staff. Furthermore, there is absolutely nothing in any of our past relationships that could possibly lead any fair-minded individual to conclude that I would so grossly abuse my powers as chief law enforcement officer for the County of York.

"To suggest that I could be motivated by anything other than the pursuit of justice to charge anyone with murder is both outrageous and ludicrous. Furthermore, it impugns the integrity and intelligence of the 29 members of the grand jury, as well as the judge who presides over the execution of their duties. Most tragically, these baseless allegations trivialize and continue to victimize the family and memory of Lillie Belle Allen."

§

At the York County Courthouse, home of the district attorney's office, the prosecutors were having the biggest press conference of their careers, defending their actions, applauding their decisions. Stan Rebert, Tom Kelley, Ed Paskey, and Tim Barker, all dressed in blue, were basking in their moment in the sun. And it was a glorious moment indeed, for they were laying claim to cracking a 32-year-old case, vowing to bring justice for an innocent African American woman who had been gunned down in the street.

Three blocks away, at City Hall, waited a battalion of media armed with a battery of microphones aimed at a podium, in anticipation of the mayor's emergence from his ornate office. They knew Robertson would not hide as long as he was mayor, and they were absolutely right. The large wooden doors of City Hall opened simultaneously, and Mayor Charlie Robertson approached the podium, flanked by Commissioner Herbert Grofcsik, Betty Atwater, Democratic nominee for the York City School Boards, and Richard Oare.

Clearing his throat, his words choked with emotion, Charlie Robertson declared his innocence. "All questions regarding the affidavit in this case will be handled by a court of law," he said.

In addition to defending himself, Charlie promised to restore the scarred city's image. "You have to remember this is the first capital of the United States," he concluded, "and I am the mayor."

And he repeated his pledge to remain in office. He was still the mayor.

The late morning news conference attracted such a crowd of media and onlookers that police closed West King Street in front of City Hall. The two major governing factions in York—the district attorney's office and the mayor's office—had declared war. Battle lines were drawn and the citizens of York were being asked to choose sides—much like the decisions some had faced in 1969.

The nation viewed a teary-eyed Charlie Robertson as he repeated the accusation in an incredulous, bleating voice: "Murder ... murder ... murder is the charge!"

3

FULL CIRCLE

May 18, 2001

I was sitting on my living room couch, waiting with a strong cup of coffee in hand.

At 7:00 a.m., Charlie Robertson was there on my TV screen, fielding questions from Bryant Gumbel on CBS's "Early Show." Gumbel went after Robertson, accusing him of racism. At 7:13 a.m., broadcasting live via satellite, NBC "Today Show" host Katie Couric grilled Robertson and attorney Richard Oare. It was just getting underway. The interviews would continue seemingly nonstop over the next few days. Oare had told me that Robertson was taking his case to the nation. I had just come on board and, at least for now, was on the sidelines. I was anxious to see how it would play out, since Robertson was still the chief executive of York. More than 80 newspapers worldwide ran stories on the arrest of Mayor Charlie Robertson.

"Are you sure about these television interviews?" asked my wife, Jill, as the morning news began to air.

"No," I answered. "I don't know how you can be charged with murder and be portrayed in a positive light by the media."

"Exactly," Jill agreed.

But he can't hide out at City Hall either, not as long as he is the mayor," I added.

Richard Oare, a sole practitioner handling medical malpractice cases, was a friend of Robertson's. They had hooked up earlier when Robertson was considering some civil litigation. Oare had gone with Robertson to the grand jury proceedings. Oare called me on May 1 and asked me if I would represent Robertson in a criminal case if it came to that. I dropped everything on a Sunday and went down to meet with Oare and Robertson in Oare's office on the south end of York.

I appreciated that they thought I was the "go-to guy." I remain indebted to Oare for bringing me in.

Prior to the election, we thought it was best to keep my name out of it. I didn't think it would help Charlie. People were being indicted in the case and the York media were in a feeding frenzy about the mayor's involvement. The fact that I was representing Robertson stayed quiet for weeks, but it got out the weekend before the election when Charlie evidently told some reporters. We agreed that Oare would handle the media.

The interviews were done with my full knowledge and consent. Privately I had some doubts. But I was, after all, the new guy on the team.

High-profile cases and courtrooms had been an integral part of my life for over thirty years. After graduating from Duquesne Law School in 1971 and getting an LL.M. from Harvard one year later, I was exposed to the real world as an assistant district attorney in Harrisburg, Pennsylvania. I was much younger then, with an attitude. I lost my youth over the years, but never my attitude.

I loved everything about the courtrooms: picking juries, trash talking, opening statements, cross-examining hostile witnesses, and closing arguments. Young and reckless, I had no other life because the law was my life. My value system was determined by wins in the courtroom. There was a direct correlation between convicting the accused and my self-esteem. Drug traffickers were easy; they usually made a direct sale to a wired undercover agent. Burglars always got caught red-handed. Pedophiles never won the credibility war when pitted against the truth-telling of a child victim, not in front of a central Pennsylvania jury they didn't.

I thought I was great in front of a jury as a prosecutor. I honestly believed that it had something to do with my oratory skills and preparation. My blue suits, exotic boots, and briefcase added to my confidence. I was fighting evil, winning the war between right and wrong, with a meaningful purpose in life as one of God's chosen. I did not have a clue.

When I was a prosecutor, homicides were my favorite cases. Usually, the victim leaves a trail of evidence that points a finger to the killer. The media's appetite for gruesome killings was insatiable. And, murder cases—where the stakes are highest—produced an adrenaline rush.

Less than 12 months after it began, without warning, my career as a prosecutor came to an abrupt end. My first cousin, John Ramos, was charged with attempted murder for shooting an African American male in Pat Patterson's bar. My father, who had never asked me for anything, and who put me through college and four years of law school by selling hot dogs in Carlisle, Pennsylvania, asked me to help out his sister, Olga Ramos, John's mother.

The shooting took place in York, Pennsylvania. A jury tried the case in York, on the second floor of the Court of Common Pleas, in front of Judge Joseph E. Erb. John asserted self-defense; an all-white jury agreed and found John not guilty.

On the morning following Robertson's arrest, waiting for the "Today Show" to come on, I realized that my life had come full circle. My career as a criminal defense attorney began in York in October 1973. Would it end there, 28 years later?

Now Katie Couric was interviewing Robertson and Oare. I took a big sip of coffee. As a mayor, Charlie had a lot of media experience, but not at this level.

Couric: Did you supply ammunition to one of the shooters that night, Mr. Mayor?

Robertson: Absolutely not and I'm innocent of all indicted charges.

Couric: Did you incite white gangs to raid black neighborhoods?

Robertson: Absolutely not.

Couric: You do admit to making racist statements back then. Can you elaborate on what kind of statements you made and on what occasions?

Robertson: Well, to say "white power" is not a racist statement. That was the language used back in '69 by both white and black. "Black power" was used by the Olympic team and "white power" was used by talk of neighborhoods where you had pockets of whites and pockets of blacks. It was used.

The "Today Show" interview veered way off track at one point. Couric asked several time whether the case was now coming to light because a York police officer committed suicide and left a tape about the events during the 1969 riots. A casual viewer might have been left with the impression that the testimony about Robertson came in the form of a deathbed statement by a fellow police officer. No police officer killed himself and left a tape. A former gang member, Donald Altland, had killed himself on April 11, 2000, and left a tape about his role as a shooter. A police officer, Dennis McMaster, a colleague of Charlie's during the riots, had given prosecutors testimony that Charlie had handed out ammunition.

But there was no cop who left a tape.

It was Robertson who corrected the record. "This was not a police officer who committed suicide, just a person . . . it wasn't a policeman," he said.

At 8:00 a.m., Robertson again faced the nation with Colleen McEdwards, CNN anchor, who confronted Charlie with the same questions taken from the affidavit that charged him with murder.

> McEdwards: The affidavit that I have seen mentions the phrase "white power," which you just mentioned. It also mentions—I'm looking here at five witnesses who say that they heard you say—you were a police officer at the time—that—and this is quoting—"If I weren't a cop, I would be leading commando raids against niggers in the black neighborhoods." Did you make a statement like that?
>
> Robertson: That's not correct. No.
>
> McEdwards: Do you—would you consider yourself to have ever been a racist, Mr. Mayor?
>
> Robertson: Excuse me.
>
> McEdwards: Are you able to hear me all right? Would you consider yourself to ever have been a racist?
>
> Robertson: Now I can hear you.
>
> McEdwards: OK. Do you consider yourself to ever have been a racist?
>
> Robertson: Yes.
>
> McEdwards: Explain that, elaborate on that.
>
> Robertson: OK. That was back in 1969 when I said "white power." That's not acceptable. That should be corrected. And it is corrected as of now, and has been for many years.

As I watched Mayor Robertson come under fire, I questioned the wisdom of doing these interviews. He was taking some serious hits, and I knew that someday we would be picking a jury somewhere, maybe even in York, hoping to find 12 citizens uninfluenced by anything they might have seen, read, or heard. These interviews weren't helping, but, on the other hand, he was the mayor and the nation demanded answers.

I also knew that this case was going to go the distance. Not many do, but I saw no way out for the prosecution and none for the defense. Charlie Robertson was charged with murder in the first degree, which is the intentional killing of another human being, with malice aforethought, premeditated, deliberate, and in wanton disregard of human life. That charge brings with it immediate public destruction of the accused.

There would be no plea bargaining; there could be no plea bargaining. There was no middle road. There was no acceptable compromise for either side.

In the American criminal justice system, most cases result in guilty pleas. It's the practical thing to do, expedient, quick, and efficient. Innocence sometimes becomes irrelevant. If you are accused of a crime, you have a right to a trial by jury; but if you exercise that right and get convicted, you get no mercy at the time of sentencing. Innocent people, on the advice of counsel, are often forced to plead guilty to cut their losses.

Great deals are also available when a defendant is willing and able to incriminate someone else in a crime, especially if that someone else is a desirable target. Some lawyers make careers out of plea bargaining, specializing in the art of negotiation, and understanding the wants and needs of the prosecution. Many of these lawyers rarely try a case, are politically connected, and excel at selling their influence.

The affidavit that charged Robertson named eight alleged shooters in the murder of Lillie Belle Allen. I knew it was time to have a meeting of all defense counsel.

The reason?

Mayor Robertson was not only the media event; he was also the *target*.

§

The defense lawyers representing all of the accused met at the law office of Pete Solymos. I had known Pete for over 20 years and knew he was a player. He was very bright and a great trial lawyer. His chain-smoking made me crazy, but that was the only bad habit he had. He could be trusted, which is something I can't say about all lawyers. Solymos and his law partner Tom Sponaugle represented Robert Messersmith, and their client was accused of firing the fatal shot at Lillie Belle Allen with a 12-gauge shotgun.

The law offices of Solymos were in the suburbs of York, near a shopping center, adjacent to a daycare center. Pete had done well in private practice, and the massive, one-floor brick building was home to eleven lawyers and a support staff. The conference room was typical of a big law office, with a long walnut table, surrounded by comfortable upholstered chairs, dominating the room. On this day, additional chairs had to be brought in to accommodate the many defense lawyers for a meeting that would prove to be very interesting.

We were going to discuss the upcoming preliminary hearing. Who was going to lead off and anchor? How we were going to be seated was no small item, since there were potentially nine defendants, a minimum of fifteen defense lawyers, paralegals, and private investigators. Add four district attorneys, detective Rodney George, and their support staff, and you've got a monster cluster in the well of any courtroom. A filing of pretrial motions was also to be discussed. We were there as well to feel each other out, and that was not a hidden agenda; in fact, that was *my* primary reason for being there.

Harold Fitzkee, former District Attorney of York County, was there on behalf of William "Sam" Ritter, accused of shooting a .22-caliber rifle at the car from several blocks away after Lillie Belle Allen was already down. Fitzkee had a great defense available to him and was a prime candidate for a sweetheart deal. I knew, however, that Fitzkee would not be so easy to roll over. York's former district attorney was also a good friend; I was glad go see him there, and knew I could count on him.

Matt Gover, another great defense lawyer, drove in for this meeting from Harrisburg, Pennslvania. He represented Chauncey Gladfelter, another alleged white shooter. Gover had recently defended a state representative in Harrisburg who was charged with vehicular homicide—killing an African American pedestrian—then leaving the scene of the accident. It was a case that had generated enormous publicity, and Matt Gover did very well for his client, with a plea that cut the representative's losses. I was glad to see Gover there for all the right reasons: he was an excellent lawyer, and a good friend.

Joe Metz, also from Harrisburg and politically connected, was there on behalf of alleged shooter Tom Smith. I had never worked with Joe before, but he had a good reputation. Whatever route he was going to take in this case, he would give all the defense attorneys a heads up.

I didn't know attorney Frank Arcuri or his paralegal Walt Trayer, but was advised that they were appointed by the court to represent Art Messersmith. In a matter of minutes I knew that Art Messersmith was well represented. I did know Greg Gettle, who represented alleged shooter Greg Neff. Gettle had been a practicing lawyer in York for almost 30 years. He was also a friend, and I respected his legal abilities and could trust him.

I noticed that Clarence Lutzinger was not represented at this meeting. When I learned that he was represented by the public defender's office of York County, I surmised that Lutzinger had probably already cut his deal.

Finally, at the table was a colorful friend of mine from the past, John Moran, who represented Rick Knouse. Moran loved to talk, and often made sense, and then he would talk some more. For years he wore his brown hair shoulder length, in a ponytail, but recently had changed it to a crew cut. He had redefined his look to run for a state representative's seat in Harrisburg, and though he lost the election, he still looked the part.

I was very interested in what Moran was going to do. He had been a defense lawyer in York his entire life, disliked the treatment he got from the young local prosecutors, and was capable of sticking it to them. In this case, whether Moran knew it or not, he owned the prosecutors because Knouse was the Commonwealth's case against Mayor Charlie Robertson. Without Knouse, the prosecution would never get Robertson past the upcoming preliminary hearing. Moran was in a position to dictate his client's demands.

After all the handshaking and pleasant exchanges, it was time to get down to business. I had been involved in multidefendant cases in the past, but never with so many. Sitting in a room with twelve lawyers, with nine defendants charged with murder, could have resulted in a ridiculous waste of time. Lawyers like to talk, assert themselves, get their positions across.

But it was time well spent.

There was a vast amount of legal talent and experience in that conference room. Everybody present realized the enormity and the complexity of what was going on. The case was much too serious for anybody to grandstand. We all knew that nobody was going to compromise his client's position out of friendship for a fellow lawyer.

"Who's going to prosecute this case for the Commonwealth?" I asked, starting things off.

"Rebert assigned this to Ed Paskey, Tom Kelley, and Tim Barker," Fitzkee answered.

"What's Bill Graff's role?" I asked.

"Graff's the lead prosecutor in the Schaad case," Fitzkee said.

The Schaad case that Graff was going to prosecute was about to break. Though the case was still in the hands of the grand jury, Graff had already promised the public imminent arrests. Henry Schaad, a young, white York police officer, who was riding in an armored vehicle during the riots, was shot and killed by African American assailants on Thursday, July 18, 1969, near midnight.

The room fell silent for a moment. I didn't know what to think. I'd never heard of Paskey, Kelley, or Barker. That didn't mean anything because I hadn't been involved in York County for years. On the other hand, I did know Bill Graff, who was Rebert's best prosecutor. He had been in Rebert's office for over 15 years and knew how to try a case. He also knew how to pick the ones to try. Stan Rebert, the elected District Attorney of York County, had been in office since 1986. He too was excellent on the courtroom floor, but his failing health understandably precluded him from combat.

"What judge is this going to end up in front of?" I asked.

"Not sure," Solymos answered. "John Uhler was the presiding judge over the grand jury, and that might knock him out; plus, he was the district attorney here in York from 1978 through 1982. Maybe Chronister, who has seniority. Dorney would be a good one. I doubt if the newer judges will get this one."

"What about Cassimatis?" I asked.

"Not likely," Arcuri added. "He's on senior status."

We then discussed whether District Justice Barbara Nixon should handle the preliminary hearing. It was decided, with everybody agreeing, that we should ask the court to assign a common pleas judge to preside rather than a magistrate. It was no reflection on Nixon's ability to hear the case, or her integrity, but we thought that a magistrate would never throw out a case of this magnitude at the preliminary hearing stage. We weren't confident a judge would either, but with a judge presiding, some of us thought it was possible. Whether it was going to be Nixon or a common pleas judge, Nixon's small courtroom would never accommodate all the litigants, let alone the media.

"I suggest," Gover said from the far end of the table, "that Costopoulos lead off at the hearing. He represents the mayor and maybe we can hide behind him. Plus, he's the oldest son of a bitch here."

Gover, with salt-and-pepper hair in a shag cut, was not always the first one to speak up. But when he spoke, in a deep baritone voice, he commanded authority. He usually cut right to the heart of an issue, with a dose of humor. He was rock-solid in the courtroom and everyone here knew it.

Amidst the laughter and jesting, the decision was made. I wasn't sure if I wanted to go first and highlight Charlie, or go last and low-key our position and his role. I surely did not want to be in the middle, and rather than risk that, I agreed to the suggestion. Matt Gover knew exactly what he was doing, and I factored that into his recommendation. His client's role was minimal in the whole thing.

We then discussed the 32-year delay at some length. Never in the history of the Commonwealth was a prosecution delayed 32 years. It was an excellent pretrial issue that could result in the dismissal of all charges for everyone. We would raise that challenge after the preliminary hearing.

Finally—and everybody knew it was coming—the question had to be asked.

"Who's going to plead out?" I asked.

The conference room fell silent. It was a tough question for the others to field. It was also too soon for some of them to know the answer, but for others, I knew it wasn't.

Like for Moran, because timing is everything. The preliminary hearing was coming up, and the prosecution needed Knouse to bind Charlie Robertson over for court action. My only hope was that Moran would seize the once-in-a-lifetime opportunity and play hardball.

"We . . . we all have to do what we have to do," Moran said cautiously.

That pretty much wrapped up the first meeting of the defense lawyers in the Lille Belle Allen case. There would be more meetings in the future, but there would be fewer lawyers attending. The plea-bargaining process had already begun.

4

TARGET

Thursday, May 24, 2001
City Hall
York, Pennsylvania

Mayor Charlie Robertson sat behind his desk in City Hall, alone, distraught over the recent events that were destroying his life. He loved his work, his city, and felt privileged to have served his community over the past seven years. He was truly proud of what he had accomplished. York was a better place now than when he had first assumed office. Neighborhoods were stronger, people were safer, and businesses were more eager than ever to invest in the city.

Charlie Robertson was on the verge of bringing a minor league baseball team back to York. His vision included a new stadium, and he would throw the first pitch to memorialize that accomplishment. Many older residents of York remembered the days when minor league teams had played in York at Memorial Stadium. Charlie knew it was good for the city and wanted to bring it back. For 20 years, Robertson had coached baseball for the American Legion, and in 1986 was elected to the American Legion Baseball Hall of Fame. His fantasy was to make that first pitch at the new stadium a smoking strike. Now, none of that was possible.

No baseball team was coming to York with the mayor under indictment for murder. No big business would invest in a city under such an ominous cloud. His accomplishments would forever be forgotten, and he would only be remembered as the mayor who had been charged with murder.

Charlie looked around his office at all the memorabilia. Photographs of his baseball teams adorned the walls. Action shots of him officiating high school football and basketball games were carefully placed on a mantel. The dark blue police hat he wore in the line of fire as an officer was plain for visitors to see behind the mayor's desk. The framed Optimist International Humanitarian Award was proudly displayed in the reception area. These were symbols of his accomplishments — his life.

Hundreds of young athletes had grown up under Charlie's tutelage. He would show up on weekday afternoons at William Penn Senior High School's baseball practice at Small's Athletic Field to help the school coaches and to scout kids for his legion team, which began practice later in the spring. Wearing a windbreaker, shorts, and long baseball socks, Robertson, then 6' 2" and maybe 180 pounds, would hit fly balls for the outfielders and warm up the pitchers in the still chilly spring air. He was an unofficial assistant coach for the school team. He was always cheerful and encouraging. His enthusiasm for the sport was contagious. During the winters, Charlie coached his own basketball team, Robbie's Rockets, in a city league. It was a team intended to provide a basketball outlet for the high school football players, who were great athletes but not necessarily basketball stars and whose prime sport cut into the basketball season anyway. He was not a coach wannabe. He knew his stuff. Some of his legion teams were damn good.

The kids were loyal as hell to Charlie. At the end of each season he'd have the ballplayers over to his house for a party, where beer, soda, hot dogs, and snacks were served. Most of the kids were drinking anyway. At least here, on one night, they wouldn't be running around York. They faced no trouble from the law. They either walked or got a ride home. There was absolutely no doubt that Charlie made a contribution to their lives. Kids respected him as a coach and a police officer. Providing an occasional beer to minors would be made much of later on, but at that time seemed almost insignificant in the overall context of Charlie's support and assistance to young athletes.

Gregarious and easygoing, Charlie thrived on the jock-banter with ballplayers on and off the field. To many, he had been one of the guys.

Now, looking back, Charlie just shook his head, disgusted. He got up from his desk and slowly walked to the main window overlooking King Street. Below his office, people were assembling for a news con-

ference to be held by the York County chapter of the National Association for the Advancement of Colored People. He estimated more
than 100 people were gathering to hear the organization's statements
on Robertson's recent homicide charge and the 1969 death of Lillie
Belle Allen. He was told that there would be national and state
NAACP officials in attendance, and he recognized Leo Cooper, York
County's NAACP president, standing on the steps of City Hall between the massive white pillars. Charlie never really liked Leo Cooper,
or his attitude.

The media were there in full strength for this African American
press conference. As the speaker beside Leo Cooper adjusted and
tapped the microphones on the podium, the camera people moved up
the steps toward him. Charlie's loyal secretary, Helen Rohrbaugh, told
him that Eric Bryant, the national NAACP assistant director of field
operations, was going to be the main speaker. Charlie assumed the
well-dressed man in a dark brown suit with a red tie was Mr. Bryant.

Everybody in attendance could hear the fiery delivery of Eric
Bryant, including Charlie Robertson in his first-floor office.

"The time has come for Charlie Robertson to evaluate the state
of his affairs and determine if he should still be in office . . . York
wants to move forward and there are grave concerns whether York is
able to join the rest of America . . . the national chapter of the
NAACP joins the York County chapter in demanding that Mayor
Robertson resign from office immediately, and withdraw from the
current mayoral race."

Many in the crowd began applauding and cheering.

It was the kind of story the media loved. The mayor hanging on
despite a murder charge. African Americans demanding justice. A
32-year-old murder case reopened, seemingly, by newspaper coverage. The national spotlight on York. It all fit into their notion of the
perfect story, which would play out over a year or more.

In the office just above them was *the target.*

Charlie felt helpless, hurt, and angry. He wondered if he would
ever get past those emotions. Nighttime was the worst, when he
would lie in bed alone, fearing what could happen. He had been a police officer for 27 years, and he knew that a conviction for murder in
the first degree carried a mandatory life sentence and a conviction
for murder in the second degree carried 20 years. He was 67 years
old, and any conviction meant that he would die in a jail cell. As the
speakers below continued to incite the crowd, demanding his resignation from office, Charlie walked away from the window and sat in

the overstuffed chair in front of his desk. He buried his face in his hands, and the voices and noises outside faded away.

Charlie recalled the events of 1969; he had lived with them for over 30 years. It was a different era then, and some of it he remembered well, but much of it was a blur. Martin Luther King Jr. was assassinated in April 1968 in Memphis, and that is when things got really tense. Two months later, Robert Kennedy, Democratic candidate for president of the United States, was assassinated in Los Angeles. That same summer, rioters were setting fires in Watts, Detroit, Chicago, and Washington, D.C. York experienced a series of racial outbreaks in 1968, but it was in 1969 that York joined the fray on a major scale.

Charlie remembered the tension in the city before the riots erupted. He had been a police officer since 1962, and for seven years before the riots he was a uniformed beat cop. He knew every back street, alley, speakeasy, drug corner, and whorehouse in York. The whites were as bad as the blacks, but every time he had to respond to a crime scene, it seemed the blacks took it more personally. They resisted Charlie, called him a fucking pig, spat at and sometimes assaulted him. Having saliva spat in his face was the one thing he could not stand. That had happened to him as an officer. The risk on the job was obvious. In really tense situations, there would sometimes be backup, and sometimes not. It all came with the uniform.

There was this 12-year-old African American kid, and though Charlie had long forgotten his name, the kid would pour lighter fluid in his mouth, and would light it as he spat it out. The child must have seen a flame-thrower when the York Fair had come to town. In any event, on one occasion when he lit the fluid, it flashed back into his mouth. His face and body caught on fire and he was immediately rushed to the York Hospital. Afraid to tell his parents the truth, the severely burned child said that an east-end gang of white youths attacked him, knocked him down, poured gasoline on him, and set him on fire. "Yes," he repeated, "the attackers were white."

The preexisting racial tension in York was already at the flash point, and when that boy's story circulated, the city erupted. A group of African Americans marched down to Newberry Street, which was predominantly white, and threw rocks at windows. The whites retaliated, and the rock throwing escalated to shootings. Whites were shooting blacks. Blacks were shooting whites. Arson erupted throughout the city. Police vehicles and fire trucks that responded to the violence were moving targets. Charlie clearly remembered his police cruiser taking machine-gun fire while he was parked at the bottom of a hill; he and a fellow police officer were almost killed.

Charlie also remembered how Officer Henry Schaad was killed in the line of duty on July 18, 1969. Henry Schaad, 22, the son of a police detective for the city of York, was riding in an armored vehicle known as "Big Al." He and two other officers were ambushed while responding to a call that a white motorcyclist had been shot. A high-powered bullet pierced the converted Brink's truck, striking Henry Schaad, and though he was wearing a bulletproof vest, he died on August 1, 1969. The funeral was attended by every police department in the county. An American flag was draped over the coffin, then ceremoniously folded and given to the young officer's wife. The 21-gun salute rang in Charlie's ears, seemingly forever.

A hundred men cried at the funeral.

Detective Russell Schaad, who had lost his son, was Charlie's good friend.

Three days later, there was a shooting on Newberry Street that took the life of Lillie Belle Allen. Charlie Robertson remembered responding to that crime scene in an armored vehicle with three other police officers. He could not remember the names of those officers when Detective Rodney George and Trooper Keith Stone interviewed him on May 9, 2000. He did recall getting out of the vehicle on the night in question, offering assistance to the survivors in the car, and then reporting to another shooting where three police officers were pinned down by gunfire. It was a night of hell, and the riots in York were out of control.

The mayor of York at the time was John Snyder. Realizing that he was losing the city, Snyder called then Governor Raymond Shafer for immediate military assistance. Governor Shafer complied, and ordered the Pennsylvania National Guard and the Pennsylvania State Police into York.

With tanks and armored personnel carriers rolling in the streets of York, order was restored.

Charlie Robertson shook his head as he relived that nightmare.

He didn't have a fucking clue why he was charged with murder.

§

Hours later, after the NAACP's news conference on the steps of City Hall, Charlie went home to rest. He lived alone in the same house he had grown up in, a small rowhouse on Princess Street in York. It was a simple house, unpretentious. It was an ethnically diverse neighborhood in 2001, with African Americans, Latinos, and whites living side by side.

Charlie kept his fenced-in backyard neatly mowed, but with the media constantly cruising the back alley, the grass would have to wait. He would stay indoors with the shades pulled, and would only answer the phone if the answering machine revealed a welcome caller.

Charlie had fallen asleep on the couch and was awakened by Charlie Bacas, a top Robertson adviser, banging at the door. Eric Mentzer, who handled the city's financial affairs, accompanied him. Dressed in a gray pinstriped suit, Bacas sat across from Charlie in the kitchen. Getting right to the point, he insisted that Charlie needed to withdraw from the race.

"You have to," said Bacas, former chief of staff for late house speaker James Manderino, who had been a legendary power broker at the capitol.

"It's the right thing to do for the people of York," Bacas told Robertson.

"It's the right thing to do for the York County Democratic Party," Bacas said.

"That's right," Mentzer added.

Tom Wolfe, who was chairman of Robertson's primary campaign, called while Bacas was there to pile on the bad news. He told Robertson that Congressman Todd Platts wanted Charlie to withdraw and resign. He told Robertson that Eugene DePasquale, chairman of the York County Democratic Party, wanted Charlie to write a carefully worded letter to the Democratic Party of York, announcing that he was withdrawing from the race for the good of the city. The letter was then to be released to the media.

Charlie Robertson, betrayed by his most loyal supporters, acquiesced.

That night, Charlie wrote a letter to the party, withdrawing from the race. "This is the most painful decision I have ever made in my life," he wrote. "I would have loved to continue serving this city for another four years in order to make sure these good things keep happening. But, I recognize that this is not possible. Someone else must now continue this work, and lead this city toward the bright future it has earned."

Charlie would not, however, resign from his present term. He would continue to serve as the city's mayor, and nobody was going to take that from him.

§

Rich Oare was shocked. He had been cut out of the decision-making process, and resented what had been done to his client and friend.

Oare called me at home, apologizing for the late hour. He needed to vent. Rich believed in the presumption of innocence; he believed that the charges were politically motivated; he believed that Bacas and the boys were only interested in themselves and their vested interests, not the city of York.

There was very little I could say. I knew how much that race meant to Charlie. Rich and I then talked about our roles in the case and agreed to stay out of the local political arena. We would defend Charlie Robertson on the murder charges, and do what we could to minimize media damage. We could not, and would not, try to take over City Hall.

Though it was almost midnight, I called Charlie at home. He picked up when he heard my voice on his answering machine.

"Hey, Charlie," I said, "I just want you to know that I understand your decision."

"It was really a tough thing to do," Charlie replied, still upset.

"Are you OK?" I asked.

"Not really, but I'll hang in there," Charlie answered.

Questions kept nagging at him: How do you defend yourself against something from 32 years ago that you didn't do? How can anyone do that? How can a mayor do that? Why was this happening to him?

For Charlie, who had given so much to his community, the nightmare was well underway. This new nightmare was far worse than the one that lingered from the streets in 1969. Only his faith, his strength as a human being, and his family would sustain him through the long ordeal.

5

JACKALS

jack-al *(1) any of several races of wild dogs of the genus* Canis, *esp.* Canis aureus, *of Asia and Africa, which hunt in packs at night and which were formerly supposed to hunt prey for the lion. (2) one who does drudgery for another, or who meanly serves the purpose of another. (*The American College Dictionary)

Let me say this up front: In the high-profile cases I have handled, I have received great press on occasion. Other times I've gotten knocked around. It comes with the territory. I have dealt with the media my entire career. By and large, the media have been fair. Even in the Robertson case, the national coverage was reasonably balanced and accurate. But I'd also say this: The sustained coverage in York by its two daily newspapers was pretty bad. The unrelenting drumbeat, the constant pounding, took its toll on Charlie Robertson—and the truth.

It was advocacy journalism gone awry.

There almost seemed to be a script for York's two daily newspapers. It was prevalent throughout much of the ongoing coverage referred to by the dailies as the "1969 York Riots Investigation" and the "1969 York City Riots Homicides Investigation." The script went something like this: Racism is evil; the papers' anniversary coverage in 1999 sparked the criminal investigation into racially related riot killings 30 years before; the DA's office was on the side of good, battling racism; the mayor, Charlie Robertson, was a vestige of York's ugly past; as a cop in '69, Charlie had been, at least, a racist; the DA's office at various stages was looking into crimes that might ... would ... should include Robertson; anyone who opposed the investigation (and by extension the news and editorial coverage) just might be a racist. Needless to say, the mayor had to go.

There was no room for dissent.

This script was not written anywhere, of course. But it was the thread throughout stories, editorials, and columns published in the *York Daily Record* and the *York Dispatch/York Sunday News*, newspapers published under a joint operating agreement. It went on for nearly two years. The York papers won plenty of awards for their coverage, but at whose expense? Surely, they would go on to more prestigious awards if someone were convicted—if the mayor were convicted—in the investigation underway by the district attorney's office.

The York papers were hitting it hard long before the national media came to town in May 2001, after Robertson's arrest for the murder of Lillie Belle Allen. Newspaper reporters and television crews from across the country swarmed over the community, scrambling to collect information from anyone connected to the case. It was understandable. A racially motivated killing during the '69 riots by a police officer who rose to become that community's mayor was truly a sensational story.

The media's relentless presence and aggressive reporting tactics were seemingly justified. The allegations were horrific, and though 32 years had gone by, it was time for the Allen family and the African American community of York to get justice. The city of York and its people would just have to deal with it. It was reported that the racial healing in York for the past 32 years would never be complete without exposing the truth.

The media have an interest in any high-profile case. The United States Supreme Court has proclaimed, time and time again, that the First Amendment guarantees this interest, which is not only constitutionally protected but also morally legitimate: The public has a right to know. The media are also the watchdogs of government, and the justice system is a branch of government. Clearly, even more was at stake for the York papers, with the city's mayor accused of murder. However, to further justice and secure the foundation of democracy, the media should seek the truth impartially, and provide a fair and comprehensive account of events and issues. They should be honest, fair, and courageous in gathering, reporting, and interpreting information; make certain that headlines, front-page teases, photos, and quotations do not misrepresent the truth; and never highlight incidents with quotations out of context.

The two York newspapers, obsessed with the violence in 1969, were having a problem with responsible reporting. They engaged in tabloid-style, confrontational journalism filled with rumor, innuendo, and irresponsible quotations from heavily biased individuals. Much of the coverage throughout seemed predisposed toward Robertson's guilt. The York newspapers had an *agenda.*

Never mind that it ruined a man's life.

The stories battered Robertson day after day. Any story containing the word "riots" was a candidate for the front-page. Some stories were meaty, but many were thin. The idea was to keep it going, no matter what—to repeat the basic allegations ad nauseum. This was, after all, a crusade.

§

The slant was there from the early days of the coverage.

In June 2000, after District Attorney Rebert announced a grand jury probe of the 1969 killings of Allen and Schaad, the *York Dispatch* ran a story quoting Rebert as saying Mayor Robertson "doth protest too much." The headline stated, "DA: Mayor Protests Too Much; Robertson's Anger Bewilders Council Members." It came in response to Robertson's suggestion that the probe was political. The paper quoted the mayor saying, "Why 31 years later? This will destroy the city. I'm hoping not. But if it does we will sure know the reason."

Tom Kelley, the first assistant district attorney, had said he wasn't surprised at Robertson's allegation of a political motive. The story went on to say that Kelley was the sole Republican city council member from 1995 through 1999, and that he had been critical of Robertson's Democratic administration. Kelley, of course, would go on to become the lead prosecutor in the Robertson case. In short, the story was implying that Robertson had something to hide. Instead of questioning whether Kelley had a grudge or political ax to grind, it used Kelley's once adversarial relationship with Robertson as a way to knock down any suggestion of a political motive. The *Dispatch* quoted Kelley as saying he would not be "dragged" into responding to Robertson's allegation, adding that it would tarnish the memories of the victims and the importance of the investigation. It doesn't come any higher and mightier than that. One council member cited in this article and many other stories as a champion of justice was Ray Crenshaw, an African American. He would later become Robertson's opponent in the 2001 Democratic primary.

"Stand Up Mayor and Tell the Truth," proclaimed a scorching *York Daily Record* editorial on May 22, 2001, shortly after Robertson's arrest for murder. The editorial questioned what the paper viewed as inconsistencies: whether Robertson, as an officer in 1969, waited until the shooting stopped before he approached the car in which Lillie Belle Allen had been riding on Newberry Street, or whether he waded in amidst the gunfire in an effort to save the passengers. "The two stories came from the same man—Charlie Robertson," the paper noted.

The editorial stated, "This is the same mayor who has taken so many twists and turns in his stories that it's hard to know if he's really bad at lying or his memory is gone. One problem with the memory theory is that some of these stories change in the course of one week." As further evidence of Robertson's inconsistencies, the paper went on to cite an issue with the handcuffs at the time of his arrest. The mayor had objected to wearing cuffs, and his brother, Milford Robertson, had talked about Charlie's worrying about the cuffs the night before. After his arrest, Robertson told a local TV station the handcuffs didn't bother him. "Which was it, mayor?" the editorial asked.

Which was it? The question sounded like something from a Watergate special prosecutor directed at a Nixon White House co-conspirator. It overlooked a basic tendency of human nature to try to brush away what has been extremely hurtful. To cover one's damaged pride, one takes a step back. Did the Daily Record *really think it didn't bother Robertson, a former cop, to wear handcuffs when he was arrested?*

The thrust of the editorial was that the charges alone were enough reason for Robertson to resign for the good of the city. "For the city, the mayor's guilt or innocence isn't nearly as important as the implications of his arrest," the editorial stated. "York simply can't walk that gangplank with him—guilty or innocent." The city had already been "subjected" to its mayor's admission that 32 years earlier he had shouted "white power" at a rally, the *Daily Record* wrote. "He recently said he wasn't sorry for saying it—a raw and unpolished moment. He tried to take it back later saying he was sorry, that his misguided past had affected his life. No tears though. No contrite apology to black residents. No concern over the family that Lillie Belle Allen left behind."

The editorial concluded, saying: "Mayor Charlie Robertson, these are the words we want to hear you utter on the steps of City Hall: 'I'm sorry. Forgive me. I resign.'"

Just days before on May 18, in an editorial entitled "Mayor, resign," they had banged him on the handcuffs "issue."

"On Thursday the mayor looked at a television camera and said the handcuffs he cried about before his arrest hadn't really bothered him. It smells false. What does it tell us about this man, who can waffle on a small matter without missing a beat? Is he under great stress, as his advisers suggest, or is it another glimpse into his character? And if this sort of distortion is due to stress, isn't that all the more reason to step down?"

Stress? Yeah, people charged with murder deal with that on occasion. It was so fucking petty.

§

It got so bad that over 100 of York's most reputable citizens—businessmen, religious leaders, and school board members; city, county, and state office holders—signed a letter to the *York Daily Record* and the *York Dispatch* expressing their concerns. It was a "who's who" list of community leaders. The guy behind it was Louis J. Appell Jr., president and CEO of Susquehanna Pfaltzgraph Company. It was a bold and courageous move, given the climate set by both of York's daily newspapers. It was copied to then Pennsylvania Governor Thomas J. Ridge. The letter stated that it was not for publication. The *York Sunday News* carried it as its lead story on June 3, 2001. It was originally intended to spark dialogue with the papers and it certainly did that.

The letter was addressed to *York Dispatch* publisher and editor Stan Hough and Dennis Hetzel, editor and publisher of the *York Daily Record*:

"The inflammatory approach which has characterized newspaper coverage threatens to undo the selfless efforts of many hundreds of citizens from all over the community who over the past 30 years have managed to heal the social wounds resulting from the riots. A continuation of the irresponsible approach by the newspapers which we have witnessed in recent weeks could open a Pandora's box of severely damaging consequences. Further, this excessive local coverage has caught the attention of the national media with results that can only be detrimental to the York community.

"It appears that the motivation of the local papers extends beyond simply covering the news in a professional, responsible way. Rather it would seem that a strong element of self-aggrandizement is playing a role. Whether or not this is the case, we urge in the strongest terms that for the good of the community and the welfare of its citizens you adopt a far more moderate, balanced approach to the coverage of these unfortunate events."

Charlie Robertson had been arrested within the previous 30 days. The critical letter to the *York Daily Record* and the *York Dispatch* referred to provocative "annual pot stirring" of the riots story every summer. The community was inundated by the recent coverage, the letter stated. "Day after day, column after column, page after page, the events, past and present, are recounted. The same limited set of facts are repeated unrestrainedly, often several times in the same issue. Your pages are filled with rumor, innuendo, intemperate quotations from heavily biased individuals and indiscriminate use of the word riots." The letter also expressed grave concerns about the voluminous and detailed coverage of the grand jury proceedings. It was obvious to me, from the articles I read, that the district attorney's office was leaking the grand jury proceedings, and that the district attorney's office and the local papers were in bed together.

The letter stated, "We believe newspaper coverage has been entirely excessive as well as irresponsible."

Dennis Hetzel was not just another name in print. I considered the *Daily Record's* publisher a friend. We were on press–bar committees together to further an understanding between the two professions. We spoke on the same panels before the Pennsylvania Newspaper Association. I still consider him my friend, but his paper's coverage of the 1969 riots, and especially Charlie Robertson's role, made *Star* magazine read like the *New York Times*.

Instead of taking the constructive criticism from the community leaders' letter, Hetzel fired back an editorial in his own newspaper. He published the critical letter and his reply on the same day, June 4, 2001. His responded with disappointment and total denial, and laid the blame elsewhere.

"There is one other point I feel compelled to make," Hetzel wrote, "because I agree that the newspaper has a role to play in the community beyond reporting a story. The signers of this letter, who are so concerned about negativity, might want to locate the real source of this concern. The negativity isn't coming from the media, it's mainly coming from the Robertson camp and some elements of the business community."

Charlie Robertson's camp? The business community? What the fuck was that all about, Dennis?

§

Stan Hough, former editor and publisher of the *York Dispatch*, had his eye on the big prize—a Pulitzer. Some at the newspaper thought they had a chance, until later—after the tragic events of September 11, 2001.

Eventually, the Pulitzer Prize was on just about everyone's mind. It is the highest, most sought-after, award in journalism. Winning a Pulitzer can be a career-maker. It forever distinguishes a recipient among others in the profession.

Hough was a small-town newspaper guy. He had been assistant managing editor at the *York Dispatch*, but left in 1996 for a stint as top editor at the *Evening Sun* in Hanover, Pennsylvania. He later returned to the *Dispatch* as editor and publisher. He had previously worked at the *Winchester Star* in Virginia.

With salt-and-pepper hair brushed back, Hough was a tyrant in the newsroom and a sight to behold when he was crossed. It was a dictatorship, not a democracy, in the *Dispatch* newsroom. Hough thought nothing of yelling and screaming at editors and reporters. He did not tolerate dissent. He demanded 100 percent loyalty from his troops.

On Saturday, June 2, 2001, the *Sunday News* was ready to go to print with the letter attacking the "riots investigation." It had been leaked to the *Dispatch* earlier in the week. They knew what was coming and they were prepared for it. By their reckoning, no one sends a letter like that to a newspaper and really expects it to be "not for publication."

A reporter had been assigned to write the story. Hough had been interviewed to respond to the charges on behalf of the newspaper. That's commonplace in newsrooms when the paper itself has been accused of something and a story is being prepared. Reading the story on a computer terminal late Saturday, Hough wanted to change one of his own quotes. "That's not what I said," he remarked to Assistant Managing Editor J. P. Kurish. Hough was advised that this story was about him, about directing the coverage, and that he should not go into the story and change his own quote. "I told him to write a letter to the editor," Kurish recalled.

He was taken outside and dressed down by Hough.

To show his impartiality, Hough brought in another editor to read the story about the letter blasting the papers' coverage. The editor, Lori Goodlin, didn't even work at the *Dispatch*. Goodlin was from Hanover where the *Dispatch* had a sister paper.

Goodlin also happened to be Hough's girlfriend, and later became his wife. Goodlin was viewed as honest and even-handed. In the end, she handled the story fairly and Hough's quote was not changed.

Still, to the chagrin of some, Hough's response to being too close to the story was to bring in his girlfriend to edit it—despite the fact that she did the right thing.

From that point on, Hough was believed by many to be "overboard" on the York story, particularly in relation to Robertson. He had been obsessed with finding the killers of Lillie Belle Allen and Officer Schaad, believing that the community collectively had turned away. Earlier, he had assigned three reporters from a staff of 18 to cover the riots investigation full-time. But after the letter from business and political leaders, Hough could not be reasoned with about Robertson or the riots coverage.

Even for the *Dispatch*, however, there was a silver lining in the opposition from community leaders: It could potentially play a key role in the paper's pursuit of the Pulitzer. Eventually, the *Dispatch* could demonstrate to the Pulitzer judges that not only had it broken open 30-year-old murder cases that no one else in the community wanted to deal with—and had taken down the city's mayor to boot—but it also had done so in the face of spirited opposition from business and government leaders. You could not write a better script for a Pulitzer—except that the mayor was innocent and never should have been charged with murder in the first place.

After receiving the community leaders' letter, Hough viewed Robertson as the head of a coiled snake out to get him. It wasn't just Charlie Robertson. It was that damned cabal. It intensified Hough's opposition to the mayor.

At one point, as York's fiscal woes began looking worse, a reporter put together a story saying in essence that it wasn't Robertson's fault. It was the economy, stupid. Other municipalities, and the state of Pennsylvania, were seeing tax revenues lag behind.

It's called a recession.

When the story was proposed at a news meeting, Hough's response was, "Bullshit." Kurish, at the far end of the table, said, "Why don't you read it?" Hough's reply? "We're not running it." That particular story did not run. A revised version ran several weeks later.

On another occasion near the end of Robertson's term, a reporter interviewed the mayor for a look back, with the headline, "Robertson Stands Tall Despite Riots, Budget." Hough went ballistic about the December 30, 2001, story and headline. He later determined that there was nothing wrong with the story. It was the headline that infuriated him. Hough was beyond angry. The editor who wrote the headline was threatened with suspension, but it blew over.

Any way you cut it, this was still a lousy headline. For a reader new to the city (which should always be the standard in editing a story), a quick glance at the headline would suggest there had just been riots.

In another matter, Kurish was suspended for insubordination. He had informed Hough that the general view on staff was that the publisher had lost his objectivity concerning Robertson and the riots. Kurish and Hough, who had once been friends and taken their families to the shore together, made up at first. But Hough stewed about it over the weekend. The following Monday morning in January 2002, Hough told Kurish he was suspended. Three months later he would be fired.

Kurish would eventually file suit against the newspaper.

Kurish, it seemed, had dared to say that the emperor had no clothes.

§

The campaign against Robertson wasn't solely driven by the quest for journalism awards. Nor was it solely political for the DA's office. It was also driven by the career ambitions of journalists and top prosecutors. Maybe, too, it was a bit personal for Tom Kelley, who as a city council member had quarreled with Mayor Robertson. Beneath it all, not just for the newspapers, but also for some young and middle-aged professionals like Kelley who had moved to York from other cities and states, was this question: Was York a progressive city, or was it still the shameful place that had overlooked racial crimes 32 years before? Charlie, while widely popular in the city (he won re-election while facing a near-certain criminal indictment in 2001), was seen by some as a clear link to that racist past.

§

The York newspapers and the DA's office clearly fed off each other. They were working in tandem. After all, they had a common goal.

This was never any clearer to me than when I sent a one-page letter to Judge Emanuel Cassimatis on May 31, 2001, requesting that the court schedule a conference of the prosecutors and all defense attorneys. I made the request in anticipation of a preliminary hearing scheduled for June 25, 2001. "This conference would be to discuss logistics, procedures, 'ground rules,' exhibits, discovery, etc., in an effort to streamline a preliminary hearing with nine defendants represented by nine attorneys," the letter stated. I copied it to the district attorney and all defense lawyers.

I was trying to move the case along and to prevent nightmarish logistics. The court granted the request on June 6. I did not believe a court filing was needed or was appropriate, and I would do it the same way today.

What happened next boggles the mind. Claiming he had never received my letter, District Attorney Rebert, along with Kelley and two other prosecutors, filed a response in court stating that our position sought discussion of the Commonwealth's evidence and exhibits. It also stated that there was no rule calling for a conference before a preliminary hearing. It went on to claim that the defense was "clearly attempting to sidestep the rules of criminal procedure by subterfuge."

In bold, black type large enough to proclaim war, the lead story in the *Dispatch* on June 7, 2001, carried the headline: "'Subterfuge' alleged in riot case." I was taken aback by the story's play and slant. "Accusing one of Mayor Charles Robertson's attorneys of using 'subterfuge' to gain access to information he is not yet entitled to see, county prosecutors are objecting to a court-ordered conference tomorrow for all legal counsel in the case of nine men charged in the 1969 murder of Lillie Belle Allen."

Obviously, I was the lawyer referred to. A casual reader glancing at the first paragraph might think I had broken into the courthouse at night and tried to rifle through the DA's files. It was absurd. The request itself had been what I call a nothing burger.

Judge Cassimatis never responded to the DA's petition.

§

Hough's leadership role in the riots investigation did not go unnoticed. He was awarded the 2001 Ben Franklin Award by the Pennsylvania Newspaper Association. The award was for an individual "who has performed an outstanding service that positively impacts the newspaper industry in Pennsylvania."

Hough was recognized for "his pursuit of an explosive story that started with the commemoration of the 30th anniversary of a race riot and two unsolved murders and ended with the arrest of nine men, including the mayor of York."

Hough and the York newspapers won their awards on Charlie Robertson's back. Hough's reporters did it with a direct pipeline from the DA's office.

The press can be an institution more powerful than government since it affects the thoughts of millions of Americans. It is true reporters can be sued for libel and slander and jailed for refusing to reveal sources in court in some circumstances. But where was the relief for Charlie Robertson? I was gravely concerned that the prejudicial coverage in York would make it impossible to pick a fair jury—"uninfluenced by anything they may have seen, read, or heard."

In June 2001, however, I wasn't that freaked out about it. The reason? I thought I was going to blow out the murder charges against Charlie Robertson before trial because they were baseless. I also thought that the 32-year delay was so prejudicial to all of the accused that we had a good shot at getting the charges dismissed for everybody at a pretrial hearing. If this case ever did go to a trial by jury, we could always move for a change of venue.

At least that's what I thought.

6

TEAM

Rich Oare had done very little criminal defense work in his 30 years of practice, but he was ready to give Charlie Robertson's case his undivided attention. That meant Rich's one-man law practice would suffer indefinitely, and that kind of selflessness is hard to find. Charlie was lucky to have a lawyer, and loyal friend, like that on his defense team.

I know I appreciated Rich's commitment. At 56, he had been practicing law in York since 1976, mostly medical malpractice, and had a lot of street sense. Witnesses had to be found and interviewed, and some would not want to get involved. Over the thirty-two years since the 1969 riots, many potential defense witnesses—25 police officers among them—had died, and the passage of time always clouds memories. The chief investigator for the Pennsylvania State Police assigned to the Lillie Belle Allen case was in the advanced stages of Alzheimer's.

Thirty-two years was a long time. I can't remember what I did, or where I was, or what I said two weeks ago. I know memorable events can leave lasting impressions, but there is a limit, especially when it comes to who said what—exactly what—and when.

Rich had his work cut out for him, but with Charlie's assistance and contacts, he would get it done.

Rich moved with an athlete's grace and he was quicker than hell on his feet. This was a guy I'd be more than happy to share a foxhole with, and that's what we were about to do.

"Here's my thinking," Rich said to me during one of our luncheons at Chaps, a Greek-owned restaurant in York. The restaurant, even at the lunch hour, was dimly lit with candles. The tuxedoed servers were polite, and because all Greeks are cousins, we got a private corner. "There's this lawyer in York who's the godfather of my only daughter Lauren. He's very bright, Bill, and really connected. The judges in York think highly of him. He's the heavyweight with Barley, Snyder, Senft & Cohen, a law firm with 75 lawyers. They have offices located in Harrisburg, Hanover, Chambersburg, York, Lancaster, Reading, and Berlin. He's a big Democrat in York, and resents the Republican district attorney's office bringing this bullshit charge against Charlie to gain political advantage. He wants to be on the defense team, but wants to stay in the background."

Rich had already introduced me to Ellen Wagner, his legal assistant and lover. Deeply committed to Rich, and to Charlie Robertson, she would get stuck with all the thankless work in preparing the case: making phone calls, getting subpoenas, serving subpoenas, typing affidavits, handling correspondence, preparing exhibits, endless photocopying, and retrieving 32-year-old photographs, reports, and newspaper clippings from the archives. Yet Ellen never complained and usually seemed to enjoy it.

This legal assistant of Rich's was a frisky little thing. She had very blonde hair, cut short, with bangs, and could swear when she got mad; actually, she swore even when she wasn't mad. She wore expensive outfits with a provocative touch, and would hang on Rich whenever they were together.

And they were always together.

Ellen insisted on telling everybody that Rich, though 56, had a very young body. She attributed that to his daily tennis workouts, a low-carb diet, and their active life together. Rich never knew how to respond, and would always smile. I didn't know how to respond either.

"You're going to like Rees," Ellen interjected as she ordered her second glass of white Zinfandel wine. "He's about your age, Bill, and a bright son of a bitch. He'll be like a real asset to our defense team."

"Who is it, Rich?" I asked.

"Rees Griffiths," Rich answered. "He's also in a position to raise some serious money, and we're going to need it."

I was willing to take all the help I could get. I knew Rees Griffiths as an adversary from a previous case. He was an excellent lawyer, a

Harvard graduate, and a bright strategist. I wasn't sure what it was going to do to the dynamics of the defense team, something you must be careful about, particularly in high-profile cases. I had seen what happened to the defense team in the O. J. Simpson case. Robert Shapiro wouldn't talk to Johnny Cochran, even during the trial; F. Lee Bailey, the veteran trial lawyer, was given a supporting role; and Barry Scheck, the guru of DNA, was just happy to be there. That team was constantly fighting among themselves, and I didn't want to go there with our line-up.

I had my own team to try a case. Nick Ressetar was my research and writing expert, a Columbia graduate who had been with me since 1985. The trial judges throughout the Commonwealth, and the appellate courts, respected his work.

With good reason.

In 1985, I represented Dr. Jay Smith, who was charged with the murder of Susan Reinert, a suburban Philadelphia high school teacher. She was found jammed into the hatchback of a car, in the fetal position and naked. Her two young children were missing. This notorious case became known as the Main Line Murders, and would grip the nation and become the target of a seven-year investigation by the FBI and the Pennsylvania State Police—the most massive homicide investigation in American history. The media frenzy was attributed in part to the fact that the children could not be found—have never been found—and that Dr. Jay Smith was the principal of Upper Merion High School in the prestigious Philadelphia suburb where Reinert taught.

Jay Smith, who had maintained his innocence from day one, was found guilty of murder in the first degree for each of the deaths and was given three death sentences by a jury of his peers. The prosecution's case was circumstantial, and subsequent to the convictions and death sentences, we learned that the prosecution had intentionally withheld critical physical evidence, which would have resulted in an acquittal.

The Supreme Court of Pennsylvania went ballistic when we argued that the trial was "fixed" by the prosecution, and in an unprecedented legal ruling, the state's highest court set Jay Smith free in September 1992. Three books were published about this case, one by the nationally acclaimed true-crime writer, Joseph Wambaugh, who parlayed his book into a TV miniseries. One of the books was my own—*Principal Suspect: The True Story of Dr. Jay Smith and the Main Line Murders*. Wambaugh's book and the TV miniseries ended with Jay Smith's being put to death; mine ended with his being set free. I liked my book better because it told the whole story—and it was better written.

I argued this case before the Supreme Court, having suffered with it for seven years, to bring about this landmark ruling. The case of *Commonwealth v. Jay Smith* established this precedent: If the prosecution fixes the trial, or engages in egregious prosecutorial misconduct, the Pennsylvania appellate courts will set the defendant free in Pennsylvania—not grant a new trial, but set him free.

Nick Ressetar alone did all the pleadings, creative research, and writing to bring about this result. I haven't been in a library for almost 30 years; I don't know how to research, and never really did. I'm computer illiterate. Though today West Law, a computerized legal research service and database, does much research, in this area of expertise Ressetar is a guru. He makes very few court appearances, but he was my law man and I wasn't going anywhere without him.

Then there was Jayme Emig. I don't know where this kid came from, but she started working for me at the young age of 21; she just walked into my office looking for a job, having graduated with honors from the Central Pennsylvania Business College. She learned how to document a case, no matter how complex, and put it together. There would not be one document in any file, photograph, or exhibit that Jayme could not produce on demand: Before trial, she would memorize the file's contents and could hit on inconsistent statements by witnesses. She would assist in the courtroom at every relevant stage. Jayme knew how to work 20 hours a day at crunch time, and was loyal. Her ability is genuine and is not something you can learn in school. You either have it or you don't, and she had it. I wasn't walking into any courtroom without her.

Rich assured me that I had nothing to worry about. He understood exactly where I was coming from.

Rees Griffiths, as the case moved forward, became truly invaluable, and a trusted friend.

§

The defense request for a common pleas judge to preside over the upcoming preliminary hearing was granted. The Honorable Emanuel A. Cassimatis, a senior judge, would be the sitting judicial authority. The preliminary hearing was going to be held in Courtroom No. 1 in the York County Courthouse, the largest courtroom in the county. And the hearing was going to take place on Monday, June 25, 2001.

The purpose of a preliminary hearing is for a neutral magistrate or judge to determine whether the criminal charges against the accused have a reasonable basis. If so, the charges get bound over for court action, and that means a trial by jury or a plea. If there is no reasonable basis for the charges, then the charges are dismissed. Judge Emanuel A. Cassimatis was capable, I thought, of throwing out the highest-profile case in the history of York at the preliminary hearing.

Naive I'm not, and I had never had a major case thrown out at the preliminary hearing in my 30 years of practice. But this case was different: Charlie Robertson was not on Newberry Street when Lillie Belle Allen was shot; the ammunition he allegedly gave Rick Knouse was not the ammunition that took the life of Lillie Belle Allen; and I didn't think Knouse was going to plead guilty to murder. If Knouse got a sweetheart deal to roll over on Charlie Robertson, he would have to "tweak" his testimony, and that corrupt source could be dealt with.

The prosecution objected to the appointment of a common pleas judge.

Their objection was denied.

The prosecution requested a continuance of the preliminary hearing.

Their request was denied.

I liked the way things were going. I confirmed in my own mind that the allegations against Charlie Robertson as a matter of law did not constitute murder. I contacted John Duke, a professor of criminal law at Yale University, and he and two Yale research interns undertook a computerized search of a national legal database. They, too, concluded that the allegations against Charlie Robertson as a matter of law did not constitute murder.

Rich Oare and Rees Griffiths agreed.

We would have to convince Judge Cassimatis.

7

SHOWTIME

June 25, 2001
York County Courthouse
York, Pennsylvania

At the crack of dawn, media trucks from television stations maneuvered into position in front of the courthouse. The technicians hoisted their broadcast antennas into the air, high above Market Street's colonial lampposts. Reporters also arrived early, and positioned themselves at the front and back entrances—notebooks and tape recorders ready. "It's more dramatic when you have the mayor under indictment," a reporter remarked from WGZ-TV, a Baltimore station.

Shortly before 9:00 a.m., Police Commissioner Herbert Grofcsik cleared a path for Mayor Robertson and Richard Oare to enter the courthouse. Grofcsik had taken an oath to provide for the mayor's safety, and as long as Charlie Robertson was the mayor of York, Grofcsik intended to honor that oath. The local papers wrote scathing editorials about a police commissioner escorting an indicted murderer, but Grofcsik willingly took the hits for his friend. I personally respected Grofcsik, and had never before had a client protected by a police commissioner.

Oare's responsibility was to get Charlie through the crowd with dignity—and "no more news conferences."

One block away, in the conference room of Rees Griffiths's prestigious law offices, we waited: Rees, dressed in a taupe Enzo suit with a gold tie, looked like a corporate lawyer. Jayme Emig, young and beautiful, dressed in a conservative business suit, was my courtroom assistant. She knew where every document was, every newspaper article published in the case, and its content. Earlier that morning, she had taken everything on a dolly to the courthouse through the back door. Jayme also made sure that the well of the courtroom was laid out as previously agreed to between the parties and the court administrator, Robert "Bob" Chuk. The defense lawyers were in the rear of the well, and would be seated with their clients behind a long row of tables; the support staff would sit in the jury box. Charlie Robertson and his three lawyers would be at the far left, closest to the witness stand, and would go first; then Harold Fitzkee for William Ritter; then Pete Solymos and Tom Sponaugle for Bob Messersmith; then Matt Gover for Chauncey Gladfelter; then Frank Arcuri for Art Messersmith; and finally, Joe Metz for Tom Smith.

The district attorneys prosecuting the case at this hearing — Ed Paskey, Tom Kelley, and Tim Barker — had two smaller tables in front of us: one for the three of them, and one for District Attorney Stan Rebert, Bill Graff, and Rodney George.

John Moran was huddling with Kelley and Paskey. His client, Rick Knouse, was waiting nervously in the front row of the gallery. Moran had cut a deal for Knouse; in exchange for Knouse's testimony, the murder charges carrying life would be reduced to conspiracy, with a maximum exposure of $11\frac{1}{2}$ to 23 months in the county jail and the possibility of work release.

Chauncey Gladfelter's deal was like Knouse's.

Greg Neff, through his lawyer Greg Gettle, cut a deal for probation.

The well of the courtroom was crowded, but we would manage. The back of the courtroom was packed, with heightened security in place. Many of the onlookers were African Americans, seated together on the left side of the courtroom; on the right side were the whites. Though the seating was obviously racially divided, there was not a hint of violence looming.

Judge Cassimatis, in black robes, entered the courtroom as his tipstaff banged the gavel and cried out, "This honorable court is now in session."

Everyone in the courtroom stood up; Cassimatis motioned for everyone to sit down and immediately took over. Peering over his wire-rimmed glasses, he issued a series of directives in a stern voice:

Only lawyers and the accused were to be in the well of the court-room; no press, loved ones, onlookers, or spectators were allowed in that area for any reason; and everyone who entered the courtroom would be subjected to metal-detection security devices.

"We understand," Judge Cassimatis added, anticipating the testimony, "emotions may run high during parts of this hearing. It is important, however, that this hearing take place in a civil, dignified, and courteous atmosphere. This is important to the Commonwealth and each of the defendants. In a larger sense, it is also important to the York community that this hearing be perceived to be, as well as actually be, fair and impartial, a hearing conducted in a calm, dignified atmosphere."

Silence consumed the courtroom. Built in 1840, it lacked modern technological amenities. Large, framed oil paintings of York County jurists hung ominously on the high, plastered walls; one of these oil paintings depicted Judge Cassimatis when he was younger, draped in robes, holding a law book. His hair had gotten thin and white, but though he was a senior judge, he was still fit and alert. I liked that politics were behind him, and I hoped he would see this as an opportunity to do the right thing without regard for public perception.

The first order of business was to put on the record the plea agreements of Knouse, Lutzinger, and Neff. He advised each of them that these pleas would be taken under advisement by the court at a later time. The defendants, and their lawyers, stated on the record that they understood what was going on.

I understood exactly what was going on. Testimony was for sale and had just been bought.

At approximately 10:20 a.m., Cassimatis said to the prosecution, "Call your first witness." That went through me like the buzzer when I wrestled in another lifetime. First Assistant District Attorney Tom Kelley stood up and dramatically called his first witness, Luis Mercado.

Luis Antonio Mercado, 73, had been a resident of Newberry Street in 1969. He spoke in broken English, but to me he had credibility. He had no interest in the outcome of the case, and he testified that on Newberry Street in 1969 he sensed violence; he could feel it. That feeling became intense because white youths were running around on the street with guns. Late on the afternoon of July 21 he drove his four children to a relative's house in Columbia, Lancaster County. Returning home, he and his wife sat in the dark of their second-floor bedroom, from which they saw Lillie Belle Allen gunned down by "a storm of bullets from all directions."

I watched Mercado carefully and listened intently. I also watched Tom Kelley do his work, focusing on his ability to do a direct examination as well as on his style and presence. Broad-shouldered and nattily dressed, Kelley cut a good figure in the courtroom. He was confident but may have overestimated his own experience and ability. One of the purposes of a preliminary hearing is for the defense to assess the strengths and weaknesses of both the Commonwealth's case and the prosecutors assigned. This purpose is not addressed in the rules, but a good defense lawyer knows how to maximize the opportunity. He will make objections to questions that he would never object to before a jury, to test the skin of a prosecutor. He will also ask a witness questions that he would never ask in front of a jury, particularly questions he doesn't know the answer to, to get the information.

Mercado was a good Commonwealth witness, and not necessarily harmful to Charlie Robertson.

Tom Kelley wasn't bad, but by the time Mercado was done, I was convinced that Kelley couldn't take a direct hit. I intended to pummel him at the right time. Litigation is a search for truth, but it's also a contact sport.

Assistant District Attorney Ed Paskey stood up to call the prosecution's second witness. Paskey was also a young prosecutor and, like the rest of his team, he was in a blue suit with a matching but odd tie. He was less dramatic and, to me, potentially dangerous because of a deliberate, unemotional, matter-of-fact direct examination. But no matter how good, or bad, you are in the courtroom, it helps when you have a powerful witness. Paskey's first witness, Hattie Mosley Dickson, the sister of Lillie Belle Allen, who was in the car on the night of the shooting, was a powerful witness. She gave testimony that I will remember for a long time.

A York resident, Dickson was 23 years old in 1969, and testified that on the night in question she was driving a 1961 Cadillac to J. M. Fields on Route 30 for groceries after a family fishing trip near Delta, on the outskirts of the city. She testified that there were no roadblocks to interfere with her passage onto North Newberry Street from Philadelphia Street. "The street was not closed," she said.

In the front passenger seat of her Cadillac was her husband. In the back was her sister Lillie Belle Allen, her father, who was a minister from South Carolina, and her mother. It was almost dark, around 9:00 p.m., when her headlights revealed a man leaning from an upstairs house window with a gun in his hands. Dickson panicked and tried to turn around on the railroad tracks, but the street was too narrow. The car stopped, perpendicular to the street, at which time Lillie Belle Allen, 27, offered to take over. When she got out of the car, Allen was hit with a hail of gunfire.

Hattie Dickson relived that night of horror on the witness stand. She could hear the storm of bullets "pinging and banging" the car, and could feel the car rock from the gunfire. Trembling and crying, she described her family's helplessness and fear as they watched Lillie Belle Allen fall to the ground. Her testimony shocked the courtroom.

"We called to Jesus. We prayed to Jesus to come help us," Dickson said.

I just sat there, without visible expression or emotion, but inside I felt the impact. I decided that I was not going to blame the victim, not in this case I wasn't. Dickson didn't mention Charlie Robertson, but her damaging testimony went beyond Newberry Street, and I didn't like it. The only note I jotted down was, "no barricades were up."

Harold Fitzkee and the other defense lawyers had their work cut out for them. He led off, very gently, and did a great job creating the visual idea that the Cadillac appeared to move into a defensive position, and that no shooting took place until after an occupant got out of the car. The defense knew that on July 20, 1969, an identical-looking Cadillac crept up Newberry Street during the daylight hours and stopped, at which time the trunk popped open and an African American with a high-powered rifle opened fire on the residents and their homes.

Tom Sponaugle, on behalf of Bob Messersmith, was excellent. I had never seen him work, but he was soft-spoken and thoroughly prepared.

Matt Gover demonstrated great talent that only years in a courtroom can bring. The defense of the boys on Newberry Street was taking on credibility. These clients had been young, very young, and frightened. They were in the midst of riots, and believed they had the right to defend their homes and loved ones. Their perceptions, though not relevant at the preliminary hearing, would become relevant later. Even with Hattie Dickson on the witness stand, the Commonwealth's charge of murder in the first degree—which requires premeditation, deliberation, and malice aforethought—was in jeopardy.

Frank Arcuri and Joe Metz had little to do by the time it was their turn to cross-examine, but they made their points.

Fred Flickinger was the Commonwealth's third witness of the day, called by Ed Paskey. Flickinger, a former member of the Newberry Street Boys, said members of the gang were on alert from two nights before when rookie York City Police Officer Henry C. Schaad was shot. He then testified about "a white power rally" at Farquhar Park to "discuss" what was happening. According to Flickinger, attending the rally were the Newberry Street Boys and members of other gangs, as well as concerned parents and citizens.

The white street-gang members believed that blacks were going to invade their neighborhood, Flickinger said.

They believed that black gangs had mounted a machine gun on the back of a pickup truck, and that there would be war, he added. That rumor had been flying around York in the midst of the riots.

"Then Officer Charlie Robertson got on the stage at the park, it was like a gazebo," Flickinger testified, "and encouraged us to protect our neighborhood. He encouraged us to look out for each other."

"Robertson then thrust his fist into the air and shouted 'white power,' " Flickinger said, pumping his right arm for the gallery to observe.

I knew all about that rally at Farquhar Park, and Charlie Robertson yelling "white power." Flickinger had testified to that event in 1969 at a civil rights hearing before District Judge William J. Nealon. It was a hearing in federal court that spanned eight days, resulting in 1346 pages of testimony. The suit was brought by African Americans in York who alleged excessive force by police, unreasonable searches and seizures during the riots, and illegal police tactics in black communities or against black people.

Judge Nealon, after touring the embattled York community within weeks of the riots, concluded that the police did not engage in a pattern of racism, antagonism, name calling, or physical abuse. Judge Nealon did note, however, that for Officer Charles Robertson to shout "white power," considering the frenzied state of emotions prevailing at that time, was outrageous and reprehensible.

Charlie Robertson never denied his misconduct on July 20, 1969, at Farquhar Park, a sprawling city park that sat at the top of North Newberry Street. Robertson willingly went to "sensitivity training," provided by the police department after the riots, as did the entire department. He publicly apologized for what he admitted was conduct unbecoming an officer. He would apologize again and again to the public for his misdeed 32 years ago.

That portion of Fred Flickinger's testimony could be dealt with. The affidavit, however, contained a recent embellishment by Flickinger. He proudly recalled another time Robertson had spoken with white street gang members. It happened either the night before or the day of the rally. Flickinger was hanging out on Newberry Street with about five other guys when Robertson pulled up in a patrol car.

"Robertson got out of the car and approached us," Flickinger said. "He again told us to protect our neighborhood and to look out for each other.

Then Flickinger testified that Robertson told them, "If I weren't a cop, I'd be leading commando raids against the niggers in black neighborhoods."

Paskey skillfully let that testimony hang in the air. He made Flickinger repeat it, emphasizing the word "niggers."

To me, Flickinger was enjoying his moment in the sun. He had been flown up from Texas at the expense of the Commonwealth to bask in the glare. His thin hair was slicked over to the side, and he would shift his portly body to give important answers. The time would come, however, when the rays from that sun would burn him.

Flickinger testified under oath before Judge Cassimatis that he had told Judge Nealon the same thing in 1969. He didn't know that I had read the entire 1969 transcript, which included his testimony, and nowhere in that transcript was there any reference to "niggers" or "commando raids." Nick Ressetar was in the process of getting that transcript from the federal archives.

In addition, Flickinger would not be able to identify anybody who could corroborate his recent recollection.

Charlie Robertson showed no emotion during Flickinger's testimony. We communicated in whispers, and he made it clear to me that there would be no corroboration because it never happened. Police officers never patrolled alone, especially during the riots.

I hate liars—especially liars who enjoy themselves in a courtroom.

Paskey knew that the credibility of witnesses was not at issue at a preliminary hearing. I knew that there was still no evidence that Charlie Robertson had anything to do with the death of Lillie Belle Allen. The media was going to have a lot of fun with Flickinger's testimony, and would put his photograph on the front page. I would learn later that the *York Daily Record* had something to do with Flickinger's embellishment.

Gary Holtzapple, Paskey's next witness, was 17 years old in 1969, and a member of the Yorklyn Boys. The Yorklyn Boys, a white gang from the east side of York, had joined the Newberry Street Boys to defend their area on the night in question. Yes, he was there when

Lillie Belle Allen was killed. He had gone there with Tom Smith, who carried a single-shot .30-30-caliber rifle.

Holtzapple told Judge Cassimatis that when the white Cadillac pulled sideways, "I honestly thought that she [Allen] was getting out of the car to get prepared to attack. I really wasn't sure. I thought she was going to pull a weapon out of the car. That's what it looked like to me. I thought these people were attacking, and they were going to firebomb us, and I didn't want to be stuck in the house with it being on fire, so I left the premises."

When the shooting stopped, the streetlights had been shot out, and Holtzapple testified that an unidentified male boasted, "I blew her right out of her sneakers."

The final witness of the day was Detective Rodney George. George, a detective with the district attorney's office since 1998, was the affiant; he was the one who had brought the charges against everybody, including Charlie Robertson. He testified briefly to several facts: Charlie Robertson was a police officer in 1969; the killing of Officer Henry Schaad was "disturbing" to Charlie; and Robertson testified before the grand jury. Charlie was asked whether he was in possession of .30-06 ammunition during the riots, and Robertson said yes.

Rodney George, like everybody else on the prosecution team, had gotten caught up in the media swirl. All detectives dream of cracking big cases, and without a doubt this case could make him a star. He looked and played the part—husky and handsome, with calculated answers—but he and I had different agendas.

Charlie Robertson, who had been passive the entire day, whispered to me, "He wasn't even born when all of this was going on."

§

June 26, 2001
York County Courthouse
Day Two of Preliminary Hearing

Ed Paskey had already given me a heads up; Rick Knouse was going to be his first witness. The day before, Knouse had already told Judge Cassimatis that he was going to testify for the prosecution pursuant to a plea agreement. He acknowledged having been a patient at the York Hospital for seven or eight days within the previous two weeks, because of post-traumatic stress, and said that the rehashing of all this caused him to think about suicide. Yes, he said, he was on medication but his mind was clear.

I dreaded what was coming.

The affidavit charging Robertson with murder alleged that he had handed Knouse .30-06 ammunition and told him to "kill as many niggers as you can." This took place, according to Knouse, on the day Lillie Belle Allen was killed. This exchange and directive took place, according to Knouse, by the railroad crossing on Newberry Street.

Knouse's sweetheart deal depended on his testimony. "Credibility is not an issue at the preliminary hearing," Paskey would assert. "The only issue is whether accepting his testimony as true, there is a prima facie case of homicide by defendant Robertson."

Well, Rick Knouse said what was in the affidavit.

He testified that he was 16 years old in 1969, and a member of the Girarders, another white gang. He testified that he was on Newberry Street on July 21, 1969, before dusk, and that approximately four to five uniformed police officers approached him. The only one he could identify was Charlie Robertson. He stated that Robertson called him "Knousie" and that Robertson "threw a box of shells— .30-06—and said, kill as many niggers as you can."

"Can you use the precise language that Officer Robertson said as he threw the shells?" Paskey asked, to drive his point into the heart of the court.

"Niggers," Knouse answered.

"Kill as many niggers as you can?" Paskey asked for the third time.

"Yes," Knouse answered, for the third time.

Knouse told Judge Cassimatis that he felt Charlie Robertson had given him "a license to kill."

A lifetime of drug addiction and alcohol abuse had taken its toll on Knouse. He had told the authorities that he had passed out for three days immediately after Lillie Belle Allen was killed. His drugs of choice for years were LSD and crank, powerful hallucinogenic chemicals. Though not yet 50, his gaunt face, frail body, and sparse hair in a tight, short ponytail made him look very old.

Yet, Knouse was no dummy. He had gone to the school of hard knocks and was a survivor. I did not believe he was mentally ill, or considering suicide. I did believe that he would sell his soul to stay out of jail.

Knouse had been in and out of prison, and knew how the plea-bargain game was played. The fundamental rule of thumb is the more you give the prosecution, the more you get in return. With minimal prodding by Paskey on direct examination, Knouse pointed the finger at Bob Messersmith and implicated him as a shooter; then at Art Messersmith and implicated him; and finally at Chauncey Gladfelter and implicated him. "The shooting at the car was like a scene out of the Bonnie and Clyde movie," Knouse said.

The defense lawyers then went to work like piranhas.

"Yes," Knouse said on cross examination, "we thought we needed to defend ourselves and our homes . . . I was there when a similar white Cadillac opened fire from the trunk . . . I know I was scared . . . I thought I saw fire coming from the hands of Lillie Belle Allen . . . I thought Lillie Belle Allen was shooting at us and that's what I told the police."

"No," Knouse said, "I didn't kill anybody . . . I didn't even fire at Lillie Belle Allen."

The prosecution acknowledged, on the record, that Lillie Belle Allen was killed by a 12-gauge shotgun slug, not a .30-06 round.

The prosecution also acknowledged, on the record, that Charlie Robertson was not on Newberry Street when Lillie Belle Allen was killed.

These "stipulations" were not out of kindness. The autopsy report, and the ballistic analysis, confirmed the cause and manner of death; and three police officers were prepared to testify under oath that Charlie Robertson was with them on the night in question, assigned to an armored vehicle known as "Big Al."

Nevertheless, the prosecution was on a roll—at least with the media, who were frantically writing as Knouse testified. The artist's sketches of Knouse and the prosecutors at their table would be the visual tease on the televised news.

Then Tom Kelley took over, and witness after witness testified that the Newberry Street Boys and others from the Girarders and Yorklyns felt they were on Newberry Street to thwart another racist attack. Hours before, or the day before Allen was shot to death beside her white Cadillac, another white Cadillac with a gunman hiding in the trunk made its way onto Newberry Street through an alley and opened fire.

Yes, they said, they felt they had been given the OK from the York police to defend their neighborhood with bloodshed if necessary.

Greg Neff, a Girarder, had cut the sweetest deal. Though he was charged with murder in the first degree, and was an alleged shooter, the prosecution agreed in writing to reduced charges and probation "in exchange for his truthful testimony." Neff, dressed in a sport coat, implicated Bob Messersmith as an organizer and shooter. Neff's testimony alone was enough to take Bob down, along with others at the defense table who shot at the car. That's assuming the boys had no defense.

Neff, repeating what he had told the grand jury on a previous occasion, a proceeding conducted by Tom Kelley, seemed to startle Kelley when he testified that Lillie Belle Allen leaned over the trunk of her car and pointed a gun up the street.

"You saw a gun in her hand?" Kelley asked, incredulous, thinking the deal for probation would have made the gun go away.

"Yes," Neff answered.

"You are absolutely sure of that?" Kelley fired back.

"I believed it to be a gun in her hand," Neff replied.

"So, are you saying you didn't see a gun in her hand, but you believed that she had a gun in her hands?" Kelley asked in another way, sensing an opening.

"I believe it was a bluish handgun, yes," Neff answered, unwavering.

"I have nothing further of this witness at this time, Your Honor," Kelley said, angry and frustrated. Kelley had just taken a hit, and was visibly shaken. He would make sure that Greg Neff would pay.

§

June 27, 2001
York County Courthouse
Day Three of Preliminary Hearing

A typical preliminary hearing, even in murder cases, takes a couple of hours. The threshold of proof for the district attorney's office to get a case bound over for court action is minimal. All testimony, prosecution or defense, must "be viewed in a light most favorable to the Commonwealth." The credibility of prosecution witnesses is not at issue.

We were into our third day of testimony when Kelley recalled Detective George to implicate William Ritter. According to George,

Ritter told the grand jury that he was on Gay Street when the shooting started on Newberry Street. Ritter said he ran home, got a .22-caliber rifle, and fired six shots in the direction of the car from the North Penn Street Bridge, 225 yards away.

"That's a hell of a long shot for a .22," Fitzkee whispered to me, incredulous that his client could be charged with murder on that testimony.

Kelley huddled with Ed Paskey and Tim Barker before announcing, "we rest."

Prosecutors in the Lillie Belle Allen case were satisfied that they had met their burden against the six remaining defendants. They were confident that Judge Cassimatis would not dismiss the charges against anybody.

Normally, getting a case bound over is a slam dunk, a rubber-stamp process.

Senior Judge Cassimatis, however, requested the submission of legal briefs before he would decide, and agreed to hear oral arguments on Monday, July 2, 2001, at 9:00 a.m.

8

GAVEL

Rees Griffiths's law office, less than a block from the York County Courthouse, was once the Bank of York. The enormous steel vault was still in place on the first floor, and the balconied second floor had a powerful look. It still had the feel of an affluent bank, with granite floors, oriental rugs, and expansive corridors. The conference room on the first floor became our "war room," and Rees possessed a wealth of combat intelligence.

I never saw Rees in casual clothes at the office. He always wore a two-piece suit, tie, and expensive leather shoes. He and Rich Oare, when they got together, were a trip; they had a special relationship, and constantly argued about money in the account and the media war that Rich was losing. Rich would remind Rees that he was in the case because of him. I referred to them as "brothers," and that made them both crazy.

The "brothers" loved each other, and were serious about the Robertson case. We spent hours together in the conference room— often with Charlie, often not—discussing the strength of the Commonwealth's case, analyzing our defense, and assessing the constant media assault. I was very interested in knowing what they thought about Judge Cassimatis, Judge Uhler, Stan Rebert, Tom Kelley, Ed Paskey, and Tim Barker.

In five days we would be presenting our closing argument to Judge Cassimatis. Rees could not see any causal connection between

Charlie's alleged actions and the death of Lillie Belle Allen. We had all been taught in law school that there must be causation.

"In other words, Bill," Rees said, "even in a light most favorable to the Commonwealth, and even though this was only a preliminary hearing, Charlie didn't do anything that can be connected to her death. The victim was killed because the shooters thought the other white Cadillac was back, the one from the day before. They didn't shoot until the car appeared to stop in a defensive position, and then only after Lillie Belle Allen got out waving her arms. Knouse thought she was shooting, Neff thought she was shooting. She wasn't shot because she was African American. She certainly wasn't shot because of Charlie Robertson."

In addition, it was inconceivable to him that a murder charge against the mayor was even brought. There was nothing to connect the mayor to the shooting. Though Charlie was accused of distributing .30-06 shells and provoking the shooting, only one witness claimed the mayor provided .30-06 shells to him. That witness was a corrupt source and was uncorroborated. Even the prosecution conceded that the .30-06 shells did not kill or injure Lillie Belle Allen, and weren't even fired at her. There was no evidence that whoever shot at the victim heard anything the mayor was supposed to have said, much less was influenced by it.

To Rees, the prosecution's duty to seek truth and justice didn't mean a damn. They chose to charge the mayor on an unprecedented theory of incitement, and to convict him they would play the race card. The preliminary hearing focused on racism in the police force, by then Officer Charlie Robertson, and among the white gangs. By portraying Lillie Belle Allen as the innocent victim of a race murder, the prosecution sought to stir public outrage within a city responsible for its troubled racial history. They hoped, without evidence, that Judge Cassimatis would bind the case over to repudiate the perception of institutional racism.

§

Monday, July 1, 2001

At 8:45 a.m., Police Commissioner Herbert Grofcsik escorted Charlie through the crush of media and surprised everybody when he pulled out a prepared statement. He scolded the press for destroying the mayor's reputation. "Individuals with their own agendas have found a way to subvert the will of the people who elected the mayor to run for a third term," Grofcsik said. "They have found a way to have him deposed and exiled from his position of leadership. They have, unfortunately, changed the course of history."

The individuals with their own agendas to whom Grofcsik was referring were the prosecutors, and, in particular, Tom Kelley. Grofcsik knew all about the venomous local politics. He firmly believed that Tom Kelley, who was the mayor's only Republican opponent on York City Council, had initiated the murder charges. Kelley's public attacks were vicious, to the point that he proposed the appointment of "independent counsel" to investigate Robertson when the mayor vetoed one of Kelley's proposed ordinances. Grofcsik had written correspondence from Tom Kelley, berating and criticizing the mayor, and threatening correspondence from Kelley on the stationery of the district attorney's office of York.

Dirty politics are tolerated everywhere, but for one's political opponent to be one's prosecutor outraged Grofcsik.

I liked Herbert Grofcsik, and always will. It took a lot of courage for the police commissioner of York to go after the district attorney's office of York.

Inside the courtroom, the defense closing arguments were presented to Judge Cassimatis. Rees and I went first, arguing what we discussed in his conference room. Nick Ressetar had provided to the judge a 43-page brief setting forth our legal authority. It was a compelling legal treatise supporting a dismissal of the mayor's murder charges.

Harold Fitzkee, York County's former district attorney, sought the dismissal of William Ritter's charges by asserting selective prosecution. Pete Solymos, for Bob Messersmith, argued the shooting was in self-defense, or in the defense of others, and the law recognized that defense even if the boys were mistaken in their belief. Matt Gover, for Chauncey Gladfelter, said the prosecution apparently decided to charge anyone who had taken up arms and had fired at Allen's car that night. That theory of murder, Gover stressed, could have been pursued 32 years earlier, but wasn't. Frank Arcuri, arguing for Art Messersmith, said that "if the prosecution's case was a skating pond, we would have to erect a sign that says Danger: Thin Ice." Joe Metz stressed that the riots had instilled a sense of fear and chaos in everyone, and that we should not pass judgment on their actions of self-defense under the circumstances.

Deputy District Attorney Tim Barker finally got his opportunity to be heard. Tim was a 1991 Dickinson College graduate who had completed law school in 1994; to me, he was a very young prosecutor. He perceived himself as knowledgeable in the law, intellectual, and bright. He approached the podium to address Judge Cassimatis—supported by much paperwork, many cases, and the confidence prosecutors have at a preliminary hearing. His thin black beard evidenced his youthfulness, as well as his intellectual self-image.

Barker spoke clearly, like a debater in a competition, and reminded Judge Cassimatis that "credibility is not an issue at a preliminary hearing, and yet, the defense invites you to suspend and overrule established law."

Barker said the sum of the testimony—witnesses who described the kind of weapon and ammunition Bob Messersmith had fired that night and who saw Messersmith shoot at Allen's car—could lead the judge to conclude that Bob Messersmith had fired the fatal shot.

Barker also described the evidence that could lead the judge to believe that the other defendants were "principals" or "accessories" in the Allen murder. The other defendants—Art Messersmith, Chauncey Gladfelter, Thomas Smith, William Ritter, and Robertson—were culpable in the murder because, he claimed, they collectively participated in a series of events that resulted in Allen's death.

Barker said that Robertson had incited the crowd and provided Knouse with ammunition. Knouse believed that Robertson had given him and others on the street a license to kill—something that Barker asserted negates the claim of self-defense: "Not a license to protect. Not a license to defend. A license to kill."

Then Barker turned around and dramatically pointed his finger at Charlie Robertson.

"He is a co-conspirator," Barker charged, raising his voice. "He is a murderer!"

Charlie Robertson stiffened, clenching his huge fists, controlling his inner rage. He was stoic throughout the entire preliminary hearing and the many closing arguments. He listened to Knouse's lies and Flickinger's imagined recollection. He had dealt with his arrest and the humiliation of handcuffs. As a police officer, he had been called a fucking pig many times, had been spat at and accosted. For Barker to point his finger at him and call him a murderer was more than Charlie could take.

"He's just a spoiled brat out of school having fun," Charlie said to me. "I feel like smacking the shit out of him for calling me a murderer. I had nothing to do with Lillie Belle Allen's death and that little punk knows it."

Barker had no idea how close he came to getting knocked on his ass.

Deputies escorted Robertson into a car that was waiting at the rear of the courthouse. I went with them to make sure Charlie didn't stop at the DA's office on the way.

§

Tuesday, July 2, 2001

York County Senior Judge Emanuel Cassimatis took the bench at 9:00 a.m. to announce whether he believed enough evidence had been presented to order Mayor Charlie Robertson and five other men to stand trial in the 1969 death of Lillie Belle Allen.

Everybody sat motionless in the well of the courtroom. I was convinced the other five defendants would be bound over for trial. I could only hope, and pray, that Charlie Robertson's nightmare would come to an end. The evidence against him just wasn't there, not for murder it wasn't. Cassimatis had mentioned on day one of the preliminary hearing that the perception of justice was important to him — and that worried me.

Two uniformed sheriffs closed the massive doors in the back of Courtroom 1. Four other deputy sheriffs positioned themselves in the aisles. Silence set in, adding to the tension.

"This is the time for announcing my decision in this preliminary hearing involving Chauncey Gladfelter, Arthur Messersmith, Robert Nelson Messersmith, William Ritter, Charles Robertson, and Thomas Smith," Judge Cassimatis began, and I immediately noted that the order was alphabetical, consistent with the caption.

Then Judge Cassimatis, in a rote, steady voice, explained that the purpose of a preliminary hearing was not to determine guilt or innocence, but to determine whether the Commonwealth had established a prima facie case. His explanation of a preliminary hearing offered more detail, but made no mention of dismissing charges.

"In the case of Chauncey Gladfelter, we find that the Commonwealth has established a prima facie case and direct that he be held for court," the judge said, and continued.

"In the case of Arthur Messersmith, we find that the Commonwealth has established a prima facie case and direct that he be held for court."

"In the case of Robert Nelson Messersmith, we find that the Commonwealth has established a prima facie case and direct that he be held for court."

"In the case of William Ritter, we find that the Commonwealth has established a prima facie case and direct that he be held for court."

"In the case of Charles Robertson, we find that the Commonwealth has established a prima facie case and direct that he be held for court."

"In the case of Thomas Smith, we find that the Commonwealth has established a prima facie case and direct that he be held for court."

And that was it; that's all there was to it. Mayor Charlie Robertson was going to trial on murder charges.

When the judge announced that Charlie Robertson was being held over for court action, I showed no emotion, but was truly upset.

9

MAYOR

Charlie Robertson, though bound over for court action by Judge Cassimatis, was in a hurry to get back to City Hall. He told the pesky reporters that he was innocent, he wasn't worried, and he really had to be going. "I'm still the mayor," he said, "and there's much to do to keep this great city progressing. I'm a little behind schedule because of this hearing, especially with the Board of Parks and Recreation. We have 23 parks in York and seven recreational facilities."

Several reporters were aghast. Charlie had just been bound over on murder charges and he was worried about the Board of Parks and Recreation.

Outside, the scorching July sun was baking the city, but it was still a beautiful day to Charlie. The short walk from the courthouse to City Hall would give him a chance to collect his thoughts. It was important for a mayor to be seen by the people of his city—standing tall and staying strong. Charlie instinctively straightened his tie, made sure the white-rose lapel pin was secure on his suit jacket, and headed for George Street. He did notice, with some annoyance, that several reporters were interviewing Leo Cooper—president of the York chapter of the NAACP—on the courthouse steps. Charlie overheard Leo say, "City Council, if it takes its responsibility to represent its residents seriously, should join us in asking for Robertson and Grofcsik to resign."

Grofcsik wasn't resigning, not for Leo Cooper or anybody else. He would remain as the police commissioner of York until Charlie's term expired in six more months.

And nobody was going to make Charlie Robertson resign his position as the honorable mayor of York.

Nobody!

He had resigned as the Democratic Party's nominee for the general election in 2001. He felt pressured into it by his supposed loyal confidants and some elected officials. He felt betrayed.

But resign outright as mayor?

Never!

Charlie Robertson had spent a lifetime pursuing that ambition. He had walked the streets of York as a police officer for 29 years, getting to know everybody. He shook a lot of hands, kissed a lot of babies, and gave talks at the many schools in the city. He refereed a lot of ball games, coached a lot of teams, and loved every minute of it. Charlie served for a decade on the city school board, the same school board that had employed his father. He became mayor the old-fashioned way, with minimal funding and damn little party support. He was both a natural politician—a gifted schmoozer—and an unnatural one, in that he placed public service first. He was a Democrat in a Republican county and he kicked their asses at the polls. The people of York just weeks earlier gave him the nod in a hotly contested primary. He was sorry he had withdrawn from that race on the advice of Charlie Bacas and his boys.

Charlie Robertson had come a long way. The son of a school janitor, Charlie and his five brothers worked each summer as caddies at a golf course for the money to heat their house during the winter. An average student, he graduated from William Penn Senior High School in 1952. But there was no money for college. His father, Milford "Hap" Robertson, died of a heart attack the day his retirement papers arrived in the mail. Hap Robertson had at times juggled three jobs to make ends meet.

It was difficult after high school for Charlie to find his niche. At the tail end of the Korean War, he worked at the Naval Ordinance Plant, but was laid off after about a year. Charlie then worked as a custodian in the city school district—like his dad—until he was drafted into the army. He served a two-year stint, through 1958, as a medic. He didn't volunteer to be a medic. He accepted the duty assigned to him. After his discharge from the army, he returned to his job in the school district, working as a "floater" custodian in the junior and senior high schools. In 1962, at age 28, Charlie found himself when he landed a job in the York City Police Department. He would serve briefly as sergeant, and, in the 1970s, as a detective.

Charlie acknowledged having been a racist at times in his life. In 1949, when his father was returning home from one of his jobs, as a doorman at the Dutch Club, three black men jumped him and robbed him of his $18 pay. Charlie was 15 when his father was mugged on the West College Avenue Bridge. His dad came home battered and bruised, according to Robertson, and he and his brothers wanted to take up arms. It had a lasting impact on Charlie Robertson. It was not an excuse. It's the way it was.

By the time he got to City Hall on July 2, 2001 — knowing he would likely face trial for murder — there were wellwishers on the steps waiting to welcome him home. TV cameramen, who had followed him there, got footage of Charlie signing autographs before entering his castle. Others shook his hand and patted him on the back, reassuring him that the charges were bullshit and nothing but dirty politics. Inside, other city workers — wary of the camera exposure — greeted him warmly as he walked the corridors to his stately office.

"Good to have you back," Helen Rohrbaugh said cheerfully as Charlie walked into his outer office. Helen was a high-school classmate and a lifelong friend.

"Glad to be back, Helen," Charlie answered, a little weary and perspiring from the walk back. The air conditioning in his office, which Helen kept on high, was always a welcome relief.

When Charlie became mayor in 1994, Helen became his receptionist. Especially during the troubled period immediately after his arrest, Helen Rohrbaugh was his trusted gatekeeper — fending off the deluge of York reporters, screening calls and relaying messages to Rich Oare. Her service was invaluable. With his life and reputation on the line, he needed a steady friend at the gate, just a few feet from the mayor's office. Rich eventually ran all media calls through his office with Ellen Wagner handling the deluge. It lightened the load on Helen. Because of the relentless barrage of calls, Rich also gave Charlie a cell phone so he could stay in constant touch with his lawyers. The initial media wave had been incredible. Oare would joke that Connie Chung called his house so often, his daughter was getting to know her.

On this steamy July day, the mail and phone messages for Charlie were again piled high on his desk. It was just two days' worth. His stack of phone messages was as thick as a deck of cards.

Most people don't understand how much responsibility falls on the shoulders of the mayor of York. It's not just cutting ribbons at groundbreaking ceremonies, handing out $25 gift certificates to city employees, or showing up at two-alarm fires in the middle of the night.

York, 60 miles north of Baltimore, is no small town; at least the problems that have to be dealt with are "big-city" problems. Urban housing, employment (thank God for the local Harley-Davidson plant), economic development, and maintaining racial tranquility in a city with many minorities are always at the top of the list. Charlie often wished that York's police officers were trained in Philadelphia rather than at the Harrisburg Area Community College.

The city's budget for 2001 was $59,691,047. Running a community for over 40,000 people requires road and park maintenance, snow removal, sanitation, economic development, police and fire protection, and much, much more. These municipal responsibilities are serious business, and don't just happen on their own.

Charlie Robertson, who had been mayor for eight years, came up with a fine organization. He appointed capable "project directors," who were required to meet with him every Monday morning at 9:00 a.m. — on time. . . in his office . . . without fail. . . no excuses. His project directors were responsible for the efficient management of their departments, but the buck stopped with Mayor Charlie Robertson.

Charlie's business administrator was Mike O'Rourke, who knew how to crunch numbers when the need arose. His economic director was Andrew Dale, assigned to revitalizing the city by bringing in business and industry. Chief John Senft, who headed the fire department, had been one hell of a firefighter. The mayor was close to getting a minor league baseball team and a brand new stadium for the city of York; it was Charlie's idea, and his dream.

Then there was the department of highways, sewer, and sanitation. Maintaining the road system — which included immediate snow removal whenever Pennsylvania's winter storms hit, sometimes unexpectedly and contrary to the weather-reporting gurus — was a huge and costly responsibility. The upkeep of sanitation and the sewer lines added to the stress of this department.

Finally, yet another department oversaw 23 parks and 7 recreation areas, not only to help beautify York, but also to avoid negligence claims. This department had a special place in Charlie's heart because he loved sports and leisure activities, and many youths in the city of York depended on its efforts.

Four hundred city employees were on the payroll. There were five labor unions representing city workers. Charlie felt personally responsible for the well-being of the employees, and because he was sympathetic to working people, he welcomed legitimate complaints from their unions. Charlie was a Democrat by registration, but believed that he was at heart neither a Democrat nor a Republican, but one of the common folk. The slogan he liked to use in his campaigns was: "He's one of us."

His philosophy on government, encompassed in the "Mayor's Vision Statement for 2001," spoke of increasing customer satisfaction; continuing to provide safer, healthier streets and neighborhoods; and giving "people their money's worth from city government." Ironically, in the year of his arrest on murder charges, his vision statement emphasized the need to "enhance and extend a positive image of the City of York through our actions and statements." Charlie Robertson continued trying to improve that image. He wasn't the one tearing it down.

For the preceding eight years, the city had been well run. By most accounts, that was not in dispute.

§

In the legal arena, Charlie Robertson left all the strategy decisions to his attorneys, never second-guessed anything, and really seemed OK at times. It was truly remarkable. I was curious about his ability—his inner strength—to deal with pending murder charges. After all, he was 68 years old, lived alone, and had given York his entire life. He was not a complicated man; Charlie kept his feelings, thoughts, and emotions to himself. He did not deserve the horrendous card that life had dealt him, and I was concerned.

Charlie and I became friends. It's dangerous for a lawyer to become close to a client, especially one who is facing a mandatory or long-term jail sentence. It gets worse emotionally if you truly believe in your client's innocence, worse yet if the prosecution is legally and morally bereft. Friendship can interfere with objective judgment calls, strategy, and decision making. It's the quickest road for a defense lawyer to get fried.

I was told in law school by Dean Lou Manderino, who went on to become a Pennsylvania Supreme Court Justice, that the average life expectancy of a trial lawyer is ten years; not that you perish after ten years, but that you can't do it anymore—you "burn out." The stress is a killer, and accelerates your death if you have a tendency to get close to your client on a personal level. I was taught that truth 30 years ago, and I was on borrowed time. Maybe I should have listened.

"How do you deal with what's happening to you, Charlie?" I asked him, wanting to know how he coped, during a personal interview with him at his kitchen table. His small home, a modest, gray-shingled, three-story row house at 828 Princess Street, is where he was born in 1934. The house was built in 1906, but new, lighter-gray siding gave the exterior a fresh appearance. From the front door, a darkened hallway led to his living room and kitchen. A "Miller Lite" clock hung on one wall of the kitchen. The room was a time capsule from 1967, the last year it was remodeled. A post-it note hung on one of his cupboards, in Charlie's scribbled handwriting: "Do Not Talk To Anyone About The Case." In his living room, the walls revealed a light orange-colored wood framework, which Charlie thought was part of the original structure. His place was not unkempt, but most of the furniture was old and worn. A reddish-orange shag carpet covered the living room floor, and framed pictures of his American Legion baseball teams and his basketball teams, year by year, lined the walls. "I'm innocent," Charlie told me, "and knowing that helps, no matter what happens to me. I know that I yelled, 'white power' at Farquhar Park, but that's all I did. I still can't believe that I've been charged with murder. I honestly thought, when my name kept coming up in the papers in connection with the grand jury investigation . . . and then when I got subpoenaed to appear before the grand jury . . . that I might get charged with disorderly conduct or conduct unbecoming a police officer."

I knew that the district attorney's office of York could not have charged him with disorderly conduct, or conduct unbecoming a police officer, or just about any other crime in the crimes code. The statute of limitations had run out on almost everything, including conspiracy to commit murder, which had expired in 1973.

Only for the crime of murder—which is the intentional, malicious killing of another human being—is there no statute of limitations. The fuckers charged him with murder—knowing that it wasn't murder—because it was the only way to get him into the case.

"But what I'm asking, Charlie, is now that you've been charged with murder, how do you deal with it? My interest is personal, has nothing to do with defending you." I asked again because I wanted to know.

"I don't know how to answer that, Bill," Charlie replied, then paused for a long minute before continuing. "I'm concerned about the murder charges, of course, really concerned; but I'm more angry at the DA's office for doing this to me than worried. I'm also upset with the local papers, and people that I thought were my friends that walk the other way when they see me. I . . . uh . . . I just don't know . . . ."

"What I can tell you, Charlie," I said when he seemed to falter, "is that I think you have a lot of inner strength under the circumstances."

"You have to stay strong, Bill," Charlie responded, coming back to me, seemingly from another zone. "It's hard at times, but you have to. You have to stand tall, especially when you're down, or you'll never get up. All I can tell you, when I get really down, is I remind myself that I'm innocent."

I had noticed, and continued to notice, that Charlie would sometimes lose his train of thought. He would either not finish his sentence or seem to drift off into the past. He also seemed to have difficulty focusing on a particular question, even the most innocuous inquiry. He would apologize, realizing my concern, and tell me that it was probably "a senior moment."

Will he be able to take the witness stand if I need him to?

§

August 31, 2001
Yorktowne Hotel

The lobby of the Yorktowne Hotel was abuzz with people dressed in their Sunday best, laughing and shaking hands. A huge, muscular African American man, with a clean-shaven head, was directing everybody up a winding stairwell to the second-floor ballroom; he looked like an NFL lineman, with a big diamond in his left ear. I liked his look and assumed he was a bodyguard.

My wife, Jill, was also dressed for the occasion in a calf-length, pearlized dress. She had had her hair done earlier by Johnny Mathis's hairdresser—an updated shag, forever blonde. Jill is almost ten years younger than I am, but that night the age difference widened. She noticed the bodyguard's oval-cut diamond and liked it; she guessed it to be almost two carats.

We were Mayor Charlie Robertson's guests at a formal dinner at York's prestigious but old-time center city hotel, in honor of Chantel

Tremitiere. Chantel, a beautiful African American woman, was a graduate of York High School and an awesome basketball player. She went on to play for Auburn University as point guard and excelled at that famous Alabama school, taking them to the Final Four. She rarely turned the ball over, was lightning fast, and had a killer three-point shot. She went on to become one of York's first females to be recruited by the National Women's Basketball Association.

Charlie Robertson was there at Chantel's invitation. Chantel's father served with Charlie on the York City School Board. Charlie recalled that he had flown out to the West Coast to watch Chantel play in the Final Four. Before the game, while warming up, she recognized him and came over to give him a hug and talk to him.

This was Chantel's night. She sponsored the dinner in an effort to ease racial tension in the city. Chantel specifically had asked Charlie to come. She had made many of the invitations from the mayor's office.

The flash of cameras lit up the second floor. Chantel was posing with admirers in the lobby. Jill insisted that we get in line to get an autographed picture for Callista. Callista was our youngest daughter, a junior at West Perry High School in Perry County, and a good basketball player in her own right. Jill knew, and I agreed, that Callista would love an autographed picture of Chantel to show her friends.

The evening was a lot of fun, and everybody was very friendly. About 250 people attended, most of them African Americans. Jill and I sat at a table of eight with Charlie Robertson, several of his office employees, and Alex Chhum. We were introduced to Alex by Charlie, and were told that Charlie was his "father"—not his biological father, but his father nevertheless. It was in the cafeteria of York's middle school that Charlie had met Alex Chhum, then a 14-year-old Cambodian refugee who had been having family problems. The troubled Alex ended up moving into Robertson's home, and Charlie became his legal guardian and raised him. Chhum was now 31, married, with two children and a stepchild. Every Wednesday night, Charlie had dinner with his son and beloved grandchildren.

Throughout the evening, everybody was coming over to our table to shake Charlie's hand, offering their prayers and wishing him well. Many of those wellwishers, recognizing me from the local media photos and footage, asked me to please "take care of Charlie . . . don't let anything happen to him."

"People make me feel better," Charlie said, and got teary-eyed before going back to his dinner after another guest came across the room to shake his hand, promising to pray for him.

Alex looked at me with deep concern for his father.

Jill felt bad when she saw Charlie's tears.

"Are you OK?" I asked Charlie quietly to avoid drawing attention, putting my hand on his shoulder.

"Yeah," Charlie said, nodding his head.

After a few moments, to break an awkward silence, I jokingly asked Charlie if he had had any more news interviews with Rich, especially with the national boys.

"As a matter of fact," Charlie answered, smiling, "I have an advance copy of a piece in the *New York Times Magazine* that will be on the stands in a couple of days. The guy that did the piece is William Bunch, a real nice guy that came to a baseball game I was watching in Mount Wolf, and then came to my house. I kind of liked the guy, and he didn't treat me too bad."

I had to laugh, for it was vintage Charlie. But another national piece this soon after his arrest made me nervous. I intended to call Rich Oare for the details and then put it out of my mind.

Chantel's speech was beautiful and touching. She knew what the situation was in York at that hour. The hotel was right next to the courthouse. She expressed her love for Charlie Robertson and asked that the people of York, black and white, stay strong to get through this challenge. Chantel Tremitiere was a class act, and she did a lot for the community that night, and it certainly meant a lot to Charlie.

Before the evening ended, Charlie went to the podium after being introduced, and gave Chantel "the keys of the city." That act of kindness and recognition generated heartfelt applause.

I was proud of Chantel, Charlie, and the people of York.

The whole thing seemed bizarre. Charlie Robertson was charged with the murder of an innocent African American woman during the York riots of '69, and here hundreds of African Americans and whites were singing his praises and praying for him publicly. I have never represented anybody charged with murder who was treated with such kindness and was thought of as a beloved community leader.

Outside, at approximately 11:00 p.m., a driving rainstorm moved in. Small streams quickly formed, racing down the gutters along Market Street. Somebody offered me an umbrella to keep—somebody I didn't even know—with the instruction to "take care of Charlie."

10

PERSONAL

The summer of 2001 put my life in high gear, in the fast lane. There was Charlie's arrest, and the preliminary hearing, which consumed weeks of preparation. Then there were meetings in York with Rich Oare and Rees Griffiths to discuss the filing of our pretrial motions. We knew we were filing a motion to challenge the 32-year delay—alleging prejudice—for such a delay makes an affirmative defense almost impossible. Key witnesses were dead, memories were lost, and the rewriting of history by the district attorney's office was legally repugnant.

I know that a defendant is presumed innocent, that he has a right to remain silent, and that he is not required to present evidence in a court of law. I also know that a defendant charged with murder is not presumed innocent, not in this world; that he had better have an explanation, or a jury is going to take him down.

Coordinating with the remaining six defense teams required more trips to York, and diplomacy. We all agonized over seeking the recusal of the Honorable Judge John Uhler, who had been York's district attorney between 1978 and 1982. He was also the presiding judge of the grand jury that issued the presentments for the arrest of all defendants in the Lillie Belle Allen case. As the presiding judge of the grand jury, Uhler was privy to the facts of the case, was instrumental in compelling testimony with his contempt powers, and was responsible for instructing the jury on the law.

Without a motion for recusal, it was almost certain that Judge Uhler would be the trial judge, and the one to rule on pretrial motions.

There were mixed reactions and emotions about keeping him. Judge Uhler was a Bucknell University alumnus, and had graduated from Dickinson School of Law in Carlisle, Pennsylvania, in 1969. He was a bright jurist with many years on the bench. Having been a good prosecutor and defense lawyer, he knew how to referee a combat trial, and how to maintain control when the objections started flying on the courtroom floor.

He was also tough when it came to sentencing. Some judges go out of their way to provide a fair trial—but if the accused gets convicted, look out.

Yet, I had some history with John Uhler that endeared him to me, so I trusted him. When he started law school in Carlisle, he lived in my brother's place, the Molly Pitcher Hotel, and we became friends. We remained friends for 30 years, though we took different career paths. I had even taken his girlfriend, whom he ended up marrying, on a motorcycle ride that she will long remember; at the time, I was riding an Indian Scout, a spirited 700 cc road burner, and didn't really know what I was doing.

Judge Uhler also had a great sense of humor, an essential quality when the gavel falls. However, he could be impatient and would not tolerate disrespect in his courtroom, or whining when he ruled against you. He insisted on keeping things moving along, especially when a jury was in the box.

The issue of recusal would wait until after the upcoming hearing on prejudicial delay. Judge Uhler recused himself for that hearing, knowing he could be a potential witness. Judge Edward G. Biester Jr. of the Court of Common Pleas of Bucks County was assigned by the Supreme Court of Pennsylvania to preside over the prejudicial delay hearing, scheduled for late November.

My summer and my life were not restricted to York and the Robertson case. My oldest daughter, Kara, 27, was to marry Matthew DiFilippo, an Italian boy from the old neighborhood. Matt was a nice young man, in the construction painting business with his father, and came from a good family. Kara convinced me that Matt was the one, he convinced me that he would be good to her, and I convinced them that this was a one-shot deal. They were to be married in the Holy Trinity Greek Orthodox Church in Camp Hill, Pennsylvania, and they arranged a formal reception at the Army War College Officer's Club, in Carlisle.

My brother Paul Costopoulos is a Greek Orthodox priest with a big church in Birmingham, Alabama. He's been married to Penny since 1969, and they have two loving daughters. He is a moving orator, with a fiery delivery, and drove up with his family to do the service.

Kara and Matt were married on July 28, 2001.

We were all there. My mother, my father, my wife and our other two daughters, three of my four brothers, my sister, their children, our cousins, our nephews and nieces, our aunts and uncles, their cousins, nephews, and nieces, plus all of the extended family. This event could have been the precursor to *My Big Fat Greek Wedding*, which would debut in a year.

The DiFilippos were all there, and though a smaller family, the Italians can also produce big numbers.

I hated giving Kara away. I know what they say, that I wasn't losing a daughter, but gaining a son. Maybe so, but I hated walking down the aisle and handing my kid over.

The reception, which was planned by Kara and Jill, was beautiful in every detail. Even the tablecloths matched the wedding party gowns, with centerpieces and burning candles, a layered cake with multiple flavors, and a seven-course menu of steak filet, chicken cordon bleu, and battered fish. The band Kara and Matt picked was a soul band that played white music. Fortunately, they had some Greek CDs for the wedding dance; otherwise the Greeks might have walked out.

Khristina, 24, my second beautiful daughter, gave a toast that brought tears to everybody's eyes. She wished Kara and Matt a long and beautiful life, and hoped that someday she would walk in her sister's footsteps.

§

The early September morning was brisk. Leaves were starting their colorful change, which looked even more vibrant in the sun at that hour. With a gentle breeze blowing, it was the perfect time for working an upland game-bird dog.

Lacy, a dark chocolate lab, was on fire. She was scouring the sorghum and switch grass, and her tail got busy when she got hot. Whenever she braced up, a bird was about to flush; she was never wrong. Within seconds, a beautiful, multicolored cockbird would rise straight up, cackling, or a chucker would take off in a straight line like a low-flying aircraft. The lab's job was twofold: to flush and to retrieve. My job was to bring down the birds with my Browning .28-

gauge over-and-under shotgun. If I missed, Lacy expressed her displeasure with me for failing to hold up my end of the bargain.

This pastime of mine was pretty cool. It was special to me because it gave me two or three hours alone in the open fields, with a loving dog that was well trained to do what it was born to do. The Book family—Mike, Carol, Jason, and Bridgette—owned the fields, hundreds of rolling acres. Their operation was known as Hyd-A-Del and was located in Blaine, Perry County, Pennsylvania, 30 minutes from my home. Mike trained my dog, and then trained me; my dog was the better student, according to Jason.

I think and philosophize out there, mostly about life. The blood of Socrates, Plato, and Aristotle is in my veins, or so I believe. I'm told there's a little of Aristotle Onassis in me, too. I try hard not to think about work in the open fields, but sometimes it's impossible.

In 1992, I represented Justice Rolf Larsen of the Pennsylvania Supreme Court. He suffered from depression, and came under fire and was indicted when a grand jury determined that his doctor was filling out prescriptions for antidepressant medications in Larsen's employees' names. The doctor did so at Larsen's request and saw nothing wrong with it, since the medications were properly prescribed and intended for Larsen. Larsen made the request because he didn't want anybody to know about his painful, embarrassing affliction.

This deed triggered a historic impeachment trial on the floor of the majestic Pennsylvania Senate in the capitol building in Harrisburg. That trial, especially the closing before the entire senate, was a high point in my career. I'm not sure the House of Representatives, which prosecuted the case, had anything to be proud about. The Pennsylvania Senate would eventually impeach Larsen on one of seven counts—not the medication charge that had triggered the impeachment, but improper communications with a litigant.

Justice Larsen knew more law than I ever will. He had also majored in philosophy, insisting that I follow the teaching of Logan Pearsoll Smith, who wrote, "There are two things to aim at in life: first, to get what you want; and after that, to enjoy it. Only the wisest of mankind achieve the second."

That quote haunted me.

The reason?

Though I got what I wanted in life when I went into the law, enjoying it was becoming a struggle. The law is truly a jealous mistress with many demands. My 30-year love affair was taking its toll; she was beautiful, passionate, and lustful, but maybe it was time for the younger generation to serve her.

Trying cases, especially when you commit your soul, is a killer. Typically, from day one, and for many years after, it is all-consuming. The Jay Smith case took seven years to close. It was not the romantic, sexy experience of *The Practice.*

But that fall day, a day to remember forever, reminded me of all the things that matter. I was on my way home with Lacy in the back of my Suburban, listening to a country radio station. The local disc jockey broke in to announce that a commercial plane, American Airlines Flight 11 from Boston to Los Angeles, had just crashed into the North Tower of the World Trade Center in Manhattan. I just assumed it was a horrific accident that would claim the 92 lives on board.

Seventeen minutes later, at 9:03 a.m., the announcer frantically reported that another commercial plane, United Airlines Flight 175 from Boston to Los Angeles, had just crashed into the South Tower of the World Trade Center. He further reported that 65 people were on that plane, all presumed dead. Both flights had originated from Logan Airport in Boston, a place I was familiar with because of my year at Harvard.

At this point, I wasn't freaking out, but I wanted to get home to the television coverage. The radio announcer then reported an "unconfirmed" terrorist attack, with no one claiming responsibility.

Jill was already glued to the live coverage when I walked in; she was visibly shaken and distraught.

Within minutes, our phone rang and it was Khristina, crying, catching her breath, calling from her cellular phone. Khristina was working for Goldman-Sachs, a giant financial institution within blocks of the World Trade Center.

"Dad," she said, "I'm really scared. I ran down 50 flights because the elevators in our building were shut down. I'm now running up a street, don't know where to, with thousands of people screaming. I don't know what's going on, but the World Trade Center has been hit. I don't know where to go."

"Khristina, listen to me," I answered, trying to control the fear in my heart, still not knowing the extent of the horror in New York. "Just get out of there, stay with friends, try to get a hold of Brian to come get you . . . and please, if we get disconnected, call back!"

Then her phone went dead, just like that, and I speed-dialed her back and redialed the digits, but all lines were busy, and stayed busy.

At 9:38 a.m., American Airlines Flight 77 from Washington, D.C., to Los Angeles, crashed into the Pentagon, killing all 64 on board. Evacuation of America's premier military fortress began immediately; the White House evacuated moments later.

The Federal Aviation Administration responded, shutting down all airports in New York City, then halting all flights in America. It was the first time in history that air traffic had been halted nationwide.

At 10:05 a.m., the South Tower of the World Trade Center collapsed as the world watched it live on television.

At 10:10 a.m., a portion of the Pentagon fell to ruins.

At that moment, United Airlines Flight 93 from Newark to San Francisco crashed into the wooded fields of rural southwestern Pennsylvania, killing all 44 people on board.

At 10:28 a.m., the World Trade Center's North Tower collapsed.

The major networks were estimating the number of deaths at the World Trade Center, and the figures were staggering and frightening.

Live footage of brave police officers and firefighters entering the World Trade Center to rescue survivors captured the hearts of all Americans.

In the meantime, there was no phone call from Khristina. All phone lines were busy or had gone dead, and the waiting and helplessness were killing me.

At 1:44 p.m., five warships and two aircraft carriers were ordered to leave the United States naval station in Norfolk, Virginia, to protect the East Coast.

Late that night, with television still reporting and updating the events of September 11, 2001, the long-awaited and prayed-for call came in.

"Dad," Khristina said, "I couldn't get through to you, but I'm OK. I stayed with friends at a restaurant uptown, and Brian got here from Stamford, Connecticut, just now. I'll be home as soon as I can get out of here, but it may be days . . . the bridges are closed . . . the trains and bus systems are shut down."

"I love you, Khristina," was all I could say. I was relieved, having felt the pain of fear and helplessness since we had been disconnected ten hours before.

Thus began the "War on Terrorism."

I still don't know where it's going.

I do know what matters. I sort of knew before those events, but I definitely do now, and will forever.

§

Surfing the TV stations days later, I saw Mayor Charlie Robertson giving the speech of his life in downtown York, attended by a crowd that included shaken police officers and firefighters. His delivery was heartfelt as he extended the prayers of the community to the families of all victims lost in the four air crashes, the World Trade Center, and the Pentagon. "Also," Robertson said, with evident anguish for fallen comrades, "our hearts go out to the families of the police and fire personnel who lost their lives while assisting with the rescue. Some fire battalions lost all of their men . . . firefighters nearing retirement within two or three days perished . . . age or rank of command made no difference . . . they were all doing their job, to achieve a safe and successful rescue . . . we applaud the selfless efforts of volunteers from across the country, doctors, nurses, police, fire emergency personnel, counselors, blood donors, and the response from York Countians which has been overwhelming . . . we have much to be thankful for."

Well done, Charlie, I thought.

No one escaped the impact of September 11, 2001.

Harold Fitzkee, one of the defense lawyers, was waiting at Heathrow Airport in London when live coverage of the planes crashing into the World Trade Center flashed across TV screens. Overcome by stress, he was rushed to a hospital and remained in intensive care for days.

Nick Ressetar, on a return trip from Russia with his father, coincidentally was detained at the same airport in London. It took them two weeks to get home because of the U.S. airport shutdown.

Khristina did make it home that weekend, stayed for a few days, then returned to her work and life in New York City, at Goldman-Sachs, in the heart of the scarred and dust-covered financial district.

I didn't know what to think. I never believed that the world was coming to an end, or that America was going to be a shackled and frightened country. Osama bin Laden and Al Qaeda could be dealt with. I was concerned about the new security measures and the possible revisions to our Constitution that might result—not necessarily opposed to them, just concerned. I was also concerned about the endless "war talk," with its global implications.

None of the foregoing, it seemed, had any impact on the racially charged trial in York. The community's taxpayers were going to pay for that prosecution, and York's local paparazzi kept Charlie Robertson on the front page.

Despite the cataclysmic events in the nation, the injustice perpetrated by the DA's office rolled on in York, Pennsylvania.

11

PREJUDICE

The lapse of 32 years had resulted in the loss of exculpatory evidence and testimony needed to mount an effective defense against the charges at trial. Witnesses had died, or moved to locations unknown, or were otherwise unavailable. Witnesses who were available were unable to remember many facts because their memories had waned over the course of more than three decades. Physical evidence had been lost, destroyed, or was missing.

The critical evidence to support the charges against Mayor Robertson was the testimony of Rick Knouse, who was 16 at the time of the shooting. Knouse was now cooperating with the Commonwealth pursuant to a deal. Recently, and only recently, had he said that then Officer Robertson had provided him with a box of .30-06 ammunition and told him to kill as many "niggers" as he could. This was supposed to have occurred on the day of the shooting, and according to Knouse's grand jury testimony, was witnessed by "at least 30 to 60 bystanders and from four to eight police officers in uniform."

The Commonwealth could not provide one of those witnesses to the defense. The explanation was that too much time had elapsed for Knouse to remember who they were. Knouse's credibility, according to the prosecutors, would be for the jury to decide.

The problem?

Charlie Robertson shouldn't have to go to a trial by jury on a murder charge without a defense. I know a defendant is presumed innocent, and the burden of proof is on the Commonwealth. I also know that a defendant charged with murder is presumed guilty as hell when arrested—and the media fuels this presumed guilt.

With the passage of 32 years, the others accused had their own crosses to bear. The slug that took the life of Lillie Belle Allen had gotten lost in 1980. And though the trajectories of the bullets hitting the car were relevant, the Cadillac she was riding in had disappeared long ago. The weapons used on Newberry Street were also gone.

Exculpatory evidence, in general, is any evidence that tends to establish a criminal defendant's innocence. It may include evidence the prosecution has that is favorable to the defendant. The prosecution has a duty to disclose such evidence to the defense if it may be material to the outcome. The evidence may not be in anyone's possession.

Or it may no longer exist.

In 1969, when witnesses' memories were very much intact, when all physical evidence was available, the death of Lillie Belle Allen was thoroughly investigated. Sergeant John Creavey, a veteran homicide investigator with the Pennsylvania State Police, was assigned the case. Teams of troopers assisted him and interviews were conducted on Newberry Street, and at the barracks, with potential witnesses to the events. Those interviews established who the shooters were on Newberry Street on July 21, 1969.

Sergeant Creavey filed a 33-page report detailing his findings.

The United States Department of Justice did its own investigation and concluded in November 1969 that no federal violations were committed in connection with the killing. Their report referenced Creavey's investigation, confirming, "They [the state police] have been able to determine the identities of many of the white youths who were at the scene, and many who fired weapons. However, they have been unable to determine who fired the fatal shot."

The Pennsylvania State Police and the Feds also documented the relevant riotous events throughout York. Those agencies noted that on July 20, 1969—the day before the Allen killing—an identical-looking Cadillac had proceeded up North Newberry Street during daylight hours, with one or two African Americans hidden in the trunk of that car. When the trunk popped open, the occupants opened fire in that white residential neighborhood. "Some of the white youths," according to Creavey's report, "told the state police that when they saw the Allen Cadillac stop with its trunk facing them, they believed they were about to be fired upon."

Sergeant Creavey believed that this earlier incident had made the residents of North Newberry Street jumpy, and when the Allen vehicle turned around at the tracks and a black woman got out of the car, the gang in the area believed they were about to be shot at from the trunk.

Sergeant Creavey based his conclusion, in part, "on the fact that the majority of the shots hitting the vehicle hit it in the right rear, particularly in the area of the trunk."

The York City Police Department assisted the Pennsylvania State Police in the investigation. Detective Tom Chapman, an African American homicide investigator who grew up in the streets of York, accompanied Creavey and paved the way for a lot of interviews.

The city police executed the search warrants on Newberry Street, which included the Messersmith home. The search resulted in the confiscation of an arsenal.

The York County district attorney's office, headed at the time by District Attorney John Rauhauser Jr., was actively involved in the investigation of the Allen and Schaad deaths, and participated in making the appropriate decisions, based on the evidence and the climate in 1969.

United States District Court Judge William Nealon held seven days of hearings immediately following the 1969 riots, and made a personal inspection of the destruction in York. He issued 129 discrete findings of fact, engaged in extensive factual and legal discussion, and then dismissed the plaintiffs' civil rights complaint. He was subsequently affirmed by the United States Court of Appeals for the Third Circuit.

Notwithstanding the intensive investigation and the Commonwealth's actual knowledge of the shooters in question, no arrests were made for the killing of Lillie Belle Allen in the ensuing 32 years. The investigating officers and District Attorney John Rauhauser Jr. were neither corrupt nor racially motivated.

Charlie Robertson's name was never mentioned by any witness interviewed in 1969, except Fred Flickinger, who said that Robertson yelled "white power" at Farquhar Park.

Now, under the authority vested in Tom Kelley and Tim Barker, history was being rewritten, and Charlie Robertson and those shooters still living were arrested and charged with murdering Lillie Belle Allen on July 21, 1969.

Thus, the motion to dismiss the charges was filed by all defendants. This was not "a mere technicality," or "a defense ploy to avoid an unpleasant task."

§

November 19, 2001
York County Courthouse
York, Pennsylvania

The courtroom well was packed again, set up the same as during the preliminary hearing. Ed Paskey, Tom Kelley, Tim Barker, Bill Graff, and District Attorney Stan Rebert talked and seemed at ease.

There were two major developments in the defense lineup. Harold Fitzkee, upon motion of the Commonwealth, was removed from the case. The Commonwealth had alleged that Fitzkee was a potential witness in the case since he was the District Attorney of York County from 1970 to 1974. Furthermore, they alleged that Fitzkee at one time had represented Sherman Spells, a potential trial witness in the Lillie Belle Allen case. Judge Uhler, in reaching his decision to disqualify William Ritter's counsel of choice, concluded that Fitzkee could not act as both a critical fact witness and an advocate for his client.

I keenly felt the loss, for Fitzkee was a great defense lawyer—and a real threat to the prosecution. I didn't know Ritter's new lawyer, Albert G. Barnes, but assumed that Fitzkee would have provided his client with a good replacement.

The second defense development was the presence of Greg Neff and his attorney, Greg Gettle, at our table. Neff, an alleged shooter, was the former leader of the Girarders gang. The prosecution had filed a motion to vacate their deal with Greg Neff, who had screwed them at the preliminary hearing. Neff had testified "the victim had a gun," and though he always maintained that belief—during police interviews, before the grand jury, and before the deal—that was not acceptable testimony in exchange for probation. Greg Gettle was fighting that motion, and since Judge Uhler hadn't ruled yet, he was covering his legal bases.

Then there was the presence of the Honorable Edward G. Biester Jr., appointed by the Supreme Court of Pennsylvania to preside over this hearing. Judge Biester had been the Attorney General of Pennsylvania in 1977 under Governor Milton Shapp. I had had some personal dealings with his office, but hadn't seen Biester for 24 years. He had gained a little weight, picked up a few wrinkles here and there, and had whiter hair. I know he probably saw me the same way when I shook his hand before the hearing began.

National Guard personnel and equipment move into the York armory during the race riots of July 1969, York, Pennsylvania. *The York County Heritage Trust, PA*

Major Rice takes command of his men, as National Guard personnel and equipment station themselves across the street from City Hall on West King Street, July 1969, York, Pennsylvania. *The York County Heritage Trust, PA*

Charlie Robertson takes his assignment on an armored personnel carrier, top left, York, Pennsylvania.   *The York County Heritage Trust, PA*

Car ablaze at the intersection of Princess and Penn Streets during the race riots of July 1969, York, Pennsylvania.   *The York County Heritage Trust, PA*

Damage on George and King Streets during the race riots of July 1969, York, Pennsylvania. *The York County Heritage Trust, PA*

Police sharpshooters leaving to do surveillance, also know as "spot watch," during the race riots of July 1969, York, Pennsylvania. *The York County Heritage Trust, PA*

National Guard looks for weapons near Newberry Street shortly after the killing of Lillie Belle Allen on July 21, 1969, York, Pennsylvania. *The York County Heritage Trust, PA*

York City police, pursuant to search warrant, seize weapons from the Messersmith home on Newberry Street, with protective assistance from the National Guard, July 1969, York, Pennsylvania. *The York County Heritage Trust, PA*

Charlie Robertson, third officer from the right, paying his respects with the York
City Police Department immediately after the assassination of John F. Kennedy,
November 22, 1963. *Wm. J. Schintz, Photographer*

Charlie Robertson, as a young police officer for the York City Police Department, 1965. *Gil Tunney Studios, Inc.*

The Honorable John C. Uhler, Court of Common Pleas, York, Pennsylvania, presided over all pretrial matters and the trial of Charlie Robertson and the other defendants.

York Daily Record *and* The York Dispatch

Right, the elected district attorney of York County, District Attorney H. Stanley Robert. Left, First Assistant District Attorney, Thomas H. Kelley, the lead prosecutor in the case of Charlie Robertson and the other defendants.

Randy Rizzutto, Photographer

Tim Barker, First Deputy District Attorney of York, was second in command of the prosecution team.

Douglas M. Demangone, Photographer

Fran Chardo, Special Assistant Prosecutor from Harrisburg, Dauphin County District Attorney's Office, assigned to the prosecutorial team in York, Pennsylvania.

Dauphin County District Attorney's Office

I had called a bunch of lawyers in Bucks County to get a read on him, and their input was unanimous. Bright jurist, affable person, will let you create a record; but if I thought for one second that he was going to throw out the biggest murder cases in the history of York, with decades of racial overtones, I was fucking dreaming.

That's not what I wanted to hear. This prejudicial delay issue was a good one, my best pretrial motion, and if he wasn't going to allow it, my belief was that the appellate courts would—before a trial by jury.

But I would need to create a record, and the court directed me to go first.

Rich Oare and Ellen Wagner had served a bunch of subpoenas, and the witnesses we had lined up would consume a day. We had former district attorneys, including Harold Fitzkee, Donald Reihart, Judge Uhler, and Stan Rebert, standing by. They basically said nothing except that they were district attorneys for their respective terms and didn't know a thing about any unsolved '69 murder cases. If anybody had brought an unsolved murder case to their attention, they would have gotten on it right away.

Rebert said he did get on it right away in 1998, though he had been in office since 1986. The district attorneys who had served before Rebert confirmed that no information about Charlie Robertson and his alleged involvement in the Allen killing was ever brought to their attention.

An exhaustive, magazine-style retrospective by *York Daily Record* Editorial Page Editor Kim Strong, published by that newspaper on December 18, 2002, said a reporter's phone call to Tom Kelley in 1999 had triggered Kelley's interest in the 1969 murders. Until that point, he "knew nothing" of the riots or of Lillie Belle Allen. "Curious after the reporter's phone call, he asked his boss [Rebert] if he could pull the case file. Sure, Rebert said, but he wouldn't find much there," Strong's article stated.

It might seem odd to the public that Stan Rebert, the district attorney prosecuting the case, was called as our witness. But this was not an effort to sandbag him. It was not unusual either. Lawyers, prosecutors, even judges, are sometimes called to the stand on procedural or substantive matters relating to a case. Rebert was one of a long line of York County district attorneys who had had ample opportunity to investigate the case, and had not. Rebert had spent at least 12 years in office before he thought it worthy of investigation. That he did launch an investigation seemed more closely linked primarily to Kelley's influence in pushing the probe forward and to the assurance that two daily newspapers would glorify his every step. In June and July of 1999, the *York Daily Record* and the *York Dispatch*, respectively, published their "anniversary stories" on the '69 riots.

The most interesting witnesses I called were the police officers who had been riding with Charlie Robertson in "Big Al" on the night in question. Rich had interviewed two of them — Ray Markle and James VanGreen — and they both confirmed that Robertson was with them in the armored car, blocks away, when the shooting occurred. They testified that they responded to the gunfire, and collectively they got the surviving occupants of the car out of there. "Yes," they said, "Charlie Robertson was instrumental that night in helping save lives."

The other police occupant of "Big Al" was Officer Dennis McMaster, the current chief of police for East Pennsboro Township in Cumberland County and a former York police detective. He had been in law enforcement for 38 years. I wasn't sure what Chief McMaster was going to testify to, but I needed to know exactly what his recollection was.

I had read in newspaper accounts that he was going to confirm Rick Knouse's testimony that Charlie Robertson handed out .30-06 ammunition, presumably to Knouse. Yet, at the preliminary hearing in front of Judge Cassimatis, the prosecutors hadn't called him. I knew that they had McMaster sitting in their offices during that hearing, and their decision not to call the chief intrigued me; they certainly didn't do that to help me out.

So I called him at the hearing and put him under oath, because I needed to know what he was going to say. There was no jury in the box, and if I was going to take a hit, it just had to be.

Chief McMaster, who had testified off and on for 38 years, was a pro. He said that he had been a patrolman in 1963 for the city of York, that he had worked during the terrifying riots in 1969, and that he was in "Big Al" with the other boys on the night in question. "We were extremely busy," he said, "and we were learning by doing."

"Four police officers had previously been injured by gunfire during that week, and I believe all of them were assigned to armored cars," he said.

I worked my way up to the question that made me most nervous: "Consistent with what you were asked before the grand jury, are you aware of any officer, specifically Officer Robertson, providing any of the Newberry Street Boys with ammunition?"

"I can't tell you," McMaster answered cautiously, "the date that this happened. There were four other police officers in the vehicle with me, and the request came from an individual by the name of Jim

Messersmith. It was my recollection he walked up by himself. I knew James Messersmith to be a law-abiding person, and I had assumed that he wanted the ammunition for home protection, and it was not illegal to give him ammunition."

McMaster witnessed nothing that was illegal; he testified to nothing that was illegal. No, he didn't file a report because there was nothing to report.

That was it. No wonder the prosecutors hadn't called him at the preliminary hearing. He didn't corroborate Knouse in any way.

Paskey and the boys were objecting to every question I asked, and maybe it wasn't relevant to the issue before Judge Biester, but I needed to know.

The other defense lawyers stayed out of that dogfight; but when their turn came, they created their own record for the court, and for possible appeals. The slug that took the life of Lillie Belle Allen was gone, and had been since 1980. The Cadillac had been scrap metal since the early '70s and was therefore long gone. The weapons were unavailable. Sergeant Creavey's investigation showed that shooters were known in 1969, but no arrests were made at that time.

Not a bad record, I thought—but Judge Biester didn't seem too interested.

§

November 20, 2001
York County Courthouse
York, Pennsylvania

We were back in court, but this time it was the prosecution's turn.

They had set up a big screen, like one for an old projector, and some kind of a machine at their table to do a powerpoint presentation. I don't know a thing about computers, but I was interested in this high-tech exhibition. At the office, I have to wait for the secretaries to turn on the photocopier, let alone use it; the same is true of the fax machine. At home, Callista accesses the channels on Direct TV and is responsible for all videotaping. I can't even set the digital clock in my truck when the time changes twice a year.

I had seen a high-tech closing argument demonstrated at a continuing-legal-education seminar. It was in Wilkes-Barre, Pennsylvania, and was a medical malpractice closing argument by a talented civil lawyer. It was impressive.

I had done a demonstration closing argument in a murder case for that same audience the old-fashioned way, and felt like a dinosaur.

The back of Courtroom 1 had plenty of spectators, not as many as before, but Leo Cooper of the NAACP was there with some of his friends. Members of the Allen family filled an entire row on one side of the courtroom—they always sat quietly on the same side—but whenever there was a break, they met with reporters to express their emotions and thoughts. Soon, they were joined by a lawyer from Philadelphia who loved having press conferences and threatened to sue the city of York.

Charlie Robertson remained expressionless, slightly removed from the other defendants, but did not miss a thing. He did not take notes, but could recall details months later, especially ones that angered him, or testimony that would impact his life.

The day began with Detective Rodney George taking the witness stand, and the day ended with George still up there. His testimony resulted in almost 300 pages of transcribed testimony, none of which meant a damn thing. He was the spokesman for this powerpoint show, with Tim Barker doing the questioning and operating the machine at the same time. The whole day was spent trying to put up on that screen the names of the witnesses interviewed in 1969 and of those interviewed recently.

During his day on the witness stand, Detective George detailed 309 names of people who were interviewed by investigators over the preceding two years. Barker put their names up on the screen one at a time, and half the time the machine didn't work; it was a major cluster-fuck. It was nothing, absolutely nothing, like what I had seen in Wilkes-Barre. It was also the most boring courtroom presentation I have ever witnessed.

And irrelevant—other than to show how hard they had worked over the preceding two years. The issue of delay was not addressed, but in the end that didn't matter.

Judge Biester tabled final arguments, allowing himself and the attorneys time to review the testimony, submit briefs, and prepare closing arguments.

We did all that. We argued that the death or absence of witnesses, fading memories, and the loss of evidence made it impossible to present a defense to the charges. We did not argue that the delay was intentional to prejudice the accused.

I don't think the delay was negligent either. I honestly believe a decision was made in 1969 not to charge anybody for the death on Newberry Street.

The reason?

Because of the facts known at the time, and the prevailing political climate, prosecutors made a judgment-call of self-defense.

Moreover, prosecution of those white boys in '69 would have resulted in an acquittal. That would have done nothing to heal a city reeling from the racial tensions and riots it had just experienced.

Four weeks later, on December 18, 2001, Judge Biester ruled against us and in favor of the Commonwealth. He wrote, "No one knows how these trials will come out. Until they are resolved one way or another, no amount of tamping them down or tamping down the terrible memories in an effort to make them disappear, is really possible. Only when they are resolved, one way or another, no one can predict, can this past be put fully and permanently behind this city."

12

WORRY

My 86-year-old mother had fallen down the steps at home. She was rushed to the Carlisle Hospital by ambulance and tests were being done to determine her condition. Fortunately, my niece Nina was home to make the calls for help, but she could only reach me. Nina remained at the house with my 93-year-old father. My brother John had left for his home in New York. My brother Paul had not come up from Birmingham for Thanksgiving. Jim, the eldest, was running around somewhere. Tom's phone was off the hook, and Ginny didn't answer.

Waiting alone in the hospital emergency room was distressing.

The small clock on the wall in that waiting room ticked away. It was 2:10 p.m., Sunday, November 25, 2001, three days after Thanksgiving. I had been there for an hour, maybe longer, and already there was nothing to do. The magazines were old—*Better Homes and Gardens*, *Redbook*, *Reader's Digest*, one *Sports Illustrated*—but I read them to kill time.

Thanksgiving at our home on the mountain has been a tradition. We would all gather there, and that Thursday there were 27 of us to celebrate the day of thanks. The golden-brown turkey was the centerpiece, surrounded by too many other dishes—mashed potatoes, sweet potatoes, Greek salad with feta cheese, peas, corn, homemade bread, gravy, cranberry sauce, a brown-sugared ham, and a dozen desserts. It was a special day, however, and my favorite holiday of the year. It was unpretentious and the meaning of it was genuine, at least for most of us. My entire family has been blessed with good health, and we know that matters. My father was getting old, but he was still ambulatory and living at home with my mother; he did require oxygen, but most of the time wouldn't use it. My mother insisted on taking care of him, for they had been married for over 60 years.

"Mr. Costopoulos," the pleasant, overworked nurse said when she finally made an appearance, "the x-rays have been taken, but the technician has yet to read them. Your mother seems to be doing OK, but she's experiencing a lot of pain on her side, around the rib area."

"Thank you," I said appreciatively, and meant it.

I hate hospitals, emergency rooms, waiting rooms, examinations, and waiting. I don't know why, not exactly. I never had a bad, bad experience with hospitals or doctors. Personally, I've been lucky enough to avoid that world, with my last complete physical having been done in 1966, when I was drafted into the army after college.

I know, I know, I know.

I also know that a broken rib is a painful son-of-a-bitch. I broke one during wrestling practice in the fall of 1965, and at that time had a good string of wins for the Dickinson College Devils. My trainer was Bruce Vogelson, and he felt that he could tape me up tight enough to wrestle the following week. My coach Bob Marshall wasn't sure, but we did it anyway. And though I will remember the pain, the next match went my way.

Five years ago when I was 53, I was skiing with Callista at a small family resort outside of Pittsburgh, known as Hidden Valley. I was chasing her down a hill, and she jumped a mogul; I missed the jump and crashed. Pride alone forced me to finish the run, and for the next several days I was in agony. Jill insisted that I go see her doctor, Dr. Blacksmith, to get checked out because she was tired of my groaning and complaining.

The pain was in the rib area, a familiar, sharp pain when I would sit up. Sure enough, the x-rays confirmed two broken ribs, and Dr. Blacksmith told me there was nothing to be done except to hang out for several weeks and heal. Good advice, I'm sure, but by the following morning I was totally depressed. His advice meant no working out at the gym, and I remembered that I was to try out a horse coming up from Virginia at my trainer's indoor barn. When Jill ran to the market, I got out our phone book and looked up Bruce Vogelson's name, figuring he would have been in his early 80s, if he was still living. I hadn't seen him since 1966, but had read that he went on to become the trainer for the Washington Redskins, a team that trained preseason at Dickinson College in Carlisle, Pennsylvania.

"Vogelson, B.," was in the Carlisle directory; there was only one, and I dialed the number.

"Hello," I heard on the line after many rings. The voice was that of a very old lady, and holding my breath, I asked, "Is Bruce Vogelson there, please?"

I was expecting her to tell me that he died years ago, or that I had the wrong number, but instead she told me to wait a moment, please.

Then, just like that, the familiar voice of Bruce Vogelson came across the line.

"Bruce," I said, happy to hear his voice, happy that he was still alive, embarrassed to tell him why I was calling, "this is Bill Costopoulos, do you remember me?"

"The Greek?" Bruce asked.

"Yeah," I answered.

"What in the hell do you want?" he asked, talking just like he did in the '60s, bossing me around, giving me shit, sounding great.

I proceeded to tell my old trainer that several days earlier I had broken two ribs while skiing, and that my wife's doctor told me to remain idle for weeks to heal. I told Bruce that I needed to get to the gym, and that a horse was coming up from Virginia that I wanted to ride. I then reminded him that he had taped me before a wrestling match, and that his taping had worked.

"Are you fucking nuts?" Bruce replied. "That was 30 years ago. You've got to be in your 50s by now."

I told Bruce that I was in my 50s, but I was still in good shape, and I wanted him to take care of me. "You have to, Bruce," I said. "Come on."

There was a long pause, a very long pause. He then gave me directions to his house. I went immediately, and Bruce taped the shit out of me. I got to work out that day, in pain, and I got to ride my horse—it almost killed me—but to this day I am indebted to Bruce Vogelson. It was also great to see him, though he did tell me if I fell off that horse, with two broken ribs, "You will die, Costopoulos."

Jill's still mad at me.

I relived that memory while waiting for mother's x-ray results. The clock on the wall kept ticking away, and by now it was going on 4:00 p.m. Either the x-ray technician was slow getting in, or something was going on. Either way, I didn't like it, but would continue to wait, and worry.

When I called home at 4:30 p.m., Ginny was at the house with my dad, as was Tom.

It was dark outside when the emergency room doctor, a young woman with a lot of stress in her face, told me the news.

The tests of my mother showed no broken ribs or other bones, but confirmed "a very large tumor" on her left kidney. The doctor called it renal carcinoma, commonly known as cancer, and when I asked how serious that was, she just shook her head.

"She can go home with you now," the doctor said, "but take her to her primary care physician first thing tomorrow."

Privately, I broke down.

My mother was OK with it, reminding me that we've all been blessed, and that she had no regrets. Her only concern was my father.

§

December 2001

Dr. Sevalina Boshnakov, my mother's caring Russian general practitioner, saw her immediately. She was encouraging, telling us that my mother was a strong woman, and that she should have that killer tumor removed. "Yes," she said, "it's a serious operation, but . . . "

Dr. Leon Sweer was my father's respiratory doctor, but he was much more than that. He had become a good friend of the family, in spite of our constant demands regarding our father's aging condition. We always called him about anything we thought was medically urgent, and no matter how busy he was, he would take our calls. Often he would come have dinner with my mother, and we loved him for it. We asked him to refer us to a urologist, either to do the operation, or to give us a second opinion.

Dr. Sweer referred us to Dr. J. Edward Dagen, a urologist with serious credentials. Dagen also saw us right away, a favor to Sweer, and with obvious caring sensitivity confirmed that the renal cancer was metastatic. Because of its size alone, he said, "the chance of curing this tumor is minimal . . . her risk for mortality is significant." Dr. Dagen was very concerned about the enormity and trauma of such an operation, especially at my mother's age. Ginny and I, with my mother sitting there in his examining room, unfairly pressed him for an estimate of her remaining life if we opted to let it go. He reluctantly told us, "maybe two years, maybe, certainly not eight."

We didn't know what to do. Two years seemed like such a short time, but to run the risk of losing her on the operating table within weeks was out of the question.

We ran back to Dr. Sweer, and since we asked, he suggested that we talk to an oncologist, a good friend of his, and a good doctor that specialized in cancer.

Dr. Scott Barnes agreed to see us on December 31, hours before New Year's Eve, 2001. My brother John had come in from New York for the holidays, as did my brother Paul, and the three of us took my mother to see Dr. Barnes. He had obviously spent time reviewing the file before we got there, and, wearing his white labcoat, showed us on a screen the image of the tumor. He explained that it was nine centimeters in diameter, and was beyond reasonable doubt a large renal cell carcinoma. Based on his experience as an oncologist, who works only with cancer patients, he estimated a possible life expectancy of 90 days without surgery.

My mother looked concerned throughout, but John, Paul, and I, though controlling our emotions, were not ready to bury our mother within the next 90 days. Dr. Barnes spent at least two hours with us out of his busy schedule. He could not have been gentler, and stressed that any decision to operate, with the attending risks, was up to my mother and no one else. He could certainly understand going either way with it, but if she decided to have the operation, he urged that we go to a teaching university.

My mother was not ready to give it up within 90 days. "Who's going to take care of your father?" was her number-one question and concern.

My mother was not only strong-willed, but she could be awfully manipulative. She knew how to play on the guilt of her children, and at that time in her life, she was back in control of all of us. It was still New Year's Eve, and she insisted that since we were all home, we should take her and my father and our uncle Charlie Mallios—all of us—to a New Year's Eve party at the Marriot Resort in Harrisburg. The party was hosted by the Greek church and included a full buffet and a Greek orchestra from Baltimore, with a great clarinet and violin. The celebration was to start at 11:00 p.m. and go all night.

Ordinarily, she could never have gotten us to go to such an affair—none of us is crazy about New Year's Eve parties except Jim, who likes parties anytime, anywhere, and for any occasion—but under the circumstances, we were glad to go.

It turned out to be a terrific time. The food was great and the band was awesome. When the Greek violinist and clarinet player got it together, we all danced, one more time, as a family. My mother was very proud of us that night and laughed the whole time, as 2002 was brought in with lots of noise, confetti, and helium balloons bouncing off the ceiling.

It would be the last New Year's that we would spend together.

§

New Year's Eve, 2001
York, Pennsylvania

The black sky was filled with glittering stars. More than 3,000 people were celebrating in the streets of York as the midnight hour approached. The bitter cold, with sporadic gusty winds, had many celebrants jumping up and down to keep warm, not to be confused with the younger crowd dancing in the streets. At the top of the York Chamber of Commerce building, three stories up, a huge, plastic white rose, emblem of the White Rose City, was illuminated with spotlights waiting to make the great descent. Twenty-four miles east of York is Lancaster, the Red Rose City. The symbols harken back to the cities they were named after: York and Lancaster, England.

The main streets of York boasted a solid lineup of entertainment, which included traditional groups and rock bands. They would have to compete with the horns and noisemakers of the crowd. Plenty of favorite poets, magicians, comedians, and vocalists from previous years were back.

Absent this year were the legendary Drifters, one of the premiere Motown groups of the 1950s and 1960s.

Charlie Robertson mingled with his people, in his city, one more time as their mayor. He was laughing and smiling on the outside, but his heart was gone. Just one year ago, he thought he would be York's mayor forever. Hell, Steve Reed, a Democrat just up the road in Harrisburg, had made it a lifetime gig.

Just one year ago exactly, he was asked by the lead singer of the Drifters, Charlie Thomas, a good friend, to sing and dance with that group to bring in the new year. Charlie smiled as he recalled singing and harmonizing with those five talented soul brothers. His dance steps were way off, but the crowd loved the show. The mayor crooned along to "Under the Boardwalk" and "On Broadway" — songs he had enjoyed immensely in his thirties and had never forgotten.

Little did Charlie know that memorable night that the year ahead would be the most horrible one of his life. He would be arrested for a murder he knew little about, except for the information he had gleaned later as a cop; pressured by his party's advisors to withdraw from the race for another four-year term; and subjected to the worst imaginable publicity by his own hometown papers.

And now, one year after the unthinkable happened, it appeared that he would be picking a jury to decide his fate. There was little doubt where things were headed in 2002. The county courthouse, where the trial would likely take place, was a short walk from where he had hammed it up with the Drifters.

What he would have given for one more night, harmonizing with the Drifters, without the shackles of this nightmare.

Loud cheering and noise directed his attention to the big white rose as it slowly descended, and then disappeared, into a makeshift vase. "Auld Lang Syne" filled the air and enormous sprays of booming, colorful fireworks illuminated the horizon. Charlie was not in the mood. He jammed his cold hands into his oversized coat and walked home.

His last official day as mayor of the city of York was five days away. Charlie had already moved his stuff out, and had never in his life — never — experienced such a depression.

§

February 26, 2002
York County Courthouse

The criminal justice system was moving forward in York.

We were back in Judge Uhler's courtroom to address outstanding pretrial issues, matters that had to be resolved before picking a jury and trying the case. Things were getting complicated among the defense lawyers as we moved closer to the moment of truth. We continued to meet at the offices of Pete Solymos to share our common work products, but we all knew the day was coming when we would go our separate ways.

I had filed a motion to sever, for I did not want Charlie Robertson to be tried with the shooters.

Matt Gover and the other defense lawyers agreed, for they did not want their clients to be tried with Charlie Robertson. They believed that without him—the target with notoriety—the media would go home, the "circus" would leave town, and meaningful discussions with prosecutors could be entered into for closure.

Gover's contention was supported by the mass exodus of media when Charlie Robertson left the courtroom, with the court's permission, before the end of the hearing. It was an evacuation that unsettled Judge Uhler, for it was a noisy departure, and left his courtroom almost empty.

Al Barnes, for William Ritter, objected to our motion to sever, taking the position that he wanted Ritter to be tried with the mayor.

The Commonwealth wanted one trial for everybody, "to save the taxpayers money, and for judicial economy."

To save the taxpayers money my ass, I thought. They're just going to play the reverse race card when the shooting starts in the courtroom, and they want Charlie in the middle of that shootout.

Judge Uhler denied our severance motion and granted the Commonwealth's motion to consolidate, concluding that "the Commonwealth has sufficiently established that the crimes alleged against each of the above-captioned Defendants arise from a single fact pattern which ultimately resulted in the shooting death of Lillie Belle Allen. Since the physical and testimonial evidence which the Commonwealth will seek to produce at trial is virtually the same with regard to each of the Defendants, the Court must agree with the Commonwealth that consolidation would obviate the need for repetitive testimony at separate trials which would thereby promote judicial economy. Accordingly, the Commonwealth has satisfied its initial burden with regard to establishing the need for joinder in the present matter."

Judge Uhler dismissed a subpoena for *York Dispatch* reporter Mike Hoover, a subpoena I had served to get Hoover's testimony on the record. Mike Hoover had interviewed Rick Knouse, and Knouse told him that Charlie Robertson did not hand out any ammunition to anybody, at any time, for any reason. Hoover's interview ran in a feature story in the *York Dispatch/Sunday News*, on October 22, 2000.

I was not looking for the source of confidential information provided to a reporter, for I was fully aware of the Pennsylvania Shield

Law, which protects reporters from disclosing their sources. I simply wanted Hoover to confirm that he had interviewed Knouse, and that Knouse told him what was reported in the *York Dispatch*, that "Knouse said he didn't see Robertson hand out ammunition."

That subpoena got the York reporters and their lawyers awfully excited. The lawyers filed a motion to quash, and to this day I don't know why Judge Uhler granted that motion.

Judge Uhler also denied our Petition for Writ of Habeas Corpus; simply stated, he concluded that Judge Cassimatis was correct in binding Charlie Robertson, and all others accused over for trial, at the preliminary hearing. That ruling by Uhler came as no surprise, but his opinion went on for pages, referring to "facts" as if he were making an emotional closing argument.

We had already agreed not to seek his recusal. I just hoped that we didn't fuck up.

Rich Oare and Rees Griffiths, and especially Charlie Robertson, convinced me not to seek a motion for a change of venue or venire. They wanted a jury from Robertson's community, from the war-torn community of York.

§

Nick Ressetar appealed the Cassimatis/Uhler ruling, challenging the sufficiency of the evidence, alleging that Knouse's testimony in a light most favorable to the Commonwealth did not rise to the level of murder. His research was well documented, and his brief in flowing legalese was compelling.

Charlie Robertson should not have been charged with murder based on the averments in the affidavit, or the testimony at the preliminary hearing.

The Superior Court of Pennsylvania denied that appeal.

The Supreme Court of Pennsylvania, the court of last resort, also denied that appeal.

With those appeals still pending, Nick had challenged Judge Biester's opinion and order of court. There was a case out of Susquehanna County, known as the "Scher case," in which a doctor was charged with killing his friend, while they were hunting together, so he could hook up with his friend's wife, with whom he was having a passionate affair. The doctor always maintained the killing was an accident, and got away with that explanation for 20 years. Though a jury convicted the doctor of murder, the Superior Court threw out the conviction, with an opinion critical of the delay. The prosecution appealed that dismissal to the Supreme Court of Pennsylvania, and that appeal was pending when Nick went after Judge Biester.

The Scher delay was 20 years.

The York riot case delay was 30 years.

Nick's authority for this appeal was not from another state or a federal jurisdiction.

Without warning, and much to our dismay, the Supreme Court of Pennsylvania reversed the Scher case and reinstated the conviction. Our appeal met the same fate—denied by the Superior Court of Pennsylvania, denied by the Supreme Court of Pennsylvania.

13

DECISIONS

Ed Paskey, the lead prosecutor at the preliminary hearing before Cassimatis and at the prejudicial delay hearing before Biester, left Stan Rebert's office for good in November 2001. The prejudicial delay hearing was Paskey's last official act as a York County prosecutor. He had accepted a position as a homicide prosecutor in Minnesota, his wife's home state.

I suspected there was a breakdown in the district attorney's office of York. Ed Paskey, a '97 Dickinson Law School graduate, started working for Rebert as an intern in his senior year, and stayed on as a full-time courtroom litigator upon graduation. He was a good trial lawyer and four years in the courtroom is invaluable experience; but he also had good instincts and a sense of fairness, which no amount of experience can give you. In fact, it was surprising, given the relatively few years he had in, that Paskey seemed so experienced. As a result of Paskey's departure, Tom Kelley moved into the lead slot and Tim Barker moved up to second chair.

From Shenandoah, in Schuylkill County, about an hour's drive north of Harrisburg, Paskey, 30, was clean-cut, with dark hair and a medium build. At 5' 11" and just shy of 190 pounds, Paskey was deceptively tough. He had a schoolboy look and a soft voice, but he had worked in the child abuse unit of the DA's office, which took some cojones. Prosecuting child abusers—dealing with the horrible consequences of their actions—could eat away at you over the years. But it was one of the most rewarding areas of work within the DA's office when you were able to nail one of those scumbags. Paskey was deliberate in the courtroom, carefully laying the foundation with each question.

He seemed obsessed with my ties. Paskey asked virtually every day where I got my freaking ties. They weren't wild-assed things. I dressed conservatively for court. They were silk ties, "power ties"—nothing unique or out of the ordinary.

Paskey always maintained that he left the York DA's office because he promised his wife that they would move back to her home state to be near her family. Giving up the highest-profile homicide case in the history of York was an act of love, he said, but I wasn't buying it. This was a career case for a prosecutor. Most lawyers dream of cases like this with national media exposure. I was sorry to see him go for he was a good man and a worthy adversary, but I was not sorry to see the DA's office lose that talent in the prosecution of Robertson.

Other decisions made in York impacted the proceedings. Judge Uhler decided that the court would not enforce Greg Neff's plea agreement with the district attorney's office. He concluded that "a defendant has no right to a plea agreement ... a district attorney may decide that a plea agreement not yet approved by the court is not in the best interest of the community."

That ruling gave Tom Kelley exactly what he wanted. Kelley was not happy with Neff at the preliminary hearing, where he had testified that Lillie Belle Allen had a gun. Prior to Uhler's order vacating the agreement, Neff had a deal for probation in exchange for his testimony. Now the murder charges were reinstated. Neff's only hope to avoid trial was to reopen plea negotiations with the York County district attorney's office, but that would require a different recollection.

Greg Neff, shaken by his predicament, felt that there was a serious communication breakdown with his lawyer, and that the district attorney's office had fucked him. Neff made the decision to get rid of Greg Gettle and seek other counsel. I was following that whole thing closely, for Neff's testimony that the victim had a gun, testimony that dovetailed with Knouse's, was critical to the affirmative defense of self-defense, or the defense of others, at least for those accused of killing Lillie Belle Allen. Even if there was no gun, if the shooters believed there was, and that belief was honestly entertained, they could go with it.

Every decision made in York was for the prosecution.

Judge Cassimatis bound the charges over for trial.

Judge Biester dismissed our prejudicial delay issue.

Judge Uhler threw out our pretrial motions.

Neff's plea agreement was vacated.

Those rulings left us no recourse. We were stuck, and were directed to pick a jury in York on September 23, 2002.

§

At home, another decision had to be made.

Dr. Louis R. Kavoussi, a urologist and surgeon who was eminently qualified in laparoscopic nephrectomy, looked at my mother with some confusion. Then he looked at Ginny and me, and then at Jeanne, my brother Tom's wife.

Dr. Kavoussi was in his early 40s. He had a charming demeanor and bedside manner. He was a distinguished Professor of Urology at Johns Hopkins Hospital and University in Baltimore. Kavoussi was a published author and lecturer on the laparoscopic procedure for removing malignant tumors from the human body. This procedure was a minimally invasive laser technique allowing for a shorter hospital stay, a faster recuperation, and equivalent results when compared with the traditional surgical procedure.

"What's there to talk about?" Dr. Kavoussi asked, looking at all of us during our first conference with him.

"The tumor is over nine centimeters, and my mother is 86," I said respectfully, grimacing.

"I can do this," Dr. Kavoussi replied, with cautious confidence but genuine optimism.

"Then do it," my mother said, smiling with charming warmth.

At that point, in the doctor's words, what was there to talk about?

We were to have my mother back in Baltimore, at Johns Hopkins Hospital, on March 6, 2002, for her pre-op examination. Dr. Kavoussi would do the operation, hopefully laparoscopically, but otherwise conventionally, if the laser procedure wasn't possible. In the meantime, she was to go home with her family and undergo a series of examinations and tests at home; the doctor wanted a current CT scan, more blood work, a urinalysis, a comprehensive metabolic panel, and cardiac clearance.

Over the next several weeks, Jill was a godsend. The number of visits and tests my mother underwent seemed endless, but Jill took her to every one, and my brother Tom took on the responsibility of our aging father.

On March 6, I drove my mother to Johns Hopkins for final testing and instructions. It was decided that my brother John and I would stay with my mother until everything was over. We checked into the Radisson Hotel, 28 blocks from the hospital. The operation was to be performed by Dr. Kavoussi the following morning, and everybody would come together to wait it out. Paul flew up from Birmingham, and, dressed in his Orthodox robes, put his hand on my mother's forehead and prayed for her; Jim and his wife Maria drove down from Carlisle; my sister Ginny joined us; and all of her grandchildren would visit.

We all kissed my mother goodbye at 9:00 a.m. on March 7, not knowing if we would ever see her alive again when she was taken down to the operating room in a wheelchair.

For all of six hours we waited, pacing, talking, and supporting each other.

If they were proceeding laparoscopically, rather then conventionally, the operation should have been over hours before. I had personally signed the consent forms for my mother, authorizing conventional surgery "if required," and acknowledging all of the potential risks and complications, including death.

I was the first to see Dr. Kavoussi enter the waiting room, wearing a white labcoat and accompanied by a nurse. He didn't look as if he was about to deliver bad news, but my heart was pounding furiously—until he smiled. "Your mother is going to be fine," he said, encouraging all of us; by now he was surrounded by Costopouloses. "We had to do it by conventional means, a decision we made once we went in, but the incision is not that bad."

Dr. Kavoussi had his hands full with my frantic family, but handled us all with patient resolve. Our mother was still asleep and we could see her, but he recommended that we wait until morning. She would be awake then, groggy but coherent, and the hospital recuperation time, "to be safe," was estimated at "four, five, maybe six days, something like that."

John and I stayed in Baltimore for eight days and nights. We slept at the Radisson and would walk 28 blocks at the break of day, and 28 blocks back at 9:00 p.m. Our mother fought to regain her health one hour at a time, one pain pill at a time.

On March 14, we took her home.

Dr. Kavoussi and the medical profession awakened in me a new-found respect and admiration. Doctors are truly healers, with a dedication I don't often see in my world.

§

My world is confrontational, argumentative, and often personal. The courtroom floor has been likened to Greek theater, not only in physical layout, but also in the drama that unfolds there. Tragedy is a common theme, comedy much rarer.

I took an elective course while pursuing my master's degree at Harvard. It was titled "Psychology and the Law." One aspect of the course addressed the personality types of law students. The most common characteristics found were unflattering: egotistical, self-centered, selfish, insensitive, type A, brash, bullish, and opinionated. These qualities are further embellished in law school, and forever ingrained in practice.

No wonder alcoholism and drug addiction are rampant in the profession.

No wonder the divorce rate is so high.

No wonder I have advised my daughters to seek a better life.

As combatants and warriors—certainly not healers who have taken the Hippocratic Oath—we engage in strategy, and if possible, pick our fights. This tactic in the defense of Charlie Robertson became pivotal, and would determine the parameters of our position.

In Rees Griffiths's conference room, we discussed the various defenses available to Charlie. Rees and Rich Oare were forever playing devil's advocate. The testimony at the preliminary hearing gave rise to a credible defense of self-defense, or the defense of others. Several witnesses—Neff and Knouse for starters—said they saw a gun brandished by Lillie Belle Allen. Others heard "she has a gun" and "she's going to shoot."

The Cadillac incident on July 20, 1969, would be easy to prove. In addition to witnesses on Newberry Street that day, Officer James Brown saw that car go up that street in broad daylight, saw the trunk pop open, and saw an African American open fire from that trunk into the residential community; in fact, he gave chase.

According to all accounts, the Lillie Belle Allen vehicle was also occupied by her father, a Southern Baptist minister from Aiken, South Carolina. We would be able to prove that many of the active racial movements in the '60s were organized and led by African American ministers.

If we wanted to go there.

We decided that we would not. To do so would have meant "blaming the victim." To do so was to rely on the unpredictable future testimony of Rick Knouse, and the unknown course of action of Gregory Neff. Moreover, Charlie Robertson wasn't on Newberry Street when Lillie Belle Allen was killed, had no idea what anybody's frame of mind was at that moment in time, and had nothing to do with her death. For all of those reasons we weren't getting in bed with the shooters.

And for all of those reasons, we would not be hostile or antagonistic to their defense.

Another possible theme was dirty politics. We had people on city council who were willing to testify to the animus and hostility of Tom Kelley toward Mayor Robertson. We had written correspondence from Councilman Kelley, scathing political communications to the mayor on the district attorney's stationery. Kelley had served on city council while he was an assistant district attorney. That, in and of itself, raised a substantial question. The district attorney's office was Republican, the mayor's office was Democratic, an election year was coming, and the word was that Kelley wanted to be an elected judge. Furthermore, one's prosecutor should never be a political opponent.

Rees, a powerful Democrat in a Republican county, insisted that theme would not fly. Though the politics of that community gave rise to heated discussions, "you'll never get a jury to believe that murder charges were brought, and have gone this far, because of political spats between Kelley and the mayor," he contended.

Politics in York could be brutal, but it was not overtly partisan. Many York Democrats share the conservative values of Republicans. Many Republicans are moderate. There's a big middle. While Republicans controlled the county, the city was heavily Democratic in voter registration. It could be argued that the Republicans running the county didn't give a damn who was mayor. Personal dislikes and allegiances were often more important than party registration.

Rich Oare, once a solicitor himself, agreed. But Rich would have loved to go after Kelley.

That left us with one compelling card to play. We would pick our fight. It would be our theme from the opening on. Charlie Robertson had nothing to do with the killing of Lillie Belle Allen, whether that killing was justified or not. He wasn't there when it happened, and had no reason to know that it was going to happen. And he did not hand out ammunition to Rick Knouse, or anybody else, or ever tell anybody to kill blacks.

That would be our defense, pure and simple.

That was our decision, and we were going to live with it.

§

By mid-2002, 15 large cardboard boxes were piled up in Jayme Emig's office. They were all related to the Robertson case, containing thousands of pages of grand jury transcripts; thousands of pages of police reports—most recent, many from 1969; all the newspaper articles that were to be put into sequence; volumes of transcripts, files, and exhibits from the civil rights case before Judge Nealon, a 33-year-old file that would become critical; plus correspondence, photographs, and memos from me and other defense attorneys.

Jayme Emig also had a decision to make.

How was she going to put it together?

She had gotten other cases ready for trial before, but nothing this monstrous.

Jayme knew what I wanted, but had lost a lot of sleep coming up with a system. The system would have to produce a single document, or a single entry, or a simple quote out of a newspaper on demand. Once that jury was in the box, fumbling around, looking for documents was not acceptable; organization and timing were everything. She needed to know what I wanted even before I knew what I needed.

Jayme was drop-dead gorgeous. A striking, blue-eyed brunette, Jayme was thin—not model-thin—but rather athletic. She had chiseled features in an angular face and stood tall, 5' 8'' in three-inch heels. Jayme oozed composure. What served me, however, were her intelligence, her drive, and her superb organizational skills—her instincts, really. This job played to one of her strengths. Jayme loved taking an absolute mess and making it neat. Here she would have to develop a rapid-fire information delivery system. It required more than organization. She would need to read thousands of pages, and she had to be familiar with exactly where key witnesses said something important, or even unimportant. She was not going to let me be caught off-guard with a witness we didn't know from A to Z. She was damn well determined about that. She would need to be prepared for any eventuality—we could not be surprised.

Jayme came up with several methods of tracking a document. She would have a file on every Commonwealth and defense witness. Detective Rodney George testified to the names of 309 witnesses he interviewed, and not knowing which ones would be called, she would need a file for each of them. All witness files would be accessed alphabetically, and everything about each witness, even references in newspaper articles, would be in those files.

She would also compile a discovery index chart, which would set forth the chronology, by date, of all witnesses interviewed. That way, I would know if one witness interviewed might have keyed off of a previous witness statement, or newspaper article.

It would get worse as time went on. Discovery documents from the Commonwealth were arriving all the time, in no particular order, mixing documents from 1969 and 2001.

Knowing where everything was, and what was in those files, was going to take some serious work. Jayme had another life, a personal life, but it would have to wait.

14

DOMINOES

They overcharged the boys on Newberry Street. They charged them with murder because the statute of limitations had run out on everything else. When prosecutors overcharge, they have room to move in the plea-bargaining process.

Especially when their starting position is murder in the first degree, which carries a mandatory life sentence.

The role of the prosecutor in the American criminal justice system is to seek justice. That honorable pursuit requires ethical and moral compliance. Prosecutors are not to overcharge a citizen to gain advantage, which is no different from stacking a deck in a poker game. In York, the prosecution's maneuvering was out of control. All the high cards were in their hand.

There was no way any competent lawyer could advise his client to go to a trial by jury on a murder charge when the prosecution was offering a plea to an ungraded misdemeanor. To sweeten the deal, the prosecutors in York were promising a sentence that would not exceed 12 months in jail, with the possibility of probation. Whether it would be probation, or something less than a year, would be up to the court, but the prosecutors could put in a good word at sentencing, "depending on how helpful the boys were during the trial against those left standing."

Prosecutors tell defense lawyers all the time, "first in, first out." That means if you are quick to plead guilty to their terms—quicker than the next guy—you'll get out before your accomplice.

Prosecutors also tell defense lawyers, "the more you have to give, the more you'll get." That means if you have incriminating testimony — good testimony for the prosecution or bad testimony for the defendants that dare go to trial — you'll be handed the prison keys for your release.

It really sucks, but that's the criminal justice system.

It sucks because there is no lower form of life than the informant, one who rolls over on a friend to save himself. Penitence is different, and for centuries has been a factor of mitigation. "An offender," according to President Judge Steve McEwen of the Superior Court of Pennsylvania, "who bares his soul and confesses all of his own misdeeds is entitled to quite some mitigation. However, the failure of the offender to implicate others must not be considered an aggravating factor that will serve to increase the severity of the sentence."

Other societies may penalize citizens who fail to tell on their neighbors. Our country, unfortunately, does the same without remorse in the criminal justice system. Prosecutors and our courts should not punish the individual who won't descend to be a rat, but they do it all the time.

Especially the Feds.

Certainly the DAs in York.

§

August 14, 2002
York County Courthouse

THOMAS PAUL SMITH, represented by Joe Metz, was the first to plead guilty before Judge Uhler.

Tom Kelley and Tim Barker also stood at the bar, neatly dressed for this important proceeding.

Courtroom 1 was only partially filled. The local media were certainly there, as was Hattie Dickson and members of her immediate family. Rich Oare and Ellen Wagner sat respectfully in the gallery to observe.

A guilty plea colloquy is required by our appellate courts. This is a transcribed dialogue between the court and the accused to assure that the plea is voluntarily, knowingly, and intelligently entered. It is also to assure that the accused is pleading guilty to a crime, for you can't plead guilty if you don't admit that you did the wrong you're admitting to. You can't plead guilty to conspiracy to commit murder if you didn't conspire to commit murder. The court is required to make sure it's done right.

Tom Smith looked out of place. Well-groomed and clean-cut, Smith, with a receding hairline and thick mustache, looked like a businessman. He had worked in environmental control at Starett's Metal. Though he only had a high school education, he was self-educated and very bright. He had no priors. He had not been a member of the Newberry Street Boys, but he had gone over to Newberry Street that steamy night in 1969.

Smith, with Metz at his side, told the court that he wanted to waive his right to a trial by jury, his right to remain silent, and his right to appeals in exchange for the dropping of murder charges. He was willing to plead guilty to conspiracy to commit an unlawful act, that act being murder, an ungraded misdemeanor that carried a minimum of one year and a maximum of two. This meant that under no circumstances could the court impose more than a year in jail; the court had the latitude to impose less, even down to probation.

"Mr. Smith, what is the basis for your plea? Why are you doing this today?" Judge Uhler asked, to determine whether Smith was admitting that he had conspired to commit murder.

"Well, because I actually feel that I'm guilty of a conspiracy," Smith answered.

"What did you do?" Judge Uhler asked, not satisfied with the answer.

Tom Smith, not sure how to answer and not wanting to blow the deal, told Judge Uhler that he had transported a rifle and ammunition to Newberry Street "and was prepared to defend the area." He said that he took the weapon and ammunition to Bob Messersmith's house. Later that night, when the shooting started, Smith said he was "hiding behind a car approximately 40 yards up from the Allen vehicle."

"And it's my understanding you did not fire any weapon?" Judge Uhler asked.

"Correct," Smith answered.

Kelley told Judge Uhler, "I'm satisfied, Your Honor."

Judge Uhler had to know he was on shaky appellate grounds. He then deferred accepting the plea pending a pre-sentence investigation, a position he would take for all pleas that were to be entered.

WILLIAM C. RITTER, represented by Al Barnes, assumed the position.

Judge Uhler methodically went through the waiver of all rights. That was the easy part.

"What is it—what conduct that you took part in do you believe warrants the Court to accept this plea based upon the charges that have been filed against you?" Judge Uhler asked.

"I shot at her," Ritter answered.

Ritter looked every bit the mountain man. With long hair, a scraggly beard and thick features, he appeared to be someone who had lived a hard life, which indeed he had. He had worked for 31 years on the production line at Harley-Davidson. Ritter had been married three times. In his first marriage, his son had died by accidental electrocution and his marriage could not hold up afterward. His third wife was disabled by a heart attack and he was taking care of her. His only prior was a DUI 12 years ago.

At least Ritter fired a shot, but Uhler knew the defense of self-defense, or the defense of others, was out there. He asked Ritter what prompted him to fire his gun in the first place.

"The bullets came at me. I hid behind the truck, and I ran up the street and got my gun. I should have kept going. I don't know why. Some dumb kid I guess, and I got my gun again and started shooting back," Ritter answered.

"What were you shooting at?" Judge Uhler asked.

"At a car," Ritter answered.

"Did you know who the occupants were?" Judge Uhler asked.

"No, I didn't see any," Ritter answered.

"Why were you shooting at the car?" Uhler pressed, to fill in an important blank.

"There was bullets coming at me, so I just shot back," Ritter answered.

"Now, did you discuss with your counsel the potential defense of self-defense?" Judge Uhler asked.

"No," Ritter said.

"No?" Uhler asked, obviously stressed.

"Never," Ritter answered.

At that point, Judge Uhler insisted that Ritter talk to his lawyer, that Al Barnes talk to Kelley and Barker, and that they all come back in ten minutes to continue the colloquy.

Ten minutes later, Al Barnes told the court that the defense of self-defense was discussed, and everybody agreed that it was not a defense available to Mr. Ritter. "He had an absolute duty to retreat. He didn't. He recognizes that, and so he misunderstood," Barnes explained, to keep the deal from slipping away. Otherwise, Ritter was going to stand trial for murder in the first degree.

Barker reminded Ritter that he had a duty to retreat; Ritter said, "Yeah," and that was it until future sentencing.

RICK LYNN KNOUSE, represented by John Moran, was the third to fold. He had thrown his hand in a year ago, testified for the Commonwealth at the preliminary hearing, and promised Judge Uhler that he would continue his cooperation.

"Yes," Knouse said, he understood the rights he was waiving.

"Please tell me what you perceive your involvement to be," Judge Uhler requested.

"My involvement was arming myself, listening to police at the rally, listening to police down on the street, listening to the elder Messersmith, discharging a weapon. That's it." Knouse answered. His lips were pressed tight and his eyes were darting.

Knousie was a piece of work.

Tim Barker, who was standing at the bar during the colloquy with Kelley, wanted more on the record from their key witness against Robertson.

"Where did you get the ammunition for that gun?" Barker asked.

"Where did I get the ammunition?" Knouse asked back.

"Yes," Barker said.

"I got it from Charlie Robertson, the mayor, a cop at the time," Knouse answered.

That was good enough for Barker and Kelley to seal the deal.

Judge Uhler then told Knouse, who was nervous as hell by now, that what he was pleading to "was the equivalent of a contemporaneous possession charge of marijuana or drug paraphernalia."

Of course, he had to take that deal, as did the others.

CLARENCE LUTZINGER, represented by Suzanne Smith, assistant public defender, stood before Judge Uhler for the grilling. He waived his rights, told the judge that he wanted to plead guilty, and the terms of the deal set forth on the record were identical to everybody else's.

Tom Kelley and Tim Barker continued to stand at the bar patiently, like two marshals.

Judge Uhler asked Lutzinger what he did on July 21, 1969, that amounted to "conspiracy to commit murder."

Lutzinger stated in open court that he had a pistol that night, believing he needed it to protect the neighborhood. He told Judge Uhler "a hundred or more" armed persons were similarly situated. He also said that he ran down behind a car and started shooting. He was not asked whether he was shooting at a person, or whether he intended to kill anybody.

He did tell Uhler that he thought he was doing the right thing, "protecting my neighborhood."

"Did you perceive any threat whatsoever from the car containing Lillie Belle Allen?" Kelley asked.

"Just what the people yelled," Lutzinger answered.

§

August 21, 2002
York County Courthouse

CHAUNCEY GLADFELTER, represented by Matt Gover, would have been there the previous week—with the others—but Matt was unavailable. Gover had given me a heads-up the week before that he was going down; he hated to do it, but he could not expose his client to a trial by jury on murder.

I certainly understood.

Matt suffered with his decision to plead, however, for he truly believed that Gladfelter had never conspired to commit any murder. He understood that he had to take the deal, but resented the overcharging by the prosecution that brought him to his knees. Matt was also uneasy; though he was hoping that Uhler would ultimately impose a sentence of probation, he knew that the judge could slam his client in jail for up to a year.

Gladfelter waived his rights on the record, under the watchful eyes of Kelley and Barker.

"Would you describe to me in your own words what it is that you participated in that led you to believe that you were part of the conspiracy to take the unlawful—or unlawfully take the life of another?" Judge Uhler asked.

With a shaven head and a trim white goatee, Gladfelter was standing tall for his 5' 9" frame. A laborer for a parts company in Lancaster, he was hard not to like personally. Gover was a veteran criminal defense attorney and he thought Gladfelter was a stand-up guy. He showed more character through this ordeal than just about any other client he had represented.

Chauncey Gladfelter, upon further questioning by the court, said that he went to the Messersmith house on the night in question, and that John Messersmith, the father, directed him "to go upstairs and watch for blacks." Chauncey said that he did so, that he remained on the Messersmith balcony "until after all the shooting was over," and that he did not leave that balcony "because I was scared. I didn't know where the shooting was coming from."

"What did you observe?" Judge Uhler asked.

"In the back, nothing." Gladfelter answered.

Gladfelter did tell the court that Mike Messersmith was on the balcony with him, and that Mike had a loaded rifle in case blacks came in the back.

"What was the—what was your understanding of the goal of the conduct that you were involved with?" Uhler asked.

"To protect the neighborhood," Gladfelter answered.

"And how were you going to be protecting that neighborhood?" the judge asked.

"Mike had a gun. We were on the back balcony," Gladfelter answered.

No wonder Matt Gover was in anguish. Gladfelter didn't conspire to murder anybody.

§

Five had pled guilty.

Four had not.

It appeared that the prosecution was surrounding the wagons, that with each plea they were strengthening their case against Charlie Robertson. That public perception depended on whether they got corroborative evidence, from either refreshed recollections or new lies.

Joe Metz told me that Smith was not going to hurt Charlie Robertson.

Al Barnes told me that Ritter was not going to hurt Charlie Robertson.

Suzanne Smith wasn't telling me anything, fearing the prosecution might pull the deal.

Matt Gover told me that Gladfelter didn't know shit.

I just didn't know whether the plea agreements were going to stop with Gladfelter. I believed that Greg Neff was another possible plea.

Neff had recently retained Harry Ness, a York criminal defense lawyer. Harry's brother, Chris, had been the district attorney of York from 1982 to 1986, and Harry had been an assistant prosecutor at that time. Harry and I had been friends for years, and we had taken road trips together on our motorcycles. He was a member of a motorcycle club in York known as the Road Dogs, a group of wealthy friends, mostly urbanites, all with new, customized, expensive Harley-Davidsons—not surprising, since they were made in York.

I was not a member of that club, nor would I ever be, for many reasons. I did ride with them twice, as a guest of Harry's, but every time they passed other bikers going in the other direction, they would wave—and that made me crazy. They were a lot of fun, however, and many of them were lawyers.

Harry Ness, in my opinion, was the best criminal defense lawyer in York. He was masterful on the courtroom floor, and a real charmer. The women loved him, for he was a smaller, better-looking version of the singer Meatloaf. In the '80s, he and I represented a police chief who was charged with murder, and together we won an acquittal. I have always believed that it was because of Harry's courtroom prowess in his hometown.

Harry was going to let me know his intentions. They were really quite simple: he was going to approach Tom Kelley and Tim Barker, and ask for the same deal the others had been given. It was too bad that Neff had lost his deal for probation, but an exposure of 12 months versus a life sentence was a no-brainer.

Greg Neff was a handful for Harry. Greg had this sense of honor and loyalty, not only to his friends of 30 years, but to himself. Whether he saw Lillie Belle Allen brandishing a gun or not, he believed that's what he saw. He may have been mistaken, maybe not, but in no event was he going to tailor his testimony to please Kelley and Barker.

That was a tough position for Harry to be in, but there's something to be said about honor, about knowing what matters—in fact, there's a lot to be said about that.

I wasn't too worried that Art Messersmith would plead guilty. For that to happen, for Art to get the same deal as everybody else, he would have to give up his brother. I didn't believe that was going to happen, and Frank Arcuri told me "Never."

I was certain that the prosecution could not deal with Bob Messersmith. The prosecution had taken the position that they believed Bob fired the .12-gauge shotgun slug that took the life of Lillie Belle Allen. From day one, they publicly said he was the killer.

I knew what we were doing. Charlie Robertson wasn't pleading to a fucking thing.

We weren't kissing anybody's ass.

We weren't apologizing for what we didn't do.

We were picking a jury, in York County, on September 23—and if Greg Neff did plead guilty, along with Art and Bob Messersmith, then we were going to trial alone.

§

August 29, 2002
York County Courthouse

ART MESSERSMITH, represented by Frank Arcuri, stood in front of Judge Uhler to plead guilty.

This plea had some changeovers. The prosecutors—and now there were three: Kelley, Barker, and Fran Chardo, an experienced district attorney from Harrisburg—told the judge that Art Messersmith was pleading guilty to conspiracy, as the others had done, and to attempted homicide, a felony.

Kelley also told the court that Art Messersmith's exposure was a minimum sentence of four and a half years, with a maximum of nine years. That meant that if Art went through with it, Judge Uhler could put him in jail for four and a half years, or anything less, but he would be at the mercy of the court.

In 1969, Art Messersmith was 16 years old; he was acting at the directive of his father, and was no more involved than anybody else. It was his brother who was the alleged killer, not Art.

Like all the others, he waived his trial and appellate rights.

Artie, as he had been called, was gaunt with sharp facial features. Dressed in his best outfit he still looked disheveled. His neck was pencil thin, his dark brown hair plastered back, his face pock-marked. He had been a wiseass, a tough kid, never afraid of a fight. If he got his ass kicked, his brothers would bail him out or take revenge. He still had that smirk.

"What is it that you understand the elements of the respective offenses are or do you wish me to review that with you directly on the record?" Judge Uhler asked.

"Pardon?" Art Messersmith answered, not having a clue what he was just asked.

Judge Uhler then read him the elements of the offenses from the law books, which was more confusing than ever to a guy who could barely read.

"What did you do?" Judge Uhler asked, trying to simplify the issue.

"I shot into the car," Messersmith answered, "with a .12-gauge shotgun with game load."

"What is it that prompted your firing the shot toward the car?" Judge Uhler asked.

"I guess fear that I'd be shot, just fear from what happened the night before," Messersmith answered.

"What the fuck was that about?" I asked Frank Arcuri when I finally got him on the phone.

"He freaked out at the last minute, Bill. He told me that he didn't want to run the risk, he just couldn't do it," Frank answered.

"Four and a half to nine?" I asked, surprised.

"They wouldn't budge. They did say that at the time of sentencing, they'll impress upon Judge Uhler that Art Messersmith was no more involved than anybody else." Frank answered defensively.

"Did he say that he fired at the car?" I asked, for it was the first time I had ever heard *that*.

"You know how that shit works, Bill. He had told them that he fired into the air. He had given them a written statement to that effect. One hour before going into court, they told us that if he didn't admit shooting at the car . . . they were pulling that deal. Art simply gave them what they wanted," Frank answered apologetically.

He was right about one thing—I do know how that shit works.

"Is he going to testify against his brother?" I asked.

"They never asked him about his brother," Frank answered.

"Does he have anything to say about Charlie?" I had to ask *that* question, and held my breath.

"I don't know," Frank answered. "They interviewed him outside of my presence . . . who knows what he's going to say."

15

PLAYERS

I thought I could blow out Robertson's charges at the preliminary hearing. I was wrong. Then I thought I could get everybody's charges dismissed at the trial level because of the prejudicial delay. Wrong.

I was sure the appellate courts would bail me out before trial, but they proved me wrong again.

I thought I would get a severance and that Charlie would not have to be tried with the others—wrong.

I never thought Art Messersmith would plead—wrong.

Finally, I was sure that after the prosecutors left Charlie twisting in the wind, that they would come to me on the eve of trial with a resolution. That resolution, they knew, could never include an acknowledgment that Charlie had anything to do with the death of Lillie Belle Allen. That resolution, they knew, would have to be a summary disposition—as in disorderly conduct at Farquhar Park, or conduct unbecoming a police officer at Farquhar Park—with zero exposure to jail, with zero jeopardy to his pension.

It never happened. They never came. I was wrong.

Three weeks before trial, with 31 years of experience in the criminal justice system, I wondered if I knew a fucking thing about anything.

§

Rich Oare and Ellen Wagner, with Charlie Robertson leading the way, were lining up character witnesses for trial. We wanted former police officers and firemen, preferably ones who had lived through the riots with Charlie. We wanted businessmen, community leaders, school teachers, local politicians, congressmen, religious leaders, and ordinary people in the community—of all races, colors, and creeds—who were willing to walk into a courtroom, face his jury and their community, and testify for him.

I told Charlie to call in every marker out there. People had been telling us all along that they were willing to help, and it was time to find out who his friends were.

Rich and Charlie were to talk to Jim VanGreen and Ray Markle, not over the phone, but in person. They had been with Charlie in "Big Al" on the night in question, and were critical witnesses.

VanGreen was prepared and ready to go, with an attitude, for that night still lived in his memory. He was furious. He could not believe that Charlie Robertson was being put on trial for murder after all he had done for the community.

Ray Markle was prepared and ready to go.

Rich and Charlie were to talk to Jim Brown, a York police officer who lived through the riots, and who had witnessed the events on Newberry Street on July 20, 1969. He saw the other white Cadillac go up Newberry Street in broad daylight, the trunk pop open, and an African American open fire in that residential community. Brown also had worked that 12-hour night shift. He would relive the '69 riots in York for Charlie's jury. He had the kind of powerful, emotional testimony we needed.

Jim Brown was prepared and ready to go.

Rich and Charlie were to contact firemen, two of whom had become chiefs of their departments, "to set fire to the city of York on a map." The idea was that they would use red markers to show where fires had burned during the riots and to show those that they helped extinguish while under gunfire. Sections of the city on the map would appear to be "on fire" after these guys were done with their red markers.

For Charlie Robertson, the young officer who stood by their side during the hell of July '69, the boys from the fire department were prepared and ready to go. They would have rolled out the engines with sirens blaring if asked.

Major Robert Rice was alive and well, and on telephone standby. He had been the captain of the Pennsylvania State Police in 1969, in charge of 3,000 men; Governor Shafer had summoned him to the Capitol in the early morning hours after the shooting on Newberry Street. We reached him at his home in Lancaster, Pennsylvania; he told us he was 87 years old, confined to a wheelchair, but he remembered the riots in York "like they were yesterday."

Yes, he added, he would be willing to appear in a courtroom one more time to tell the truth. He requested a subpoena, which he would honor, but we would have to make arrangements to get him to the courthouse, and then to the courtroom, for he was unable to walk.

Sergeant John Creavey, who had investigated the riots for the Pennsylvania State Police, was retired and living in Dillsburg, Pennsylvania. Creavey's son brought him to my office, and though the old sergeant looked great, a hulk of a man with flowing white hair, his Alzheimer's rendered him unavailable. I was sorry to lose him as a witness, for he better than anyone—including Rodney George, Tom Kelley, and Tim Barker—had known what happened in York in '69, and why. He knew who the shooters were on Newberry Street, and why no one was charged. He also knew that Charlie Robertson's name was never mentioned as having anything to do with any unlawful killing of an innocent black woman. Creavey's 33-page report documented all of the foregoing, but would be considered inadmissible hearsay.

The prosecutors would object, to make sure the jury was denied his findings and conclusions.

Ellen got the dirty work. She was to type up the subpoenas and get them served. She was to do the necessary photocopying of documents. She was to retrieve 1969 photographs from the archives: of the riots, of the National Guard moving in with the Pennsylvania State Police, of the York City Police executing search warrants in riot gear, and of buildings destroyed by fires. She did it all, frantically, but got it done.

Rees Griffiths, Oare, and Robertson were to review the names on the prospective jury lists. They were to look for names they recognized and mark them "yes," "no," or "?". They were to identify prospective jurors who lived in the city of York, and we would question them during voir dire to determine whether they, or their loved ones, had lived in the city during the riots. We wanted city residents, especially ones who had lived there in July 1969. We also wanted prospective jurors related to law enforcement personnel. We wanted prospective jurors who would believe a police officer over an ordinary citizen. Actually, we were looking for a jury the prosecution would ordinarily want.

But this was not an ordinary prosecution, and our roles would be reversed during the jury selection process.

Rees Griffiths was to review Nick Ressetar's legal research memos, and be prepared to argue motions in limine. A motion in limine is a matter brought before the court, either orally or in writing, for a ruling outside the presence of the jury. These motions, whether brought by the prosecution or defense, can be pivotal during a trial; and they were piling up on Judge Uhler's desk.

The prosecution wanted no reference made to Kelley's animosity toward Robertson; "not relevant" was their assertion.

The prosecution wanted no reference made to their "selective prosecutions"; they had the right to prosecute certain individuals, and not others similarly situated, or so they argued.

Pete Solymos and Tom Sponaugle wanted Bob Messersmith's prior conviction for shooting Taka Nii Sweeney, kept out. The victim was an African American who was wounded during the riots. That shooting took place on a different date, under different circumstances. He was shot with a .12-gauge shotgun. "Not relevant, too prejudicial" was their position.

Rees was to handle those legal issues, and anything else that was certain to come up. Such legal issues are resolved in the judge's chambers, or at side bar, and often get heated. Rees had the legal background, the credibility, and the constitution to take the heat. He could also deliver it, at melting temperatures.

This was no time for a lawyer like Rees to be in the background. He was to suit up from day one of the trial, call shots, and take shots. He and Rich Oare would be responsible for calling the impressive array of character witnesses to the witness stand, and with oratory flair, conduct their direct examination.

Nick Ressetar was assigned to purgatory. The anticipated legal issues were to be briefed. The jury instructions for Judge Uhler were to be prepared ahead of time. Nick was to be on telephone standby day and night. He was not to leave town, and his cellular phone was to be on at all times.

Jayme Emig was to be in court every day. She was to arrive early, and be the last one to leave. She was to sit beside her wall of cardboard boxes, six in all, and know exactly where everything was.

§

Seven Days Before Trial

The prosecution team, in the trial mode, subpoenaed 150 witnesses. Their exhibits, mostly posterboard photographs of Newberry Street, depicting different angles and distances to where the Cadillac came to rest, were pre-marked. Their many files were color-coded and divided three ways, most of them to be handled by Tom Kelley.

The prosecution team included First Assistant District Attorney Tom Kelley, and he would be lead counsel, responsible for the opening, the closing, and many key witnesses. First Deputy Prosecutor Tim Barker would handle the direct examination of others, some cross, and most objections. Dauphin County Assistant District Attorney Fran Chardo, on loan to the York County office, was to organize the complex prosecution case. Chardo would be responsible for the direct examination of Rick Knouse and Chief McMaster, critical witnesses to the prosecution's case. The cross examination of Charlie Robertson would be Chardo's.

Tom Kelley had graduated from Dickinson College in 1987, having majored in history and dramatic arts. To him the courtroom was a stage, and he had the lead role. He said that when he's in front of a jury, he knows that "I'm also the writer, the director, and the producer. It's up to me to craft my story for maximum effect."

For ten years, Kelley was a trial prosecutor. He started out prosecuting domestic violence cases, where most young prosecutors begin their careers. He then moved to child abuse prosecutions, and finally to homicide cases.

By all independent accounts—and I checked them all: defense lawyers, other prosecutors, judges, sheriffs, tipstaffs, stenographers, and other courthouse personnel—he may have had a flair for the dramatic, but he was to be respected. He would interview his witnesses, practice his opening and his closing, and write out his direct examination and his cross. He would appear in court well dressed, groomed, and fit. A Clark Kent look-alike, he had sex appeal, and this case was going to make him a star.

Kelley had huge shoulders and a well-developed upper torso. He had done some serious weightlifting and still worked out. Because of his size, he needed custom-made clothes. He'd done some boxing and played football for a while. Because of his blue eyes, dark hair, and a story-telling ability traced back to ancestors on the Emerald Isle, women thought him handsome, personable, and sensitive. Kelley was said to have been "hurt" by various allegations made in the York community, some by Robertson's supporters, that the case was born of politics or personal animosity. Stoically, his supporters say, he bore that burden, since as the prosecutor he couldn't respond—much less fire back—while the case was underway.

Kelley's right-hand man for several years, and certainly for this case, was Tim Barker. Barker was also a Dickinson College graduate, class of '91. They didn't get to know each other until Tim joined the York County DA's office in 1997. Barker remembered Kelley as a sort of big man on campus, someone whom he had looked up to. Kelley recognized that Barker was "legally bright and detail oriented." The two had tried petty cases, serious cases, and even murder cases together—they were a successful team.

"When we're in court we both feel like we're unbeatable—unstoppable—because we're confident in each other. It's not arrogance, we just know we can bring it to the table," Barker said during an interview with *Dickinson Magazine*, published in the autumn 2002 issue, shortly before the trial.

"Tim and Tom" some called them.

While Kelley considered himself the "idea guy," others believed Barker was the brain trust of this partnership. He looked like a former geek. He was a deep thinker and enjoyed philosophy. Barker was slightly overweight with a low-slung beard, like an Amishman's, and very dark hair.

Kelley had the charisma and served as the front guy, while Barker, with his knowledge of case law, served as his alter ego.

The prosecution of Charlie Robertson, however, was on a level they had never reached before. The game they were now playing was at a bigger table, with higher stakes, and they were so warned by their newest backup, District Attorney Fran Chardo.

Chardo had gone to Gettysburg College, and knew all about civil wars and bloodshed. In the fall of 2002, he had been out of law school nine years, having graduated from Widener in Wilmington, Delaware. His entire career was spent prosecuting cases in Harrisburg, Pennsylvania. He was responsible for all career criminal prosecutions, including the classification of offenders. His job description included supervising several deputy district attorneys, advising and critiquing their performance. I estimated that he had over a hundred jury trials under his belt; most were successful.

Chardo, 34, was brought in to add depth to the York lineup. His last name was French in origin, though most of his ancestors had been Irish. With a strong, almost rugged face, Chardo had the prominent Gallic nose of some distant French ancestor. He had a full head of brown hair—worn a shade over the tip of his ears. Chardo was 5' 11" and 165 pounds. He had that look of experience from nine years as a trial lawyer. Kelley considered Chardo a cross between himself and

Barker, a blend of trial lawyer acumen and case law expertise. Chardo enjoyed the latter but loved doing the trial work.

Harrisburg is five minutes from my office, across the Susquehanna River. Chardo's office is where my career started, and I had heard about Fran and his good work. I followed closely, for I had a personal interest in his handling of the Crawford case, a case he inherited from years past.

In 1974, Steven Crawford, at the young age of 14, was charged in Harrisburg, Dauphin County, with the bludgeoning death of his friend, John Eddie Mitchell, 13. Mitchell was a newspaper boy for the *Harrisburg Patriot*, and Crawford was accused of killing him to take his nickels and quarters. The body was found in the garage of Crawford's family, and the sole evidence that convicted Steven went something like this: Steven's fingerprints were on his father's car, near the body. The fingerprints of a child are often found on the outside of a parent's car, particularly an abandoned one in a garage; however, the Crawford prints had blood on them.

The prosecution needed to prove that the prints weren't innocently on the car before Mitchell's spattered blood hit them. They needed to prove the prints and the blood were put on the car simultaneously.

Otherwise, the prosecution had no case, for there was no other evidence to convict young Crawford.

To get over this hurdle, the prosecution's fingerprint experts said that "there was blood only on the ridges of Steven's prints, not in the valleys . . . the valleys were devoid of blood, totally clean . . . therefore, the blood was the medium of transfer, which means the blood acted like fingerprint ink . . . this opinion is premised on the valleys being totally clean . . . you can't throw a bucket of red paint on a zebra and only hit the stripes."

Steven Crawford was promptly convicted by a jury in Harrisburg and sentenced to life. I was his defense lawyer.

The Supreme Court of Pennsylvania granted Crawford a new trial, and I represented him a second time in Harrisburg in 1977. We lost again, based on the same expert testimony—"the valleys were totally clean."

I couldn't get around the valleys being totally clean. There was simply no explanation.

Judge John C. Dowling, who handled the second trial of Crawford, granted him a third trial for unrelated reasons.

I tried it a third time, in 1978, and lost again based on that expert testimony—"no blood in the valleys, they were totally clean."

After 28 years in jail, after 28 fucking years in prison for a murder Crawford always maintained he did not commit, there was a break. Some say it was divine intervention, and I believe it, for there can be no other explanation.

In 2002, two youths found a briefcase in a trash can, the briefcase of a police officer involved in the case. It was found seven years after that officer's death. Apparently, the briefcase had recently been thrown out. That briefcase contained the original lab reports *confirming blood in the valleys*.

When Fran Chardo was handed the file, he was put under a public microscope. Many in the law enforcement field wanted a fourth trial, but the Supreme Court ruling in the Jay Smith Case, and that court's ire, hung over their heads like a huge guillotine. The public outcry was to set Crawford free. Chardo was in the middle.

I watched with great interest the press conference and public announcement approved by Dauphin County district attorney Ed Marsico. The decision of that office was to set Crawford free.

My thoughts, the flashbacks, were in vivid color.

They put that kid through three trials. I know they wanted to win that case, and celebrated three times. The whole time, they sat on the lab notes, knowing their "expert" testimony was a fucking lie. Crawford did 28 years. How's he going to heal? How's his family going to heal? How do the wrongdoers live with themselves? Aren't they afraid of facing a higher order?

My feeling of vindication was real, for Steven Crawford's convictions haunted me for years. I could still hear his mother praying in the courtroom, his father crying. The announcement of Chardo and Marsico was met with applause on the courthouse steps of Dauphin County—mostly by African Americans, some by whites. Their applause paled compared to the thunderous ovation in my heart.

Thanks, Chardo, I thought, as I turned the television off.

Fran Chardo was a good choice for the boys in York. He took the oath to honor their cause in April 2002, and was going to see them through it.

§

For 17 months—day and night—it was like a drumbeat in the back of my head, sometimes louder, but always there. Working my dog in the game lands helped, as did running broke horses on a mountain trail. The local ski slopes in the winter would call, but not as often.

Training in the early morning hours at Gold's Gym in Carlisle, often before daylight, was much needed, but the slow pounding rhythm could not be denied. Callista's basketball and field hockey games were a godsend. Callista was a godsend—as were Kara, Khristina, and Jill. My mother's slow recovery and my aging father were a daily concern, but I had much family support.

A case like Charlie Robertson's consumes you, plagues you, won't let you alone. The closer you get to the trial date, the more overwhelming it becomes. Representing an accused, one whose innocence you truly believe in, is stressful. I did not want to lose this case—not for Charlie Robertson, not for those who believed in him, not for myself.

Doing it for myself mattered.

When I was a young defense lawyer, I believed the only bad publicity was no publicity. It was important to get exposure; even if you lost the case, at least your coverage reflected a good fight. In many criminal cases, high-profile or otherwise, the prosecution has all the cards. They have the eyewitnesses, the smoking gun, the fingerprints, the victim's blood on your client's clothes, and a taped confession. You can't win a case like that, you aren't expected to, and therefore "you can't lose a case that you can't win."

Charlie Robertson's case was different, for two reasons.

I wasn't young anymore. I had been doing this for 30 years. Maybe I shouldn't have said yes when I got the call, but I did. A lawyer at my self-imposed level of play has to win the big ones. Losing a big one, one that you *should* win, is not good, not good at all, especially when it might be your last go-around.

Second, this wasn't a case that cried out for a conviction. The prosecution didn't have shit. They had no testimony that rose to the level of murder. Their key witness was a worthless liar whose brain had been fried on drugs. All they had was a race card. The prosecution had no corroboration, no physical evidence, no confession. The defendant had been a good police officer during the '69 riots in York, who had put his life on the line for the community in which he was now being tried. The thought of losing the Robertson case made me crazy.

In my mind, and in my heart, it was still there—the attitude. I had tried more cases than the three prosecutors put together. They wanted a trial by jury in York, in a high-profile case with the big boys watching. They were going to get what they asked for. There would be no holding back. I was putting everything on the line.

16

JIHAD

September 23, 2002
Perry County, Pennsylvania

My body clock went off at 3:45 a.m., before the alarm clock as usual. It was here, the opening day of trial in the Robertson case. I had spent a lifetime's work preparing for this trial—much of it in the courtroom and much of it in the gym. Staying in shape physically went hand-in-hand with mental preparation for trial and it was the key to endurance. The ancient Spartans knew more than a little bit about this. I was up at least an hour and a half earlier than normal, but there was still no time for Gold's Gym in Carlisle. There would be no light banter or upbeat music like during my workout at Gold's Gym. The time constraints meant using my own weights in the basement. It was a lonely but necessary endeavor, with the rest of the countryside still in darkness.

One thing remained the same: I went to the kitchen first thing and put on three cups of coffee—an absolute must to kick-start the workout and my day.

In the weeks of preparation for trial and during the trial, I increased my workouts considerably, expanding the time and the number of sets that I do. Weightlifting actually releases a chemical in the brain that has a sedative effect on the body. To withstand the rigors of trial, more "sedative" is needed. The workout schedule had to be ramped up. Instead of a 70-minute workout, I'd do an 85-minute workout. Instead of 20 sets, I'd do 25 sets—working two major body parts a day, at least five days a week. It was a routine designed by my "personal trainers" John Spade and Matt Nicastro at Gold's Gym. Matt was the former chiropractor for the Baltimore Ravens. I didn't employ them as trainers. These guys were friends and they helped me out. They knew what they were doing. Every workout had to include 20 minutes or so of abdominal crunches. Over-working the abs? There's no such thing. Being strong through the middle is important any day, especially this day.

A battle for someone's life was about to be waged. It just happened to be my client. I needed every edge, every ounce of energy to defend Charlie Robertson against charges that never should have been brought in the first place. These young, hungry, misguided prosecutors in York were pulling out all the stops. Despite all the rulings against us and in the state's favor, our defense team was calling their bluff. But it would be combat, every minute of it. Blood would be spilled. I had no intention of allowing it to be mine or Charlie Robertson's.

The beard was gone. I shaved, usually two days before trial or any court appearance to avoid any rough spots or swelling. I kept the moustache. Conservative with a capital C would be the theme of the day for the clothing I had selected—a solid blue suit, a crisp white shirt, a red-blue-and-gold tie, and my most unobtrusive, dark cowboy boots—but I always wore a gold bracelet and a gold ring.

It was 52 miles from my house to the courthouse in downtown York—a roundtrip of 104 miles per day. It meant thousands of miles in the weeks leading up to trial and through the trial itself. I had to al-low an hour and a half for the drive. The trip down local roads, then I-81, the 581 Connector, and I-83 South was a chance to renew my fo-cus on jury selection. How long would it take? Would we even get a jury in York or have to move it elsewhere? What kind of hand would I be dealt and what could I do to shape it in our best interest?

The bloodletting would soon begin. It was a nice day, as I remem-ber. No overcoats yet, but the heat of summer was wearing off. The trip down to York in my pearl-red Cadillac Eldorado, with its palomino leather interior, was an opportunity to find the zone I needed to be in for effective courtroom work.

Jury selection quickly becomes mundane to many observers. It's not like opening arguments or the first day of testimony. But this was it. We'd come all this way on a trumped-up murder charge. But it wasn't going away. The breaks were not going our way. We were going to trial. I pulled into the garage of the Yorktowne Hotel with a glimpse of the pandemonium that awaited us.

The local jackals had been unleashed. They were howling, hungry, and ready for a kill.

§

September 23
York, Pennsylvania

It was crazy on Market Street. Media trucks had been double-parked since early dawn. Reporters were milling everywhere. A Philadelphia television news team was camped out on Rees Griffiths's nearby office steps, hoping that Charlie Robertson would make an appearance, and maybe give a comment. Swarms of cameras were in front of the courthouse; at least a dozen others were positioned at the back entrance.

We waited in Rees's conference room—Charlie, Rees, Rich, Jayme, and I—having arrived early, feeling surrounded, saying very little to each other. Minutes would pass in total silence, and I could hear myself breathing. Soon, Rich and Jayme would escort Charlie out the back door, and enter the courthouse from the alley. Rees and I would walk up Market Street and enter through the front to act as decoys. We laughed at our plan, knowing that it wouldn't work, and it didn't.

The camera people and teams of reporters almost knocked Charlie down the minute he crossed the street. Jayme, who was supposed to be Charlie's bodyguard, got knocked in the head with a reporter's extended microphone—and got her hair messed up. Oare ended up taking another route to protect himself.

Jury Selection

Judge Uhler told all of the lawyers in chambers how we were going to proceed. The first 100 prospective jurors would be brought into the courtroom, sworn in, and given general instructions by the court. Thereafter, they would be taken to a waiting room to be called into the courtroom one at a time for individual voir dire. Once on the witness stand, they would be questioned by the prosecutors, then by Robertson's lawyers, then Messersmith's, then Neff's.

"Only one lawyer from each team will do the questioning," Uhler instructed. "We will rotate...Prospective juror 1 will be questioned by the prosecution first . . . Then prospective juror 2 will be questioned by one of Robertson's lawyers . . . and so on down the line."

"What if we have an objection to a question?" Barker asked.

"Then object, and I'll make a ruling," Judge Uhler answered, rolling his eyes. "But let's keep this thing moving. I want to be home by Thanksgiving."

Jury selection in one of the most notorious trials in York County history got underway at 9:55 a.m. We were to pick 12 jurors and 6 alternates from a pool of 800 York County residents. The prosecution did not want jurors who were related to, or who had any connection with, law enforcement personnel. The prosecution did not want jurors who expressed displeasure or concern regarding the 32-year delay. It appeared that they were looking for younger, college-educated women, or anyone who was not male.

The defense, contrary to the pundits, was not looking for older male jurors with a high school education. Our profile did not discriminate between men and women. We were looking for prospective jurors who might have lived through the riots. We were looking for jurors who had strength and courage, for their verdict would have a lasting impact on their community as well as the accused. We wanted a jury that would render a verdict based on the evidence, not one that was going to send a message. We were looking hard for jurors uninfluenced by anything they might have seen, read, or heard about the case—and because of the media's coverage, especially that of York's papers, this was the most troublesome matter for all of us.

Juries are hard, if not almost impossible to predict. People—whether male, female, married, single, young, old, black, or white—are much too complex to figure out in five minutes. I know everything written on this subject; I have used qualified jury consultants and psychologists, and I have decided for myself for over three decades.

People are definitely much too complex to figure out in a matter of five minutes.

Instincts are also important.

And in a case like this one—emotionally charged, politically motivated, and racially layered—only the strong would survive in the jury room, for it is no place for the faint of heart.

Picking a jury in a high-profile case is a slow process, painfully boring for all concerned. Individual jurors who are conscripted suffer indignities—long periods of waiting, sparse accommodations, meager pay, and personal questions they must answer in public. Yet it is an important process, a critical institution, for only they can end a criminal prosecution that should never have been brought.

From early in the morning until late afternoon, for six days, we pressed forward.

In the end we picked 12 jurors and 6 alternates to determine the fate of Charlie Robertson, Bob Messersmith, Greg Neff, and the Commonwealth. This is who they were, with some notes:

Juror 1: White male, county corrections officer, young, single.

Juror 2: White male, middle-school world history teacher, lived in York in 1969, married, recalled armored vehicles rolling down George Street.

Juror 3: White male, state unemployment specialist, lived in York County eight years, was 15 in 1969, married with five children.

Juror 4: White female, hospital volunteer coordinator, married.

Juror 5: White female, worked for a surgeon, lived in the county since 1978.

Juror 6: White female, retired phone company administrator, lived in Springettsbury Township since 1980.

Juror 7: White male, supervised a chain of retail stores, lived in York since 1979.

Juror 8: White male, mechanical engineer.

Juror 9: White female, childhood neighbor of murdered York policeman Henry C. Schaad, married.

Juror 10: White male, 33, worked in Lancaster County, originally from Michigan.

Juror 11: White female with two friends in law enforcement.

Juror 12: White female, lived in Jacobus in 1969, married.

Alternates: The first of the six alternates was a husky, sensitive, African American male. The other five alternates were white.

During the jury selection process, we were not to refer to the prospective jurors by name, only by number. The artists in the courtroom were instructed by Judge Uhler to do no sketches of the jurors, and the other media representatives were ordered to "stay away from them with cameras, and they are not to be identified in the paper."

There were very few moments of levity while picking the jury. The objections started early, and the first one came from the prosecution after we picked our second juror. The prosecution accused the defense of "engaging in a pattern of gender discrimination." Their reason was that we had two males in the jury box, and had challenged a pretty female who was next.

That objection was ridiculous, and was summarily denied.

The prosecution then accused the defense in open court of "engaging in a pattern of racial discrimination." That objection hit a nerve with Judge Uhler, and the media went wild with it.

There was no pattern of racial discrimination engaged in by the defense. That was bullshit. The entire panel included five African Americans, and three were excused for cause; that left two potential African American jurors.

The defense had nothing to do with the potential racial composition of the jury. It simply reflected what had been the basic racial composition of York County, and central Pennsylvania, for as long as I can remember. The prosecution is generally gleeful over such a composition, since most defendants in the criminal justice system are African American.

It's true that the principal jury consisted of six white men and six white women, and that's an "all-white jury."

Did the defense get rid of the two potential African American jurors in this case by exercising peremptory challenges?

Yes, in this case, but why wouldn't we?

§

October 1, 2002
York County Courthouse

Opening Statements

We are taught in law school to "set the hook" in the opening statement. Social psychologists believe that many jurors make up their minds in the openings, and though they may be willing to change them, the burden is on the losing party. Without a doubt it is your first opportunity to state your position, to make an impression, to get their attention. "Tell them what you're going to tell them," future trial lawyers are taught, "and when you close, tell them what you told them."

Spending six days picking a jury may have been boring, but opening statements were not. The gallery had thinned out during jury selection, but it was packed for the opening exchange. Tom Kelley, the lead prosecutor, would go first. The prosecution team had two tables pressed against the bar, and they would be facing the jury. Charlie Robertson and his three lawyers were next to the jury box, uncomfortably close, facing Judge Uhler. Bob Messersmith's table was to my right. Greg Neff's was to the right of Messersmith. The defense lawyers agreed that I would go on the heels of Kelley, that Pete Solymos would follow me, and then Harry Ness. We had also discussed deferring one of the openings until the close of the Commonwealth's case, but decided against it.

It takes great restraint to be expressionless when opposing counsel opens. You know the prosecutor is going to be pointing his finger at you, telling the jury he will prove your client is guilty of murder.

And that's what Tom Kelley did.

He told the jury how the Allen family drove into "the bowels of hell" and how the young men armed on the street opened fire. To get the jury's attention, Kelley backed up from the jury box, then rushed toward it, holding an imaginary shotgun and yelling "bang, bang, bang!"

I know that made me jump, along with the jury and everybody else.

It was too much drama, though—way too much—and it didn't work. This jury had already made up its mind that it was going to render a verdict based on the testimony.

Tom Kelley not only told the jury that Charlie Robertson had aided and abetted the death of Lillie Belle Allen, but that "the York City Police were in an uneasy alliance with the Newberry Street Boys" who took her life.

Unbelievable, I thought. He's not only accusing Robertson of murder, but now I've got to defend the entire York Police Department for their actions in '69.

I had to make some quick adjustments to my opening, an opening I had spent weeks preparing.

"Our battle, ladies and gentlemen," I told the jury, "is not with the Lillie Belle Allen family or the African American community of York, and never has been . . . Our battle is not with the boys on Newberry Street for we were not there when the shooting took place, and were not in their shoes . . . Our battle *is* with the prosecutors in this case, who weren't born in 1969, and who have unilaterally decided to re-write history . . . based on the uncorroborated, and disproven testimony, of one Rick Knouse, premised upon an unprecedented theory of murder."

I asked Charlie Robertson to please stand and face his jury, and when he did so, I introduced the former mayor and police officer who had given his life to their community. That moment drove rivets into the proceedings, impressing upon the jurors his life's work and the gravity of their oath.

I promised the jury that I would prove his innocence, but to do so, they would have to relive the riots of '69. One of York's darkest hours would be described by their police officers and fire department personnel, and by retired Major Robert Rice of the Pennsylvania State Police. They would be shown photographs of streets occupied by the military, and state police transported in tanks and armored personnel carriers, in the effort to restore order to a city out of control.

"The barricades were up, blocking Newberry Street on the night in question. This incident would never have happened," I told the jury, "if the occupants of the Lillie Belle Allen car did not insist on passage, and if the police officer in charge, Officer Ron Zeager, did not make the mistake of his life . . . a mistake that has only recently surfaced, a mistake that Charlie Robertson knew nothing about."

The jurors were told during voir dire to use their common sense, that they had the right to bring it with them into the jury box. "If you're wondering why Charlie Robertson was brought into these proceedings," I said, "you may find the answer by looking around this courtroom." The jury instinctively focused on the mass of media occupying the first several rows of the gallery, and for one brief moment the media was in a glass box.

If nothing else, one thing was made clear in my opening. Our position was that Charlie Robertson was innocent, the victim of prosecutorial zeal, and that this trial was a holy war. It would be fought under the careful supervision of Judge Uhler, but in the end there would be casualties — many, many casualties.

Pete Solymos opened for Bob Messersmith, and in my opinion, it was his finest hour. Pete's style is folksy, and for him it works because it is genuine. He stood at the podium and talked to the jurors as if they were guests in his living room. He asked them to sit back and listen.

Solymos is a guy to whom you would want to listen without reservation. Bespectacled, with gray hair turned white at the temples, and experience etched into the lines of his face, he looked every bit the law school professor. He wore white shirts with button-down collars. His outward appearance was non-threatening. His easygoing manner kept your attention.

Pete told them that this case was not about murder, but about fear. "It's about young men who were acting in self-defense, or who believed they were acting in self-defense, and who were encouraged to do so by the police," he said. "The police told them to protect their neighborhoods, their loved ones, and that they had the right to do so."

Pete then described the day before the killing, explaining that an identical Cadillac came up Newberry Street in broad daylight, and someone opened fire from the trunk. "On the very day of the killing, two African American brothers—James and Sherman Spells—went to the Messersmith home, angry that a firebomb was thrown into their mother's house, promising to return."

"This case is about fear," Solymos repeated.

With the passage of 32 years, memories have faded, the killing slug has been lost, the forensic evidence is gone, and there is no way to determine who fired the killing shot, Solymos told the jury. "Robert Messersmith has been charged, and singled out, because of his father's sins," Pete said, and would prove that Messersmith's father, now deceased, was yelling what to do back then. John Messersmith, Robert's father, had been directing a makeshift command center from the basement of their Newberry Street home, where an arsenal of rifles, shotguns and handguns was handed out to the beer-drinking boys.

Bob Messersmith sat quietly and listened, knowing the rest of his life was on the line. At times, he still had the impish grin and cocky look he'd had as a youth. A recovering alcoholic the past 15 years, Messersmith found it difficult to sit for long stretches because of the severe back injury he had suffered years ago that left him on total disability. There's no question he had been a bad ass. He had a prior conviction for shooting a black youth, Taka Nii Sweeney, in the opening rounds of the '69 riots. He had served nine months in prison. The former leader of the Newberry Street Boys, Bob Messersmith had been a bully, a carouser, and a manipulator. He was also a son who listened to his dad. A hard life had taken its toll. He walked into court like an old man and looked like he was in his 60s rather than his 50s. At the time of his arrest, Bob, who now lived in Montgomery County, outside Philadelphia, wore a thick gray and white beard. For trial, he'd cleaned up with buzz-cut and a suit. His neckties came halfway down his protruding belly, which seemed like a barrel on his 5' 8" frame. Even in his best outfit, Bob appeared disheveled.

Messersmith's life had been a contradiction. To many he was the stereotypical violent racist. But he'd been trying to make things right over the years, and he considered himself a good husband and dad. He'd been a victim of drunken abuse as a child and he was trying to break that cycle. Escorting him to court each day was an African American friend, the Reverend Raymond Brown. He had other black friends from his days on Newberry Street who greeted him at court.

Harry Ness's opening and delivery were flawless.

He brought to life the fear that swept over York during the riots. His description of the reciprocal shootings, rock throwing, molotov cocktails, arsons, and vandalism was vivid. Ness painted a picture of a neighborhood nervously awaiting the return of a Cadillac that had carried gunmen into the area the day before Lillie Belle Allen's murder. "Tragedy struck," Harry said, "when Allen and her family arrived in a similar car, getting past barricades that were in place."

He told the jury not to look at Greg Neff as a middle-aged man in the safety of the courtroom, but to envision him 32 years younger, in the midst of riots out of control.

Harry described Greg Neff as "a conscript in that war . . . a buck private . . . encouraged by police to protect each other."

Harry identified with the jury, and they felt his sincerity. His blond hair, confident manner, and a face that exuded strength and character made it hard for the jurors not to like him. Harry had connected with the jury. I believed that he had leveled the playing field with his opening.

Neff watched, completely detached. It seemed as if his hair had turned grayer in the past year than in the last ten combined. Tall and lanky, with a long face and high cheekbones, Neff sat there stoically, holding it all in. His oversized hands held a cigarette at each opportunity outside court. Thick lines creased his forehead from worry. Neff came from a good family. Save for that one awful night in 1969, he was no different from most other kids who had grown up in York during the '60s—a kid from Middle America. He was convinced he knew the truth of that night, and no one, no way, no how, was going to get him to say anything different.

§

Most nights during the trial, Charlie Robertson would go home for dinner. Generally, he'd cook something—mashed potatoes, a vegetable, and whatever meat he had available. For Charlie, a lifelong bachelor, cooking was not an issue. He'd go over documents, looking for holes and contradictions in the Commonwealth's case. It came from his days as a police officer and a detective. Some nights he would catch a college football game on TV. He would take one sleeping pill before turning in for the night, and mostly he got a good night's sleep. He felt mentally exhausted. He kept wondering "why I was even there" in court, on trial for murder. He'd get up around 5:00 a.m. to shower and shave. Rich Oare would pick him up at 7:00 a.m. each morning to prepare for another daily ordeal.

§

If the courtroom is a theater, and it is, there are role players—prosecutors, defense lawyers, judges, witnesses, sometimes a runaway jury—and there are self-serving individuals who thrust themselves into the proceedings. A white supremacist group, the World Church of the Creator, came to York to make its presence known. An address to the group's members by their leader "Reverend" Matt Hale triggered altercations and protests in the community.

The group's appearance did nothing to further Robertson's cause. In the court of public opinion, it helped brand York as a racist town and Charlie as an unwilling hero to white supremacists. It was absurd and it made me sick to my stomach.

It played into the hands of the prosecution.

As always happens in high-profile cases, the presence of the media began luring other opportunists. Two white civil rights lawyers from Philadelphia came to York, and representing the Allen family, held press conferences on the courthouse steps at every available moment. On Monday after the opening arguments, surrounded by the Allen family, one told the media that the Allens "were led into an ambush and [Lillie Belle Allen] was murdered. Those doing the leading were the York City Police and the State Police on duty the night of July 21, 1969."

The lawyers promised to sue the city, and wanted Robertson convicted.

They sent me a message through the York papers. They would be willing to discuss a guilty plea from Charlie Robertson if Charlie would accept responsibility for the death of Lillie Belle Allen, and apologize.

I had no intention of negotiating with those civil rights lawyers about anything. As far as I was concerned, they could go fuck themselves.

17

RACE CARD

Tom Kelley was ready to go, and he was not fooling around.

His leadoff witness, Debra Marie Taylor, Lillie Belle Allen's daughter, was 11 when her mother was killed. She recalled her mother had been fishing that day; Debra left that evening to go to a store and later heard "fireworks." She remembered the car returning on flat tires, and only later was told her mother had been killed.

Debra, 43 when she took the witness stand, had a remarkable memory, but nobody was going to cross-examine a child who lost her mother, for any reason.

Hattie Dickson was next, and she repeated her preliminary hearing testimony in a heart-wrenching fashion. The jury was visibly shaken when she told them about the shooting. Dickson testified that the booming and banging and pinging against the car were terrifying. She said, "I heard my sister. I heard her cry out to us. I heard her cry out, help me. Would you please help me?"

Contrary to her testimony at the preliminary hearing, Hattie Dickson now recalled that the shooting had started before her sister got out of the car. At the preliminary hearing, it was after her sister got out of the car. To me, she had "tweaked" her testimony to cut off any meaningful claim of perceived self-defense. Though it would be cleared up by Tom Sponaugle and Harry Ness, it was the first of a series of tweaks.

"No," she insisted, "there were no barricades up. We passed some that were on the sidewalk, and saw police officers at the corner, but we were not stopped by the police, and there were no barricades blocking Newberry Street."

Something wasn't ringing true to me, but I would later develop the truth about the barricades through Officer Ron Zeager.

I wasn't going to start the trial off by attacking this woman. Dickson had evoked enormous sympathy from this jury, and Kelley knew it. He and his boys had a natural masterpiece on their canvas.

Luis Mercado, Jacob Berkheimer, and Steve Noonan added their own strokes to the mural in the courtroom. Newberry Street on July 21, 1969, was a ticking bomb, with armed kids running up and down the block screaming. It was obvious that there was danger in the air. Why didn't the police do anything about it?

For two days, a parade of witnesses marched into the courtroom, and with each witness the number of armed teens and young adults grew on Newberry Street. Robert Stoner, a former youth worker, called the police twice for help on the day in question. "Yes," he said on cross-examination, "I was there all day, and I did not see Robertson handing out ammunition, or exhorting anyone to kill black people."

I believe the Commonwealth called more witnesses to testify to the fusillade of shots fired than there were actual shots fired, and there were many. However, it was an effective direct examination. Though some witnesses on Newberry Street heard "gun, gun, gun . . . she has a gun," nobody, it seemed, saw one.

Those witnesses did see Lillie Belle Allen go down, and testified that white youths celebrated the killing. "They were just yelling like they won something," Russell Wantz, who lived on Newberry Street, told the jury.

Sponaugle and Ness were in this line of fire, for Bob Messersmith and Greg Neff were shooters. Those two defense lawyers brought out on cross-examination, through the prosecution's witnesses, the shooting assault from an identical Cadillac the day before. They developed the threatening confrontation at the Messersmith home by the Spells brothers. Using the prosecution's diagram, they showed how the Allen Cadillac appeared to move into a broadside defensive position at the railroad tracks. They proved beyond any doubt that no shots were fired until after Lillie Belle Allen got out of the car and walked around the trunk. They marked an "X" at the barricades, knowing they were put up by Officer Zeager.

Pathologists who performed autopsies on Allen in 1969 and in 2001 testified that she died from a single shotgun wound, in their opinion made by a .12 gauge slug removed from her body. That critical piece of evidence was lost over the years.

Judge Uhler had his hands full with six defense lawyers and three prosecutors in the well of the courtroom. Any objection resulted in "talking heads" at side bar, and Judge Uhler hated "talking heads."

"One at a time," he admonished on the record. "I can't get anything done when you're all talking at the same time."

Tim Barker was running in and out of the courtroom with stacks of books, most of which had nothing to do with anything. Tim truly had a lot of knowledge, but he couldn't stay focused. If you would ask him what time it was, he would tell you how to make a watch.

In addition, the prosecution's theory of culpability differed for each of the defendants. Messersmith was their killer; therefore he was a principal in the first degree. Neff was a backup shooter; therefore he was an accomplice. Robertson was neither; therefore he had to have aided and abetted.

My defense was that Charlie Robertson was not guilty of anything, for any reason.

I was not hostile to Sponaugle and Ness, for Charlie wasn't on Newberry Street when the shooting took place. He didn't know why it took place, and for all he knew it might very well have been in self-defense. On the other hand, I was not in bed with them either, for the same reasons. Still, I was sympathetic to their position, because their defense made sense to me; it had a lot of merit, and I personally liked the defense lawyers I was working with.

Their defense was self-defense, or defense of others, with a mix of "the police encouraged us to do it." That little bit of mix was dangerous to me, so I had to keep my eye on them. Frendship only went so far in the courtroom.

Judge Uhler was in the middle of all this, calling balls, strikes, and fouls—some technicals, a bunch below the belt. It became apparent to me, early in the trial, that he was going to call them the way he saw them, without fear or favor to anyone. I was glad he stayed on, for a good trial judge in a heated, knockdown, drag-out, high-profile case keeps the system from becoming a zoo.

"The gang meeting at Farquhar Park the day before the killing was not meant to be a race rally," said Stewart Aldinger, a 15-year-old Newberry Street Boy in 1969. I knew that when Aldinger got off the witness stand, the groundwork had been laid for my buddy from Texas.

Fred Flickinger was back, and on a mission. Bald on top with short, brown hair circling the back of his head, Flickinger was a heavyset man—not fat, but his clothes were bulging at the seams. He had a thick neck with a light set of jowls beneath. His baldness made his forehead seem broader and his entire face seemed fuller and rounder. Peering over his glasses, he testified that in 1969 he saw a police officer on the bandstand "pumping his fist in the air and shouting 'white power, white power, white power.'" Flickinger identified that officer as former York mayor Charlie Robertson, and pointed a pudgy finger at him when asked by Special Prosecutor Fran Chardo.

Flickinger said that "within a couple of hours prior to Lillie Belle Allen's death," Robertson drove a squad car to the North End Cigar Store on Newberry Street, a hangout for the local gang. Flickinger said he was with a group of teens, maybe six in all, when Robertson remarked, "If I weren't a cop, you know, I would be out leading commando raids against those niggers in the black community."

That worthless motherfucker, I thought. This recent recollection of "commando raids" and "niggers" has moved to the day in question, within a couple of hours of Lille Belle Allen's death. Robertson's arrest affidavit placed the conversation on the day of the rally. Somebody in the DA's office had tweaked Fred, needing to move the racial incitement up a day.

No, Flickinger acknowledged, he had never said a word about commando raids or blacks before Judge Nealon at the civil rights hearing in Harrisburg. His explanation was that the plaintiff's lawyers failed to ask the right questions to bring out police racism.

Yes, Flickinger said, he could identify one of the six gang members who overheard it. He then identified a gang member who was dead.

Yes, Flickinger said, he reported Robertson's incitement to the York city police. He then identified a detective who was dead.

Yes, Flickinger said, he had been communicating a lot with Mike Hoover of the *York Dispatch*, and had told Hoover about the "commando raid/nigger" incitement by Robertson. That recent recollection— probably before his grand jury appearance—made the front page, which included Flickinger's photograph.

Outside, at the conclusion of his testimony, Fred Flickinger had another press conference on the courthouse steps, and posed for more photographs.

Throughout the prosecution's case, the reverse race card was played with passion. The prosecutors would use the word "nigger" on direct, repeat it on re-direct, enunciate it, and say it loud. If sensitive witnesses referred to the "N word," the DA's would make them say "nigger." In the back of the courtroom, the Allen family was growing in numbers and sat stoically through it all.

By the end of the first week, I was sick of it.

I believe the jury got the point.

The prosecutors, however, kept flashing that card, and would until the end.

Charlie Robertson remained expressionless, an impossible read, in this high-stakes game with his life on the table. Rich and Rees were unfazed.

Fran Chardo then called Dennis McMaster, and it occurred to me that Chardo was given the Robertson witnesses to handle. That meant he was responsible for their direct examination and preparation for trial.

That certainly didn't preclude Kelley or Barker from jumping in at any time, especially behind closed doors. Rodney George was also on my "tweakers" list.

McMaster, however, was a master—and nobody was going to tweak him. His testimony tracked what he told the grand jury, what he told Judge Biester, and what he told the prosecutors after another debriefing. Charlie Robertson yelled "white power" at Farquhar Park on July 20, 1969. Four police officers in an armored car were approached by Jim Messersmith for .30-06 ammunition on July 20, 1969, "to protect his family . . . a request that came from a law-abiding citizen, and former neighbor . . . a request that was not a crime to comply with."

Rick Knouse was never given .30-06 ammunition by Charlie Robertson, or any other police officer, at any time.

Charlie Robertson was not on Newberry Street when Lillie Belle Allen was killed; he was the driver of "Big Al" on the night in question, and they — Charlie, VanGreen, Markle, and McMaster— risked their lives to save the other occupants in the Allen car.

"We did the best we could, under the circumstances," McMaster said.

"We risked our lives, together, for this community," he added.

"No," McMaster said, "we didn't investigate the scene . . . that wasn't our job that night. . . we were immediately called out to extract three pinned police officers at another location . . . and came under much fire."

§

"Do we call Charlie to the witness stand, or don't we?" I asked.

"They haven't proven anything yet," Rich Oare answered.

"I say no," Rees Griffiths added.

"What do you think, Charlie?" I asked, since it was his decision.

"I'll do whatever you guys tell me," he answered. "I'll just answer the questions, and if I don't remember something, I'll say I don't remember."

The four of us stayed together at every break. We camped out at Rees's office over the lunch hour, and that's where we ate. We would regroup before going home for the evening, assess the damage, and go from there. McMaster was the 22nd witness called by the prosecution, and we estimated 40 more.

Rich assured me that the character witnesses were ready to go.

Rees was ready to argue the dismissal motion at the close of the prosecution's case.

I was already thinking about my closing. I told Rich about the Powerpoint demonstration I had seen in Wilkes-Barre, and wished I knew something about computers. Rich wanted me to meet two of his friends on the outskirts of York, "and just hear them out," he said.

Whether or not to call Charlie to the witness stand was a huge concern. I knew all about the right to remain silent, and that the exercise of that right is not to be used by the jury against the accused. I also knew that juries want to hear from the defendant in any criminal case, and this wasn't just any criminal case.

"Charlie, if you're asked the following question on the witness stand, what's your answer going to be?" I said to Charlie, and he sat up. "Did you refer to blacks as niggers in 1969?"

"Not all blacks," Charlie answered, "just the ones that were causing trouble."

"What if Kelley or Barker get in your face with your answer?" I asked jokingly, but I wanted to know.

"I might get down off the witness stand and smack the shit out of them," Charlie answered, half serious.

Oh brother, I thought. We have some work to do.

Rees couldn't contain himself, and burst out laughing.

§

The testimony of Art Messersmith, brother of Bob, was a disappointment for the prosecution, but they got what they paid for. The others who pled guilty were paid off with misdemeanors and a one-year exposure to jail. But poor Art, who was 16 at the time—and no more involved than anyone else, probably less—had to take a felony and an exposure of four and a half years. He was jacked up because he was a Messersmith, and because he refused to dime out his blood brother. One hour before he entered his plea, the prosecutors insisted that he change his recollection from "shooting a gun in the air" to "shooting at the car"; otherwise, they were going to force him to trial on murder charges.

I felt sorry for Art as I watched him take the oath. He was uneducated and, in fact, could barely read. His greasy black hair was slicked back, and his light suit with an oversized tie made him look like a '70s disco dancer right out of the movie *Saturday Night Fever*. Art could have gotten his deal sweetened if he had been willing to lie about Charlie Robertson, but he refused. He recalled Robertson having rifle ammunition in his squad car, but never saw him hand out bullets to anybody. The most Robertson ever did was to warn him that Black Panthers were in town and that blacks with machine guns were driving around the city. To Art, Charlie Robertson "seemed like a good cop."

That testimony left the prosecutors, with five accomplices who pled guilty pursuant to deals in exchange for their truthful testimony, in the tank. They were Tom Smith, Clarence Lutzinger, Rick Knouse, Chauncy Gladfelter, and Tom Ritter.

But Clarence Lutzinger would not be available, maybe ever, for he had suffered a severe heart attack and was in intensive care at the York Hospital. The prosecutors tried to have him deposed from his bed, but were unsuccessful.

That failure took them down to four and Charlie refused to believe that Rick Knouse would be corroborated. "Damn it, I didn't do what Knouse is saying. I had nothing to do with the death of Lillie Belle Allen, nothing . . . I didn't hand out ammo, and I didn't tell anybody to kill blacks," Charlie reminded me. Charlie didn't believe, or want to believe, that the other boys were going to lie. "Unlike Knouse," he said, "who sold his soul to the prosecutors to stay out of jail."

Charlie Robertson was right, at least about Tom Smith. Called by the prosecutors, Smith said Bob Messersmith shot at Lillie Belle Allen, then implicated others; he testified to the events on the night in question, but said nothing about Charlie Robertson. Tom Smith appeared credible on the witness stand; dressed in a sport coat with a white shirt open at the collar, he looked like, and was, a law-abiding citizen. His only crime was to take a .30-30 rifle to Newberry Street on the fifth day of rioting in the city, a weapon he never shot.

Rick Knouse, on the other hand, delivered for the prosecution. Convinced the prosecutors were his ticket, his testimony tracked verbatim his preliminary hearing testimony. He must have spent hours reading his transcript, for it was repeated word for word. "Yes," he said, appearing distraught and remorseful, "Charlie Robertson called me 'Knousie' . . . threw me a box of shells — 30.06 — and said, kill as many niggers as you can."

Rick Knouse used the word "niggers" so much in his direct testimony that at one point I thought he was stuttering.

Knouse told the jury that Charlie Robertson had given him "a license to kill." But according to Knouse, on cross-examination, he didn't kill anybody, or intend to, with .30-06 ammunition, or any other ammunition. "Absolutely did not," he said. "She was already down," he insisted, when he fired a shot into the cigar store.

Prior to his trial testimony, Rick Knouse always maintained that he believed Lillie Belle Allen was armed; he had told the authorities more than once, "I thought I saw fire coming from the hands of Lillie Belle Allen . . . I thought Lillie Belle Allen was shooting at us."

At trial, he said that he saw no gun, that there must have been shooting coming from behind her.

And that is what I call tweaking — big time — as in suborning perjury.

§

The civil rights lawyers for the Allen family took turns giving press conferences on the courthouse steps, generally at the lunch break or at the end of the day, always with multiple members of the family in the background.

At the conclusion of Rick Knouse's testimony, they focused on Charlie Robertson, for they needed him convicted in order to sue the city.

"Does he investigate?" the lawyer asked the media. "Does he confiscate all the weapons we've heard about today — rifles, machetes, guns, Molotov cocktails? Did any member of the police force do that? The answer is absolutely not. Why didn't the police do that? Because they were active participants in the murder of Lillie Belle Allen."

§

I first introduced former York police officer Ronald Zeager to the jury in my opening. That forced the prosecution to call him as a witness; otherwise, it would have looked like they were withholding a material, credible version of what happened at the barricades. Officer Ron Zeager took the stand on the fifth day of testimony. You could feel the tension in the courtroom—and in his heart, I'm sure.

Ronald "Moon" Zeager had retired from the York police department years before. The passage of time, over three decades, had aged him. Once physically fit, he had gained weight; the wrinkles at his eye line were deep; his voice was raspy, but could be heard. He hated taking the witness stand, but at this point in his life, and with Charlie Robertson on trial for murder, he had no choice.

Zeager, facing the jury, said the barricades were put up to prevent passage onto Newberry Street because of the tension and violence in York between the African Americans and whites. The police were directed to man those barricades with the understanding that no blacks were to go up Newberry Street. There had been reports throughout the day that Newberry Street was volatile, and Zeager himself knew of the situation.

"The barricades were up," Zeager said emphatically, "when the white Cadillac approached."

"I stopped the car myself," Zeager testified, "and advised the family to go another route because of 'some trouble.'"

"They didn't listen, and wanted to go through, to visit relatives," he said.

Ron Zeager was reluctant to let them through, but because of the "racially sensitive times," he acquiesced.

"I then moved the barricades and they drove through," he said.

Within seconds, he heard the shots—many, many shots—and realized that he had made the mistake of his life. He never told anyone, and lived with that nightmare for over 30 years. Zeager initially denied moving the barricades before the grand jury, but returned in December 2001 and acknowledged that he had moved them to let Lille Belle Allen's family drive through.

"That was the most wrong decision I've made in my life," Zeager said.

"Yes," he said, "I think about it often, all the time."

"No," he said, "I never told Charlie Robertson."

§

After eight days of testimony from 63 witnesses, the prosecution rested its case.

I thought the prosecution's case against Bob Messersmith was their best one. They had called multiple witnesses who identified Bob as a shooter, as the one brandishing a 12-gauge shotgun. The prosecution had expert testimony that Lillie Belle Allen was killed with a 12-gauge shotgun slug. They called two witnesses who testified that Messersmith claimed credit for the killing; one of them, Chuck Fidler, testified that Bob said in his presence, "I blew that fuckin' nigger in half . . . I blew that nigger in half."

Tom Sponaugle, instead of Pete Solymos, did most of the cross-examinations. He spoke to the jury about the unavailability of the forensic evidence and the unfairness of the position he was in. The claims of responsibility by Bob Messersmith were cast into doubt, for there was much bragging going on years after the fact. Sponaugle did everything possible to create a reasonable doubt, and he may have done so.

He effectively developed for the jury the fear on Newberry Street on July 21, 1969.

There was the Cadillac incident the day before.

There were the Spells brothers' threats on the day in question, in Bob Messersmith's face, on the porch of his home.

And there were riots throughout the city, which terrorized the entire community. As Sergeant Creavey said in his report, the boys on Newberry Street were jumpy.

§

The entire case against Greg Neff was his grand jury testimony, which prosecutors read to the jury. Tom Kelley read the questions, and Detective George read the answers.

Greg Neff acknowledged that he was on Newberry Street on the night in question. He said he was a Girarder, not a Newberry Street Boy, but had gone to Newberry Street to help his friends protect their neighborhood.

"This lady gets out," George read, "and someone said 'She's got . . . they've got guns.'"

Neff told the grand jury that Allen moved to the rear of the car and "appeared to have a gun in her hand."

Neff said he retreated up the street past three or four parked cars, crouched, stood up, and fired.

Neff recalled that there was a shotgun blast before he fired.

That was the hand Harry Ness was dealt, and there was nothing he could do to change his cards. It wasn't the best hand, but maybe—he thought, we all thought—it would hold up. Harry certainly played it like a pro.

§

To bolster their case against Charlie, the prosecutors showed the jury a film clip dated May 18, 2001. It was an interview of Charlie by a Fox News reporter, held outside City Hall days after his arrest. Robertson admitted yelling "white power" to the crowd at Farquhar Park. He told the reporter about the assault and robbery of his father by African Americans. He told the reporter that 32 years ago he "believed in white power." He also told the reporter that he had nothing to do with the death of Lillie Belle Allen.

Charlie had been advised by all of us not to talk about the case. He didn't think those questions were about "the case."

The reporter from Fox asked him whether he had given ammunition to gang members.

Charlie replied, without saying it was on the advice of counsel, "I can't answer that question."

To the viewing audience, and now his jury, that answer sounded terrible.

Before resting their case, the prosecution tried to introduce Charlie's infamous quote that had appeared in *Time* magazine: "Everyone knew who was involved. But everyone thought it was even. One black had been killed, one white—even."

Judge Uhler made the appropriate ruling, and kept it out. It was an accurate quote, but way out of context, and without an explanation.

The prosecution's first witness was Debra Taylor, Lillie Belle Allen's daughter. Their last witness was Michael Allen, Lillie Belle Allen's son. They wanted to end on the emotional note they began with, and did. Michael Allen said that he remembered the night in question, even though he was just a little boy, and that he missed his mother.

I truly believed there was no case that Charlie Robertson had aided and abetted the murder of Lille Belle Allen.

I was feeling the pressure, however, for I had been wrong before—many times—especially in this case.

York County NAACP President Leo Cooper stands on the steps of York's City Hall Thursday, May 24, 2001, calling for the resignation of York City Mayor Charlie Robertson for his alleged role in the shooting death of Lillie Belle Allen, a black woman, during the York City race riots of 1969.

AP Photo, York Daily Record, *Christopher Glass*

York Mayor Charlie Robertson arrives at York County Courthouse in York, Pennsylvania, Monday, June 25, 2001, for a preliminary hearing. Robertson and eight other white men are accused in the 1969 shooting death of a black woman during 10 days of race riots. Robertson, a police officer at the time of the shooting, is accused of providing bullets to white gang members who allegedly shot 27-year-old Lillie Belle Allen on the fourth night of the riots.

AP Photo, Paul Vathis

William Ritter is seen arriving at York County Courthouse in York, Pennsylvania, Monday, June 25, 2001, for a preliminary hearing on murder charges in the 1969 shooting death of a black woman during 10 days of race riots in York. Ritter is one of nine white defendants, including York Mayor Charlie Robertson, accused in the death of Lillie Belle Allen of Aiken, South Carolina. *AP Photo, Paul Vathis*

Clarence "Sonny" Lutzinger, in this May 17, 2001, photo, in York, Pennsylvania, is one of four white men who pleaded guilty to conspiracy charges, Wednesday, August 14, 2002, in the shooting death of a black woman during the city's 1969 race riots. The four were among 10 people, including former York Mayor Charlie Robertson, who were charged with murder in the killing of Lillie Belle Allen on July 21, 1969. *AP Photo,* York Daily Record

Arthur Messersmith, center, is escorted from the rear of the York County Courthouse by Walter Trayer, right, assistant to Messersmith's attorney Frank Arcuri,
Thursday, August 29, 2002. Messersmith pleaded guilty to attempted murder and
conspiracy, Thursday, August 29, 2002, admitting in court that in 1969 he fired a
12-gauge shotgun at a car in which Lille Belle Allen, 27, was riding as the car
entered a white neighborhood. Four defendants remain charged with murder in the
case. Three of those defendants, including former York Mayor Charlie Robertson
and Robert Messersmith, Arthur Messersmith's brother, are scheduled to stand trial
together beginning September 23.   *AP Photo,* York Daily Record, *Christopher Glass*

Former York Mayor Charlie Robertson, left, and his attorney Richard Oare depart
the York County Courthouse, in York, Pennsylvania, Monday, September 23, 2002,
following the first day of jury selection in his trial for the 1969 killing of Lillie Belle
Allen. Robertson is one of three men charged in the crime.   *AP Photo, Brad C. Bower*

Media surround former York Mayor Charlie Robertson as he makes his way into the back entrance of the York County Courthouse Tuesday, October 1, 2002, in York, Pennsylvania. Robertson is one of three men charged in connection with the death of a young black South Carolina woman during York's 1969 race riots. An all-white jury, whose first alternate juror is black, is set to hear opening statements in the case Tuesday. *AP Photo,* The York Dispatch, *Jason Plotkin*

Former York Mayor Charlie Robertson, left, and his attorney, William Costopoulos, leave the York County Courthouse, Friday, October 18, 2002, in York, Pennsylvania. Jurors trying to decide whether Robertson, a policeman who went on to become York's two-term mayor, and two other men are guilty of murder in the shooting death of a young black woman, Lillie Belle Allen, during race riots in 1969, broke off deliberations for the night Friday without a verdict.

AP Photo, Brad C. Bower

Defendant Gregg Neff, center, and his attorney, Harry Ness, left, speak with Rees Griffiths, one of the attorneys for co-defendant Charlie Robertson, Friday, October 18, 2002, at the York County Courthouse in York, Pennsylvania. Jurors trying to decide whether Robertson, a policeman who went on to become York's two-term mayor, and Neff and Robert Messersmith are guilty of murder in the shooting death of a young black woman, Lillie Belle Allen, during race riots in 1969, broke off deliberations for the night Friday without a verdict. *AP Photo, Brad C. Bower*

Defendant Robert Messersmith, left, and his attorneys Tom Sponaugle, center, and Peter Solymos arrive at the York County Courthouse on Friday, October 18, 2002, during the second day of jury deliberations in the trial of Messersmith, Charlie Robertson, and Gregory Neff. The three are accused in the shooting death of a young black woman during race riots in 1969. *AP Photo, Brad C. Bower*

Former York, Pennsylvania, Mayor Charlie Robertson, listens to questions at a news conference outside the York County Courthouse in York, Pennsylvania, Saturday, October 19, 2002, after being found not guilty of second-degree murder in the death of Lillie Belle Allen, a preacher's daughter from Aiken, South Carolina, who was gunned down by a white mob on July 21, 1969. Two other men, Robert Messersmith and Greg Neff, were convicted of second-degree murder and face sentences of 10 to 20 years in prison.   *AP Photo, Paul Vathis*

Hattie Dickson, sister of murder victim Lillie Belle Allen, right, holds up two fingers during a news conference, Saturday, October 19, 2002, outside the York County Courthouse in York, Pennsylvania, as Allen's son, Michael Allen, comforts Dickson, left, and Allen's daughter, Debra Taylor, background center, listens. The former mayor, Charlie Robertson, who had been a policeman at the time of the murder, was acquitted and Robert Messersmith and Greg Neff were convicted in the shotgun slaying of the young black woman, during race riots that tore apart York in 1969.
AP Photo, The York Dispatch, *Greg Mahany*

Arriving for sentencing in the Lillie Belle Allen murder case, Rick Knouse, left, and his attorney John Moran enter the York County Courthouse Wednesday, November 13, 2002, in York, Pennsylvania. Plea agreements for Knouse and five other defendants call for prison sentences in the 1969 murder of Lillie Belle Allen. *AP Photo, Brad C. Bower*

Arriving for sentencing in the Lillie Belle Allen murder case, Tom Smith, left, and his attorney Joe Metz enter the York County Courthouse, Wednesday, November 13, 2002, in York, Pennsylvania. Plea agreements for Smith and five other defendants call for prison sentences in the 1969 murder of Lillie Belle Allen.

AP Photo, Brad C. Bower

Defense attorney Matthew Gover, left, with his client, Chauncey Gladfelter, right.

York Daily Record

18

ACES

Thursday, October 10, 2002
York County Courthouse
York, Pennsylvania

Before Charlie Robertson's defense would take center stage, we
wanted to ask Judge Uhler to dismiss Robertson's charges. The challenge would address the sufficiency of the evidence. We knew we were
dreaming, but Rees went after it.

Rees Griffiths stood at the podium, facing Judge Uhler, and made
an impressive legal argument for exoneration. His command of the
law and the facts flowed with conviction, supported by the record and
legal precedent. "There is no evidence," Rees argued, "that Charlie
Robertson committed an act that caused the death of Lillie Belle
Allen." Rees went down the line of the alleged co-conspirators, impressing upon the court that none of them was incited to kill, including Rick Knouse. His delivery should have been filmed for future trial
lawyers, for it was truly a classic oration.

"Denied," Judge Uhler said without hesitation, impressing upon
Rees that this case was going to the jury for resolution.

"You fucked that up," I whispered to Rees jokingly as he returned
to our table.

Pete Solymos and Greg Neff didn't have a prayer.

"Denied," Judge Uhler said two more times, without further explanation, and promptly ordered that the jury be returned to the courtroom.

Outside, a heavy rainstorm was drenching the city. Occasional thunder could be heard in the distance, and I was starting to worry. I had sent Jill to Lancaster to pick up Major Robert Rice, our first witness, who was confined to a wheelchair. The sheriff's department was on standby to offer assistance once they arrived. There would be no time for the two of us to meet, or to discuss his testimony, though we had talked on the phone many times.

Judge Uhler told the jury in open court that he would honor their request to visit the crime scene. Under supervision, they would all be taken there on a bus, including the alternates, at the conclusion of defense testimony. None of the lawyers or defendants would be going along. The media were to keep their distance, and not interfere with this delicate mission.

"Mr. Costopoulos," Judge Uhler said, "call your first witness."

And with that, on cue, the back doors of the courtroom swung open, and a uniformed sheriff wheeled Major Rice to a microphone in front of the jury box.

Rice, 87, was frail and crippled, the victim of a disabling heart attack. He had difficulty hearing, his speech was slurred, but his mind and memory were beyond reproach. Major Rice wrote the final State Police report on the York riots, and had that 42-page document on his lap. He listened to each question carefully before answering, for an old-time major with the Pennsylvania State Police knew how lawyers worked.

He told the jury that he was summoned to Harrisburg by then Governor Shaffer, at 2:00 a.m. on July 22, 1969, along with a ranking officer of the National Guard, whom he had never met. "We were told by the governor," he said, "that there was a problem in York that needed to be taken care of."

Rice described for the jury a war in that community—the shootings of civilians and law enforcement personnel, the raging fires of businesses and homes, the rampant vandalism—and the reinforcements needed to restore order. Troopers were sent in to assist the York City Police, along with 200 National Guardsmen supported by six armored vehicles, to end the disturbance. "A stockpile of dynamite was retrieved from a black militant faction," he told the jury, "but it was a voluntary surrender, with the understanding that no questions would be asked."

Major Rice had enormous credibility with the jury, and they were listening intently.

"No," he said, "nobody ever reported to me that Charlie Robertson, or any other police officer for that matter, was handing out ammunition and inciting white gang members to kill."

"No," Rice answered, under cross-examination by Tom Kelley, "Officer Robertson never provided me or other investigators under my command with information on the Allen murder."

Ray Markle had left the York City Police shortly after the riots, but he recalled the night in question.

"Yes," he said, "the four of us were assigned to 'Big Al' that night, and we were not on Newberry Street at any time until after the woman was killed."

Ray Markle was apprehensive on the witness stand; he gave short answers and required some prodding on direct examination. There was no detail, no elaboration, no emotion. There was nothing wrong with what he said, but it was flat and a slow start for a defense that promised the recreation of history.

§

"Get me Matt Gover on the phone," I said to Jayme before we broke for the night, "and then get me Al Barnes."

There was a reason the prosecution rested without calling Chauncey Gladfelter and William Ritter. Their plea bargains were premised upon accepting responsibility, and their truthful testimony. The prosecutors may have been holding back, intending to call them in rebuttal after we rested, but I didn't believe that.

I believed Gladfelter and Ritter weren't called because Kelley and company didn't like what they were told, or not told, about Charlie Robertson. There was no way they were debriefed and not asked about him.

That evening, after everybody went home, I drove to the outskirts of York to hook up with two friends of Rich Oare's. The sign in the parking lot of 6864 Susquehanna Trail South read Mirtech Consulting. Dan Rippon and Jerry Westerhold greeted me at the door, and they were a trip. They were both wearing black turtlenecks and black slacks with dark, checkered sport coats. If they had sported black sunglasses, they would have looked like the guys in the movie *Men in Black*, or *The Blues Brothers*.

I liked them immediately.

They didn't care if I couldn't turn on a photocopier or set a digital clock. They told me "we can do this." Though they had never furnished their high-tech equipment for use in a court of law, they said "it would be no problem." I was to get them the photographs and exhibits I wanted shown to the jury, having put them in the order I wanted, and they would make them appear on a 90-inch screen "on command."

"We will need to practice, though, with you," they said, "for buzz words and timing will trigger the images on the screen."

§

Rich Oare wanted to do the direct examination of our next witness. Rich had found him, interviewed him several times, and was confident that it would go smoothly. He understood that this witness was necessary to get into evidence the 8' x 10'' black-and-white photographs of the '69 riots. Those photographs depicted the National Guard's armored personnel carriers rolling into the city, manned by soldiers wearing army helmets and military attire. They depicted guardsmen, Pennsylvania State Police, and York City Police dressed in protective riot gear, looking like army personnel with high-powered rifles slung over their shoulders. Two photographs confirmed the York City Police executing searches and seizures on Newberry Street; one of them, dated July 24, 1969, showed the retrieval of rifles and ammunition from the Messersmith home. There were also great photos of burning cars turned over on their sides, and buildings destroyed by fires.

Oare's witness was to examine a map of the city of York, identify the five troublesome districts, and mark them with yellow labels; then he was to identify the locales of the major fires and mark them with red labels.

After admitting the exhibits into evidence, my intention was to turn them over to the men in black; delivering them would be Ellen's job, and she was waiting patiently in the corridor.

"I call to the witness stand Officer James VanGreen," Rich Oare announced, and with that began one fine direct examination. Trial advocates insist that cross-examination is the "great engine of truth." It is often exciting, the stuff that television and the media thrive on. The art of cross-examination is like the ability to destroy a painting by ripping it to shreds. Direct examination, on the other hand, requires great talent and preparation, for it is more difficult to create a painting than to destroy it.

It's true that a great witness can make a lawyer look great, but Rich had done his homework, and he nailed the task.

Officer VanGreen had presence, a big man with the aura of a Winston Churchill. He walked into the courtroom with a cane, but would not speak softly. He had retired as a police officer, but was the current chief deputy sheriff of the county; that made him the boss of the uniformed sheriffs in the courtroom, with offices one floor below, down the hall from the district attorney.

VanGreen relived for the jury the horror that still dwellled in his heart. He clearly remembered how Henry Schaad had fallen, how other officers were wounded in the line of duty, and how the city of York "was a war zone." Identifying the photos was no problem, for he clearly remembered those images. The map was a given, for VanGreen not only grew up in the streets of York, but gave that community his life.

"As did Charlie Robertson," VanGreen added, angry at what he, the mayor, and the police were being put through. VanGreen had read in the papers that Tom Kelley told the jury in his opening "that there was an uneasy alliance between the York City Police and the white gangs." He resented that unfair portrayal.

Officer VanGreen described in detail, for he remembered it well, the night of July 21, 1969: "The four of us were in 'Big Al,' and we responded to the gunshots that we heard, and Charlie Robertson was the first one out of that vehicle . . . . That took some courage."

"We helped save the lives of the other occupants [of the Allen Car] . . . . We called for the ambulance," he said.

"I say the four policemen in the armored car, in my humble opinion, were heroes," he added.

"No," VanGreen answered Kelley, "we didn't investigate the crime scene . . . we were ordered out of there immediately to extricate three fellow police officers who were pinned down in another section of town."

"We took more bullets that night than most police officers take in a lifetime," he added angrily.

"Of course we responded to the major fires on West Hope Lane. Four houses were ablaze. We went there to protect the firemen who were getting shot at, that was our job," he stated.

On direct examination, VanGreen made it clear that Charlie Robertson had been a good police officer who acted courageously and unselfishly throughout the night. He was adamant that Charlie Robertson never handed out ammunition to Rick Knouse, or anyone else, and that Robertson never incited any white gang members to kill.

On cross-examination, he was unshakable, and resented the insinuation that the York City Police did not do their job. Tom Kelley made a big mistake in front of that jury suggesting that VanGreen may have been a racist himself.

Thank you, Jim, I thought. You finally got it out there where it counts, here and now in front of this jury.

Former officer Jim Brown was next—another great witness—another ace.

The boys in blue had much to say, for they had lived through the riots and had put their lives on the line to restore order, "as did Charlie Robertson," said Brown, a retired officer who still kept himself in good shape. With a full head of charcoal-gray hair, Brown looked to be about 5' 10", with a stocky, athletic build. He had a reputation as a good guy, an honest cop.

Brown specifically recalled that Robertson had exposed himself to death or serious bodily injury, never refusing a dangerous assignment. "We were dispatched to a hot spot" in the South End, Brown said, "and there was this guy on a balcony with a rifle ... and Charlie yelled 'get the hell inside before you get killed.'" Brown was clearly saying, as a police officer, that Charlie Robertson was a guy you wanted beside you when it got tough.

Brown described an incident the day before Lillie Belle Allen's death. He said a car drove down Newberry Street, chased by 20 to 35 white people. The trunk popped open, and a black person within started firing. He said police chased the car until it crashed, and the occupants jumped out and ran away. "Yes," he added, "I witnessed it ... I was in uniform."

"I almost lost my life, probably four or five times, during the riots," Brown recalled, and broke down in tears, reliving the horror in his past. He added that it was the young guys, the single guys, that were the first to get the high-risk assignments.

Brown knew all about guns and firearms, for he grew up with them. He said that Robertson had a .300 Savage rifle, not a .30-06. He said that Robertson never handed out .30-06 ammunition, or any other kind, to any white gang members. "No, he didn't," Brown answered, when asked if Robertson had incited gang members to kill.

Brown was shown three photographs by me for identification. One depicted York police in riot gear scaling the wall of a warehouse on Newberry Street, searching for a cache of arms. Another depicted military personnel carriers surrounded by National Guardsmen, and Brown pointed to a soldier sitting on top of one. "That's Charlie Robertson," he said. The third photo showed York police removing rifles, shotguns, and other weapons from the Messersmith home. The search warrant authorizing that seizure was dated July 24, 1969; the inventory list itemized everything taken, including knives and letter openers, but not one single .30-06 rifle or casing was found on the premises.

§

Over lunch in Rees Griffiths's conference room, the question of whether to call Charlie Robertson to the witness stand came up again.

"I say no," Rees said, "they haven't proven anything."

"I agree," Rich Oare added.

"What do you think, Charlie?" I asked.

"I don't have any problem with it, but I'll do what you guys tell me," he answered.

§

After the break, I had a little surprise for the prosecution.

Matt Gover and Al Barnes gave me the green light. Though I had not talked to their clients, I trusted these lawyers as my friends. Barnes was a little nervous, fearful that William Ritter's truthful testimony for the defense might cost him at the time of sentencing.

Chauncey Gladfelter, dressed in a suit, told the jury he had pled guilty to conspiracy to commit murder. He had agreed to cooperate fully and truthfully concerning the events on Newberry Street. He said he was there, and at no time did Charlie Robertson hand out ammunition to Rick Knouse, or anybody else; nor did he encourage or incite any youth gang members to kill blacks.

"Didn't happen?" I asked, standing up to face Gladfelter.

"Didn't happen," he answered.

William Ritter, still looking like a bearded mountain man in a plaid shirt, had pled guilty to conspiracy to commit murder. He had agreed to cooperate fully and truthfully. He said he was on Newberry Street, and at no time did Charlie Robertson hand out ammunition to Rick Knouse, or anybody else; nor did he encourage or incite any youth gang members to kill blacks.

"Didn't happen?" I asked, standing up to face Ritter.

"Didn't happen," he answered.

Gladfelter and Ritter were two of the six defendants with whom the Commonwealth had made deals. Yet the prosecution did not call them to the stand. Here were the Commonwealth's witnesses offering testimony that buttressed our defense. They would not have testified if we had not called them. It showed the jury how weak the prosecution's case was in general against Charlie Robertson, and it refuted Knouse's claim that Robertson had given him ammunition.

Our case could not have been going any better. It's rare for a defense to have aces to play. It was the best hand that I've ever been dealt, and when dealt such a hand it's best to put it all in—everything—or not to play at all.

We needed those aces. Every major pretrial ruling had gone against us. Kelley and company had not proven a murder charge against Robertson—not even close—but they had mounted a credible overall effort. Every lawyer in that courtroom with some experience under his belt would tell you that anything can happen before a jury and that you can lose your best cases. It happens.

Rich Oare and Rees Griffiths took over Charlie's witnesses from that point on. They would take turns, calling an impressive mix of character witnesses one at a time. The law recognizes that character testimony alone may raise a reasonable doubt. The jury would be given that charge by Judge Uhler, and that hour was fast approaching.

Former United States Representative Bill Goodling testified that Robertson's reputation was "outstanding." From Goodling that meant a lot. He had served as chairman of the House Education Committee and was a respected figure in Washington, D.C. Though he might have outlived his time in national politics, narrowly winning a primary challenge a few years before, Goodling's stature in York politics over the past two decades stood second to none. This was a congressman who slept in his congressional office to avoid charging taxpayers for a hotel room. Goodling had been the basketball coach at Spring Grove High School and had known Charlie since his days as a referee.

Art Gladfelter, founder of Gladfelter Insurance Group, echoed Goodling's testimony.

Then there was Tom Landis, a former York Fire Department chief, who was not only a character witness but also a fact witness; he recalled the many fires, put more red labels on the map, and confirmed Robertson's assistance.

George Kroll, a retired city fire chief who had been an assistant chief in 1969, backed up Landis and added more red labels to the map.

"I think [Robertson] has an excellent reputation in our community," said State Representative Stephen Stetler. This came from a rising star in Democratic circles at the state capitol. At the time, Stetler was on the verge of breaking into the House Democratic leadership. For years, he had co-chaired the House Democratic Campaign Committee. Yet he still maintained that fresh-faced, open demeanor that York County loved in its politicians. Stetler was known for his smarts and his integrity. He would become an early supporter of Democrat Edward G. Rendell, and was a key player in his November 2002 election as Pennsylvania governor.

"Excellent," said Robert Bowers, former York County Commissioner, speaking of Charlie.

York police officer Ron McClain joined the march, as did Carol Downs-Brady, a former member of York City Council, and Reverend Robert Stone, who had known Robertson for more than 50 years.

"Excellent," said Herbert Grofcsik, former York Police Commissioner, who stood by Charlie from day one.

Rich Oare and Rees Griffiths got into a rhythm, and it was working. Such a presentation can sometimes turn into a cluster-fuck, but not this time. You also have to know when to shut it down, but we weren't quite ready for that. There were eight more character witnesses waiting in the hallway; they were sequestered, and some of them had been out there for days.

James Scarborough, retired from Metropolitan Edison Company, had known Robertson since 1947.

Parker David Lerew, a realtor with Jack Gaughen Realtor, had known Robertson since 1969.

David Mohler had known Robertson since 1959 and had played on his youth basketball team.

"Exemplary reputation," said Gladys Plank, who had known Robertson since 1971.

"Very respectable," said Beverly Atwater, a York school board member.

"Outstanding," said Terry Bupp, a math teacher and sports coach at West York High School, who knew Robertson and played on his basketball team.

Jim Stock, an employee of Seven Valleys sprinkler systems, also knew Robertson from his involvement in sports, and was a character witness.

Scott Davidson was our final character witness. He was York's current deputy fire chief, appeared in uniform, and said he had known Charlie since 1968.

And that was it. After conferring with Rich Oare, Rees Griffiths, Jayme Emig, and Charlie Robertson, we rested.

Tom Kelley and Tim Barker looked at Fran Chardo. Chardo had spent weeks preparing the cross-examination of Charlie Robertson, and was visibly amazed.

It was our decision, not Charlie's, and we had our reasons. The big one was that the prosecution hadn't proven anything.

Judge Uhler summoned Robertson to the bar, and in open court, on the record but outside the presence of the jury, he insisted on the waiver. "I am willing to testify, Your Honor," Robertson said, "but on the advice of counsel, I elect not to do so."

"Is this your decision?" Judge Uhler asked.

"Yes, Your Honor," he answered.

19

EXPERTS

Tuesday, October 15, 2002
York County Courthouse
York, Pennsylvania

It was Bob Messersmith's turn to present evidence.

Dr. Vincent Di Maio, a forensic pathologist and chief medical examiner in Bexar County, Texas, was called by Tom Sponaugle. This witness was a heavyweight because of his credentials. He had written numerous articles and textbooks, taught at the University of Texas Medical School, was a consultant to the United Nations, and had contributed to the investigation of President Kennedy's assassination.

Di Maio testified that in this case, based on the incomplete and absent evidence, the victim's fatal wound could have been caused by a number of weapons. In his opinion, beyond reasonable medical and scientific doubt, she could have been killed with a large caliber revolver—a Colt .45 or .44 magnum—or with a shotgun or a rifle.

Tom Sponaugle next called Dr. Cyril Wecht to the stand and began the direct examination.

Dr. Wecht and I knew each other from my law school days in Pittsburgh. He taught a course titled "Legal Medicine" and was impressive 32 years ago. We exchanged nods once he took the witness stand, and I knew he was going to deliver for Messersmith. Wecht had done an extensive study of the Kennedy assassination and was sharply critical of the government's autopsy procedures. He was internationally known for his forensic work. As Allegheny County's coroner, he had performed thousands of autopsies. His expertise has been utilized in high-profile cases—from Mary Jo Kopechne and Dr. Jeffrey McDonald to the Waco Branch Davidian fire and the Vincent Foster death. As an expert "talking head," he has appeared frequently on national television shows about the O.J. Simpson case and most recently, the JonBenet Ramsey murder. He was the author of a book about the Ramsey case. Wecht held a law degree from the University of Pittsburgh and a medical degree from the University of Maryland. He was a clinical professor at the University of Pittsburgh Schools of Medicine and Dental Medicine and the Graduate School of Public Health, and was an adjunct professor at the Duquesne University Schools of Law, Pharmacy, and Health Services. In forensic pathology circles, Wecht was an all-star.

Dr. Wecht testified, based on the state police analysis done in 1969, that Lillie Belle Allen "was likely killed by a rifled shotgun shell, but I cannot rule out a large-caliber handgun or rifle."

Furthermore, he said, "without having any other evidence from the scene, it is nearly impossible to determine where Allen or the shooter were at the time of the shooting."

Fred Wentling, the former head of the Pennsylvania State Police firearms department, also testified for Tom Sponaugle. Wentling was a ballistics man, and a good one, for most of his career. His expert opinion was that it could not be determined with scientific certainty whether the bullet that killed Lillie Belle Allen was fired from a 12-gauge shotgun.

His reasons certainly made sense to me. The slug retrieved from the body was lost in 1980, and there was never a slug that matched a gun of any gauge.

Sponaugle's final witness was an African American, named John Henry Atterberry. The Atterberry family lived on Gas Avenue during the riots and never had any problems with the Newberry Street Boys. In fact, he drove through the neighborhood to and from work for 23 years, and never ran into problems on Newberry Street.

"That's because," Pete Solymos would argue to the jury in his closing, "the boys on Newberry Street weren't racists. Atterberry himself became a Newberry Street Boy three years after the riots. The killing on the night in question was out of fear, not hate."

A black Newberry Street Boy was not something you heard about from the media.

Bob Messersmith also elected, on the advice of counsel, not to take the witness stand. The shooting of Taka Nii Sweeney by Messersmith, though on another occasion and under different circumstances, would come into evidence if he took the stand. The shooting had happened in the opening rounds of the 1969 riots. Though Messersmith was convicted of that crime and sentenced to jail three decades before, that prior conviction was damaging to his present claim of innocence. I agreed with his defense lawyers to keep him off the witness stand.

Before the Messersmith defense, I was pretty sure that Bob was going down. I wasn't positive about it, for the defense of self-defense or the defense of others was out there. Jury nullification—a jury verdict based on what the jury wants to do, in spite of the evidence, out of their sense of fairness—was also a possibility in this case.

After Tom Sponaugle's defense, I really thought he had a shot.

There was no more that Tom and Pete could have done with the hand they were dealt. They didn't have any aces, that's for sure.

§

Harry Ness had no aces either, except himself.

Harry Ness had no experts, except himself.

The reason I say this is that the jury liked Harry a lot. Harry was a good lawyer; he knew when to question a witness and when to keep his mouth shut. Whenever he approached a witness, he was respectful when he needed to be and ruthless if necessary. But even his ruthlessness was gentle, like a stiletto knife that makes a deep cut without the victim's knowing it until it's too late.

The jury appreciated Harry's style and occasional humor.

His client, Greg Neff, also had a likeable appearance. Greg, 56, maybe because of his heavy smoking, had a slender build. His salt-and-pepper hair was combed to the side, and his thick mustache was neatly trimmed. Greg did not wear suits to court; he always wore dress slacks and a sport coat. The jury would never know that Neff had given up a plea for probation on principle— his refusal to be tweaked.

Harry's first witness, and only fact witness, was Douglas Bredbenner. Doug was a Newberry Street Boy, and testified that he was shot at by an unknown assailant the night of July 18, 1969, on Newberry Street. The bullet shattered the window of his Volkswagen, nearly killing him. It was an unprovoked terrorist act, if not attempted murder, by a carload of African Americans who came to Newberry Street looking for trouble.

Other acts of violence—the throwing of Molotov cocktails, makeshift bombs, and rocks, along with arsons and similar shootings—had been brought to the attention of the jury throughout the trial. Many of those rampant incidents on Newberry Street and throughout the city were reported to the overwhelmed police, and had been testified to before Judge Nealon. Since the prosecutors and all defense lawyers agreed that these violent acts took place, a list of stipulations was read to the jury; a stipulation is simply a fact the jury is told to accept, for the city's history of violence was not in dispute.

Doug Bredbenner, however, brought a piece of that history to light. He recalled sitting in his parked car when another car pulled up beside him. "The back window of that car was rolled down, a rifle barrel was pointed at me, and then there was this blast almost killing me," he said.

Harry Ness wrapped up his case, producing a series of character witnesses. They included Neff's employer, John Z. Barton, Inc.; his uncle; two teachers; a neighbor and two friends, one who knew Neff from playing sports with him when they were kids.

Harry agonized over calling his client to the witness stand. Neff's grand jury testimony had been read to the jury, and there was really nothing more to tell them. Neff had admitted firing at the car, believing he saw the victim brandishing a gun. To put his client up there would add nothing, and at the last minute Harry advised Greg to remain silent. Like Robertson and Messersmith, Neff told Judge Uhler that he was waiving his right to testify, and his waiver was voluntary.

Harry Ness, on behalf of Greg Neff, rested.

§

The big yellow bus moved slowly through the city, transporting the fate of many in this notorious case.

Bob Chuck, the court administrator, sat by himself in the front of the bus. He was responsible for the jury's safety and for assuring that no juror discussed the facts of the case on this road trip. The testimony was in and all the exhibits were admitted, but until the closing arguments were concluded—I was going first, then Solymos, then Ness and Kelley—and until Judge Uhler charged the jury on the law, the jurors were instructed not to discuss the facts with anyone, including each other.

It was a gloomy day, damp and rainy. The jury sat quietly, looking out the streaked bus windows as they journeyed to where Lillie Belle

Allen was gunned down on North Newberry Street. The bus creaked to a stop, and all 18 fact-finders exited in an orderly fashion. Escorted by deputy sheriffs and court personnel, they walked north from the Philadelphia Street intersection, which reportedly was blocked by barricades the night Allen was killed.

The jury stopped momentarily at the railroad tracks and looked in all directions. Residents and curiosity seekers stared at them, for they knew who they were and why they were there.

The solemn entourage walked slowly to the former Messersmith home in the 200 block of North Newberry, and were permitted to examine the prosecution's posterboard photos to see and compare for themselves the different angles and distances.

Two or three sheriffs guarded each location. This trip was Chuck's responsibility and he was making sure it went off without a hitch.

The jury was then taken to nearby Farquhar Park to see the gazebo and the bandstand, sites of two gang rallies held the day before Allen died. It was here that Charlie Robertson had yelled "white power" 32 years ago. It was here that people were told to unite to protect their homes and their families.

In his 22 years as a court administrator, Bob Chuck had never seen anything like this. He came to York in 1994 after working in Media, the Philadelphia suburbs, as a court administrator. Organizing the well of the courtroom and dealing with the media and the lawyers had been a monster undertaking in the Robertson case. By all accounts, Chuck had handled it flawlessly. He was glad it was winding down. The lawyers would close the next day. There was a chance it might be over in a day or so. At least that's what he hoped. But until the verdicts were read, Bob Chuck had to remain on his toes, protecting the integrity of this jury.

§

Inside Judge Uhler's chambers, all the defense lawyers and prosecutors had gathered. They sat respectfully as the judge pored over his points for charge. The court reporter was poised, with her stenographic machine ready to go, for she knew what was coming.

Rees Griffiths would request jury instructions favorable to our position. The court was certain to give the general instructions regarding the burden of proof, the presumption of innocence, the right of the accused to remain silent, and the need for the verdict to be unanimous. The applicable law in the instant case required charging the jury on "aiding and abetting," and Rees wanted to assure that the charge on that point was carefully worded and legally correct.

Pete Solymos would focus on the definition of principal in the first degree.

Harry Ness would take on the definition of principal in the second degree.

Tim Barker and Fran Chardo were there to make sure the Commonwealth got the best charge possible, knowing that a good charge can go a long way in making the prosecution's case.

And Judge Uhler, who wrote the book on points for charge, would have the last say.

"Where's Costopoulos?" Uhler asked, noticing my absence.

"Practicing his closing in the courtroom, Your Honor," Rees answered.

20

ZONE

Thursday, October 17, 2002
York County Courthouse
York, Pennsylvania

The enormous 90-inch screen was set in place across the well of the courtroom, facing the jury. Dan Rippon and Jerry Westerhold of Mirtech Consulting had done all the wiring and technical work and placed the screen in the courtroom the evening before. We had moved the screen together, like a piece of furniture, to exactly where we wanted it for maximum visual effect. On cue the main lights in the courtroom would be dimmed.

Of course, we needed and got court approval, and cooperation from Bob Chuck, the court administrator.

Earlier that morning, however, the prosecutors were objecting to this Powerpoint closing, distinguishing its high-tech format from "the traditional approach." I had been summoned to Judge Uhler's chambers, by all three of them to answer their objections. Their main objection was not knowing what the jury was going to be shown on the screen. The answer was photographs admitted into evidence, selected testimony that I had the stenographer transcribe as I heard it, and charts that they could review from the hard copies printed out.

Judge Uhler saw nothing wrong with that, and it was time to get this case into the hands of the jury.

"This is going to be prejudicial," Barker said, insisting that his objection be put on the record.

"You can count on it," I answered.

For weeks, I had worked on my closing argument. Believing it might be a final moment, a great opportunity to do something that mattered, I wanted it to be the best closing argument of my career, surpassing anything I had ever done. Only my final remarks in the 1992 impeachment trial of Justice Rolf Larsen came close in preparation time; my audience was the entire Pennsylvania Senate, and I spent endless hours and sleepless nights putting the closing together. A mental goal that motivated me was that Charlie Robertson's jury would decide not only his fate and on some level the fate of York, but also that of the world. It was about truth and justice prevailing.

My prime time for preparation was early morning, and as the trial days ticked away, I would get up at 3:30 a.m. to summarize 33 years of history, 63 prosecution witnesses, and three defenses. I laid out in my mind the screen presentation, and made countless trips to 6864 Susquehanna Trail South in the evenings and on the final weekend.

I wanted to recreate York's riots—live—and the '69 photos from the archives said it all. Without having to turn around as I spoke, I wanted those images flashing in the background, supporting my remarks. Dan Rippon would work the computer, and certain words would trigger the image I wanted, but I needed to have a series of photos flashed in consecutive order, every 20 seconds. My final dress rehearsal with Rippon was the evening before, in the courtroom behind closed doors, and it worked.

It really worked.

But the question for me was, could we do it again?

I had made many closing arguments over 31 years, but never a choreographed presentation that depended on a computer operator. The thought of a wire going bad or becoming disconnected was enough to blow my fuse. This was either going to work again or it would be a day to forget.

I could feel the jury's gaze as I walked to the podium.

They knew what this case was about, what was at stake.

The 11 days of hell in 1969 left the city in ruins. The number of wounded was an unknown. There were two deaths. Those events resulted in three major law enforcement investigations. The jury had heard from Major Robert Rice; they were told about Sergeant Creavey's effort 33 years ago, an investigation that spanned weeks, if not months, resulting in the interviews of 58 persons, most of whom were from Newberry Street. They had learned that the civil division of the United States attorney's office had conducted its own inquiry. In addition, a civil rights action was filed in federal court immediately after the riots, alleging police misconduct—a hearing that took eight days and resulted in 1,000 pages of testimony.

"And Charles Robertson, ladies and gentlemen," I said, "was not identified or mentioned as having anything to do with the death of Lillie Belle Allen—in any of these investigations—undertaken 33 years ago when everybody's memories were fresh."

I impressed upon the jury that these law enforcement agencies, and the predecessors of our young prosecutors, "were neither inept, or corrupt, nor did they exercise bad judgment, or fail to investigate and interview properly and aggressively."

Yet this new team of prosecutors elected to charge Charlie Robertson with murder; a veteran police officer of 27 years with the York City Police, a two-term mayor of this city, "based on the uncorroborated testimony of Rick Knouse, who saw things nobody else ever saw, who heard things nobody else ever heard . . . and coupled that testimony with an unprecedented theory of murder . . . . Not only was Charles Robertson publicly indicted, but this prosecution team indicted the entire York City Police Department, alleging 'an uneasy alliance with white gangs to murder African Americans.'"

That was the trigger Don Rippon was waiting for, and at that moment the prosecution's entire witness list appeared on the screen—all 63 names—and Rick Lynn Knouse was highlighted in red, emphasizing the paucity of the Commonwealth's case.

The jury was reminded that Knouse alleged "30 to 60 onlookers witnessed Robertson handing out ammo . . . inciting him and others to kill blacks . . . in the presence of four to eight police officers." But Knouse could come up with no names, no corroboration, not even from alleged co-defendants who pled guilty for deals in exchange for their truthful testimony. "Otherwise, there would have been more names on the Commonwealth's witness list that appears before you."

The reason there were no other names on that witness list?

It didn't happen.

Thomas Smith, a co-defendant, was there and testified "it didn't happen."

Chauncey Gladfelter, a co-defendant, was there and testified "it didn't happen."

William Ritter, a co-defendant, was there and testified "it didn't happen."

Art Messersmith, a co-defendant, was there and testified "it didn't happen."

According to Officers VanGreen, Ray Markle, Dennis McMaster, and Jim Brown, "it didn't happen."

"Yet the prosecution wants you to believe that Charlie Robertson drove Knouse to murder . . . which is their theory . . . when Knouse himself testified that he never killed anybody, and never intended to," I said.

During my reference to testimony from key witnesses, their actual testimony provided in court, heard by the jury—with reference to line, page number, and date—appeared on the screen, confirming my representations.

The closing argument then shifted to the state of hell York was in, for 11 days, in 1969.

What Charlie Robertson, the York City Police, and the York Fire Department had gone through was about to be recreated—live—for this jury.

A map of their city appeared on the 90-inch screen, and the five main areas of disorder were identified, with a red laser, going counterclockwise: Parkway Homes, Cottage Hill, North Newberry Street, Penn College, Penn Commons, Queen and Maple.

With that backdrop, the jury was reminded that in 1969 the York City Police Department had fewer than 100 men, responsible for 55,000 citizens, and that on any given night during the 11-day period, "especially at night, in each of these five areas, there were shootings of whites by blacks. There were shootings of blacks by whites. There were fire bombings, Molotov cocktails, arsons, vandalism, rock throwing, false alarms, police officers being shot at, police department armored vehicles being shot at, and the storage of dynamite for later mass destruction . . . ."

I was facing the jury, telling these truths, my back to the screen, hoping that Rippon was timing the photo images, every 20 seconds, recreating this history—and I could tell he was.

The jury was listening, but their eyes were fixed elsewhere, riveted on the screen. I wasn't even there, only my voice and my words, as the jury watched their city burn, their police putting their lives on the line, the armored personnel carriers rolling in to restore order. I told the jury that what they were witnessing represented only a portion of the wave of horror and panic that gripped the city.

"Police officers, firemen in their vehicles and engines were subjected to heavy gunfire when assigned to the troubled areas," I said.

"The entire citizenry were subjected to vicious and numerous attacks, and their homes were threatened by roaming arsonists, both black and white," I added.

"This was the hot spot. Remember Jimmy Brown? That's where he almost got it," I said, knowing that the photo depicted a burning car on its side and burning buildings, a photo that had brought Jimmy Brown to tears on the witness stand.

I knew it was working; it was fucking working. It was a precious moment, a key moment, that I had worked hard to get. It was a type of euphoria, a strange feeling of invincibility. I was living in the present, but it was taking place in slow motion—tranquility was setting in. Yuri Vlasov, the Russian weightlifter; Pele, the Brazilian soccer great; Tony Jacklin, the British golfer; Bill Russell, the NBA standout; and Billie Jean King, the tennis player, had all talked about it. I was in the zone.

Words don't accurately describe it. It's hard to understand it unless you have been there.

"On Friday, July 18, at 11:10 p.m., Officer Henry Schaad, riding in an armored vehicle, 'Big Al,' was shot. An armor-piercing bullet went through this vehicle, through his flak vest, and mortally wounded him, and he died days later," I told the jury, knowing that the ominous image of "Big Al" was on the screen behind me.

The jury then revisited the map of York, this time marked with red labels depicting the major fires, and on the screen the city looked ablaze.

"On July 22, in the early morning hours, Mayor John Snyder realized that he had lost control of the city, and called Governor Shafer for reinforcements," I said, and Don Rippon rolled in photos of the National Guard and the Pennsylvania State Police in armored personnel carriers, brought to the scene to restore order.

And they did.

The screen went black. There was a moment of silence in the courtroom—deafening silence.

It was time to wrap it up.

I told the jury that Ron Zeager did not come into this courtroom to lie about the barricades, for his disclosure that "they were up, in place," that "the occupants of the car wanted through, despite my effort to send them another way," and that "I had made the greatest mistake of my life," exposed him to great criticism.

Facing Charlie Robertson, I told him that he deserved better, for he loved his community. I told him that the York City Police deserved better than what they got in this courtroom. I told him that the York Fire Department deserved better than what they got in this courtroom. I told him that the people of York deserved better than what they got in this courtroom.

Charlie Robertson could hold on no longer, and broke down in tears.

After thanking the jury, with a sincere appreciation from the heart, I promised them that when they reached the only appropriate verdict—a verdict of not guilty—the sacrifices they had made would be worth it for a lifetime, "for you will have served your community well . . . and the American criminal justice system . . . and will have risen to a higher level to do the right thing."

§

There was a 15-minute break after my closing, and the friends and supporters of Charlie Robertson waited for us in the rotunda. They could not have been more appreciative or hopeful. Charlie was still shaken, but the many hugs and kisses and handshakes brought him back. I personally felt that with the help of many—especially Rich, Rees, Jayme, Ellen, Jill, and Charlie—we had done everything that could be done to exonerate an innocent man, Charlie Robertson.

Always, with closing arguments in the past, there were things I wished I had said, or said differently, or remembered to include. Once you close and sit down, you're out of it.

But not this time.

At that moment, at that very moment, I was confident—everything felt right.

It took over a year and a half to get there; in some ways it took over 30 years of practicing law.

But the high didn't last long.

It would only take the next closing to bring me down, to undermine my confidence, to bring me back to reality. I knew only too well, and should have remembered, that it was not over till it was over.

§

Pete Solymos went to the podium, cleared his throat with a drink of water, and invited the jury back into his "living room."

He impressed upon the jury that critical physical evidence was lost, that memories had faded and become distorted with the passage of time.

Pete went back to what he told them in his opening, that this killing was out of fear, not hate. "There had been no racial turmoil in the Newberry Street neighborhood prior to the riots," he said.

Pete described for the jury the events of the prior day, of the prior week, brought them forward to the Spells incident, and described the Allen Cadillac as "identical-looking to the other one . . . a Cadillac that appeared to move into the defensive position on the night in question."

I was OK with all of that, and felt the jury was listening.

Then Pete's theme suddenly changed, and he turned.

"Messersmith is being offered up as a sacrificial lamb to the gods of political correctness," he said.

He told the jury that Bob Messersmith and the other boys were encouraged by the police to protect their neighborhoods and their families. This encouragement was emotionally charged, Pete said, and he blamed the police who yelled "white power, white power, white power" at Farquhar Park.

Pete told the jury that law enforcement officers urged white youth to "draw the line" against black people who came to Newberry Street.

Solymos framed the alleged lack of police action before the murder as an enabling factor that brought a hail of bullets down on Lillie Belle Allen and her family's car. Pete reminded the jury that Robert Stoner, who was on Newberry Street in the hours leading up to the shooting, called police at least twice to warn them of what was happening.

"There was no response from York Police Captain Charles McCaffrey other than, 'Stay out of harm's way,'" Pete said.

"If someone would have done something with a phone call, a movement of an armored truck, or refusal to move a barricade," he added, "we wouldn't be here."

Solymos placed the blame for what had happened on Newberry Street the night Allen was killed squarely on the shoulders of the York City Police Department.

Well, Robertson was the only police officer on trial for murder, and I was taking this huge hit from Pete without Kelley even having his turn.

Maybe I'm too sensitive, I thought, but I think Pete just fucked me.

§

"What was that all about?" Jayme asked at the break, before we went to Rees's office over the lunch hour.

Outside, on the courthouse steps, a lawyer for the Allen family was having another press conference. "Stripped to its basics, Mr. Messersmith's lawyer said this: The police made us do it. That was the message. They armed us, they incited us, we were young kids, we were influenced by our elders, by the cops that we looked up to, so we shot indiscriminately, and a 27-year-old woman was murdered. That was the message, and I hope the jury got it, because we got it," said the lawyer, lobbying the public for the conviction of Robertson.

§

For Harry Ness, nothing about the year 2002 had any relevance to the events that had happened in 1969.

Ness told the jury—and he too had their attention, for this jury was on a mission—that it was unfair to judge Greg Neff with today's values. "It was the late '60s . . . change was underway . . . and change can lead to violence . . . violence that is not murder."

Harry then hammered away at the prosecution's ability to tweak testimony by buying what they want in the plea-bargaining market. "For 32 years," he pointed out, "Knouse claimed he saw a gun in Allen's hand before the shooting started . . . but when investigators came calling, that story changed . . . quickly . . . and the gun disappeared."

"It took, I don't know, 10 or 15 minutes with Detective Rodney George for that gun to disappear," Ness said, explaining that the most likely cause of that new version was Knouse's deal.

Like Solymos, Harry Ness also turned—not a 180, but there was a little hook there—and argued that his client was the victim of the police. "Had they done their jobs," he said, "no one would be here today."

Harry's little hook didn't put it on Robertson directly, but I could tell the jury liked Ness—with good reason; he was a good lawyer. I didn't want the jury throwing him any bones, the bones of my client.

§

It was mid-afternoon. The courtroom was still packed, the tension lingered, and no one was leaving

Tom Kelley waited patiently through three closings, but when Judge Uhler finally gave him the nod, the lead prosecutor in the case came out swinging, both fists blazing. Tim Barker and Fran Chardo would sit this one out, but cheer him on. District Attorney Stan Rebert and Detective Rodney George had ringside seats.

Kelley went after Bob Messersmith first, delivering hard body blows, describing him as a self-styled John Wayne. Except, Kelley said, to Messersmith, the bad guys were the black people of this community—all of them—the ones he referred to as "niggers."

Kelley mocked Messersmith, who had stood in the middle of the street with a .12-gauge shotgun, "thinking, no one is getting by me . . . I am not afraid."

He reminded the jury that two other large, light-colored sedans with black occupants also took gunfire on Newberry Street the day before Allen was killed. Pretending to hold a shotgun, Kelley said that both times the call went out, "Nigger, nigger, nigger." He argued that alone established that whites had gathered on Newberry Street for the sole purpose of shooting black people.

Kelley then gave Greg Neff a smashing left jab, pointing out for the jury that Neff admitted to shooting that night. "Neff wasn't even from Newberry Street, or a Newberry Street Boy," Kelley said.

"Self-defense?" he asked the jury.

Kelley argued that Neff didn't go over to Newberry Street to protect its residents. He said that Neff went over there with some buddies to kill black people. He pointed out for the jury that the summer of '69 was truly contentious. "But there is no 'It was a riot' defense," Kelley said. "There was no 'It was a crazy time' defense."

Charlie Robertson was still standing, and Tom Kelley did his best to knock him down. Charlie was still the big man, a true heavyweight, the one Kelley wanted most. Kelley's adrenaline surged, and he rose to another level as a courtroom fighter.

He would be cheered on by the York newspaper reporters, for they also needed a conviction to validate what they had done to Charlie Robertson and to their community. What's more, a conviction of Robertson would go a long way toward a Pulitzer Prize.

Kelley's fans, loud and boisterous, included the activist lawyers from Philadelphia and members of the Allen family. They were in the courtroom, day in and day out, sitting through the testimony and meeting with reporters outside the courtroom. They needed Robertson's conviction in order to sue the city.

Tom Kelley, with much support from his gallery, argued that Charlie Robertson did not simply suggest to the young white men that they band together to protect their neighborhoods and loved ones. Instead, the lead prosecutor said, "Robertson handed out .30-06 ammunition . . . Robertson told the gang members 'kill as many niggers as you can.'"

"Kill 'em," Kelley quoted. "Not to protect yourself. Kill 'em."

In the final round, Kelley took a shot at Ron Zeager, and called him a liar.

His closing, and I hated giving him credit, was extremely well done. I hated what he did to Charlie Robertson, but there was no denying it—Kelley finished up strong, and I was worried about it. Especially on the heels of Pete Solymos, and to some extent Harry Ness.

I just hoped we were OK.

21

VERDICT

Judge Uhler was not a passive observer, having to deal with nine lawyers in the well of his courtroom, consisting of prosecutors and three defense teams, all with different agendas and needs. The crowded gallery had to be dealt with, its noise level a constant, annoying problem. The media thought they could come and go as they pleased, talking to whomever they wanted, whenever they wanted, but Judge Uhler took care of that early on.

"Should the jury be charged today, or should we wait until tomorrow morning?" Judge Uhler asked at side bar at the end of Tom Kelley's closing. He looked tired, for the four closing arguments took all day, and exhaustion was setting in.

Everybody wanted to get it into the hands of the jury and asked Judge Uhler to do it without delay.

He consulted the jury for their input, and without hesitation or needing to confer, they voted unanimously, "now."

The judge took almost two hours to charge the jury on the law.

He was patient with his instructions, clear of voice, and authoritative, as he laid out the groundwork for six men and six women to use in determining the guilt or innocence of three men in the 33-year-old killing of Lillie Belle Allen. Uhler explained, again, that the prosecution must prove its case beyond a reasonable doubt, that the burden is upon the Commonwealth, and that the jury cannot consider the defendants' decisions not to testify as evidence of guilt.

"You are the sole judges of the facts presented and the credibility of the witnesses," he said. "You will reach separate verdicts for each of the defendants, and your verdicts must be unanimous."

That was the easy part.

It would get more confusing, not because of Judge Uhler but because of the multiple defendants and the complex legal issues that needed to be defined.

Uhler advised the jury that former gang member Robert N. Messersmith was charged with first- and second-degree murder as a principal in the first degree. Messersmith was alleged to have fired the single fatal shot that killed the 27-year-old South Carolina woman on July 21, 1969. The court then defined the elements of murder in both degrees.

At the request of his attorneys, a count of voluntary manslaughter was added to Bob Messersmith's verdict slip. Though the statute of limitations had run out on that crime, it was up to the defense to add it or not. The decision to add it was made by Pete Solymos and Tom Sponaugle, with Messersmith's consent. It was a lesser crime, carrying six to twelve years, but if the jury was going to convict somebody for something— no matter what— this might give them an out. The elements of voluntary manslaughter were defined by the court. This gave rise to the definitions of self-defense, defense of others, and mistake of fact.

Greg Neff also requested the voluntary manslaughter charge. He really suffered with that decision, for he wanted to gamble. Harry Ness leaned on Neff to take it—a difficult decision, but the right one.

For Charlie Robertson, we refused the voluntary manslaughter charge, adding more confusion for the jury. Our position from day one was all or nothing. Charlie was either going down on murder or he was going home. There was no middle ground, no compromise verdict, not for Robertson.

The definition of aiding and abetting was then defined for the jury.

"The charge of murder, as an aider and abettor, does not require you, ladies and gentlemen of the jury, to determine that defendant Robertson was present when Lillie Belle Allen was shot, only that he had a direct role in her death," Judge Uhler said. This put Charlie in the cross-hairs, and I sweated and gulped with every word coming from the bench. I just prayed that we hadn't fucked up by refusing the lesser charge.

Even before Judge Uhler dismissed the alternate jurors, the soul-wrenching stress of waiting for the verdict was setting in.

And it would get worse. With each passing moment—with each passing hour—until they reached a unanimous decision on each of the defendants.

The stress of waiting for a jury verdict is horrible, a living hell on earth, and if I never have to wait for another verdict in my life, then good; it has aged me enough. Waiting for the verdict in this case was the most stressful, frightening, and sickening time of my career.

That evening, after 24 days in the courtroom, we waited.

There was nothing to do except wait and worry.

Rich Oare had to go home, maybe to hook up with Ellen Wagner. He had his cell phone with him and left instructions with the tipstaff, the court administrator, and us to call him immediately if anything came up.

Rees Griffiths and I walked down to The Left Bank, a nice restaurant on South George Street, three blocks from his office. It was dimly lit, with candles on linen-covered tables and a fine menu. The bar in the front was busy, and the two televisions overhead were showing the evening news, hyping the fact that the jury was out, with old footage of Charlie Robertson entering the courthouse.

Harry Ness needed company, and he joined us with his beautiful friend, Jane.

Several patrons at the bar had recognized Harry when he walked in, and wished him well. "How long do you think they'll be out?" Harry asked, after ordering a glass of Mouton Cadet wine.

"No clue," I answered, since he was looking at me. Actually, I didn't think they would be out that long, but didn't expect them back until the following morning.

"The jury will have questions," Rees warned, still worried about Uhler's charge on aiding and abetting.

"I hate questions from the jury," Harry said, shaking his head at the thought.

We all agreed there would be questions, and we hated them with a passion. Every question from a jury is a telegraphed verdict, a quiz—enough to put your stress level off the chart. Answering questions is a juggling act, for you don't want the court suggesting a verdict with the answer. Plus, every time the phone rings you think there is a verdict.

We were discussing that very subject when Harry's cellular phone rang at the table.

Our hearts nearly stopped.

It was the tipstaff, advising us that the jury was retiring for the evening. They were reporting to the Yorktowne Hotel, next to the courthouse, where they were being sequestered until they reached a verdict.

§

I had no other life.

I had missed four of Callista's field hockey games—and I never missed field hockey games. I hardly saw my teenage daughter. I was getting up before daylight and was gone before she awoke; by the time I got home from York, she was in bed. Kara and Khristina had become voices over the phone. Jill was supportive, but a stranger.

I had abandoned my law offices and my law partners, Dave Foster and Leslie Fields.

My 94-year-old father was not doing well. I missed him and felt guilty about not getting to see him. My mother was from the old school and insisted on taking care of him at home, but she had recently undergone a major cancer operation, and it was a struggle. They were living in another world, with family support, and I should have been there.

Everything about my personal life had been on hold, not only for the preceding several weeks, but also in some ways for the preceding year and a half since I had first gotten the call from Charlie Robertson. I had had enough of my possessive mistress, the law, and was ready to leave her. Yet during the Robertson trial, especially the closing, she had come to me again, this time dressed in scant red lace, and seduced me. She was beautiful and had taken me into her sexual world, reminding me that she would not give up so easily.

Waiting for the Robertson verdict, however, was too much for me. And I wished the bitch would leave me alone.

§

Friday, October 18, 2002
York, Pennsylvania

Judge Uhler had sent word to the parties that there would be "two hours of lead time to get to the courthouse once the jury reached the verdict." He explained that time was needed to secure the courthouse with additional law enforcement personnel "just in case." A spokesman for the media had also requested this time to give them an opportunity "to get there, and set up."

That left Rees Griffiths and Rich Oare on their own during the morning; I had dumped any possible juror questions on them to handle.

Little did I know, little did anybody know, the enormity and complexity of their undertaking.

First thing in the morning, the jury asked to review defendant Greg Neff's grand jury testimony, Officer Dennis McMaster's trial testimony, reports made by the defense and prosecution forensic experts, and Charlie Robertson's televised interview with Fox 43, in which he said he couldn't answer whether he had given ammunition to gang members.

Jurors also asked Judge Uhler to redefine first- and second-degree murder, and voluntary manslaughter.

The judge brought the jury back into the courtroom, spent about 30 minutes redefining the requested crimes, and denied their request to review testimony. He told them that they would have to focus on their collective wisdom and recollection, for they were getting no transcripts, forensic reports, or media films.

When Rees called me with that development, I couldn't take it anymore and rushed back to York. I didn't like their request for McMaster's testimony, or their request for the interview with Fox 43. That meant that Charlie's guilt was being discussed, I thought, and I was freaking out.

So was Rees.

So was Rich.

Jill didn't like it.

Charlie had nothing to say.

Almost immediately upon my arrival, Judge Uhler summoned us to his chambers. The jury had more questions. They wanted to know if there was a difference between participant in the second degree and aiding and abetting. They also asked if there was a difference between accomplice and aiding and abetting. In addition, the jurors asked the judge to again define voluntary manslaughter.

Judge Uhler brought the jury back into the courtroom and reread his charge on those points.

Now I was really freaking out. I felt like throwing up. I remembered my aces, but I had a flashback sitting in Rees's conference room alone. Steve McQueen, in the movie *The Cincinnati Kid*, was playing five-card stud with Edward G. Robinson. It was just the two of them, and McQueen put everything he owned on the line. With good reason: he had a full boat—aces full, three aces and a pair. Robinson stuck it out and gutted him with a low straight flush.

Remembering that movie added to my anxiety and I felt sick.

For I too had put it all on the line.

Including, in many ways, my career.

More importantly, Charlie's freedom and his life.

At 3:53 p.m. the phone rang again in Rees's office. The jury had more questions.

"What's a person's obligation to claim self-defense?"

"What is the unreasonable justification for self-defense?"

"Do you need to know the actual killer to render a verdict of voluntary manslaughter?"

"Can someone be an accessory to voluntary manslaughter?"

At 4:38 p.m., the jury sent word that they were tired. Although it was early, they were retiring for the night. They had not yet reached a verdict, and said that they would resume deliberations in the morning.

That evening, Charlie and I went to dinner, just the two of us. We met at the Hillside Cafe outside of York, a Greek-owned steak and seafood house. The restaurant was standing room only, but the owner— a cousin—got us a private table immediately. Having once lived on Newberry Street, he also recognized Charlie Robertson and wished us well. Throughout our evening, patrons kept coming to our table to shake Charlie's hand, wishing him the best.

"You OK, Charlie?" I asked.

"I don't like it." he answered.

And neither did I, but said nothing.

§

Saturday, October 19, 2002
York, Pennsylvania

Rich and Ellen were having breakfast in the dining room of the Yorktowne Hotel. Pete Solymos and his devoted wife, Barbara, joined them. Harry Ness soon walked in, alone, to wait it out.

Rees and I hung out in his conference room, but things were too quiet, and we joined the vigil at the hotel. Jill arrived, unable to wait at home for my call. ESPN was on the television above our heads, and we watched a football game that nobody cared about.

Charlie Robertson was nowhere around, but on telephone standby.

Before noon, Rees's cell phone rang, jumping our heart rates.

"No," Uhler's tipstaff said, "the jury doesn't have a verdict, but the judge wants to see everybody in chambers."

11:44 a.m.

A tired, stressed-out-looking jury convened in the courtroom and asked Judge Uhler if it was too soon to be deadlocked.

Uhler told them this case was an important one. It was important to the Commonwealth, which had brought the charges; it was important to the accused who were on trial; and it was important to the community of York. He urged them to go back into the jury room to discuss their differences and to reconcile them based on the evidence, without violating their consciences.

As he charged the jurors, everybody was checking them out, looking for a read, but there was nothing there. They had isolated themselves as if in a cocoon. They knew that no matter what they decided, there would be many casualties; there was no way to make everybody happy. The system had put in their hands a hot dispute, emotionally and racially charged. They also knew they were an all-white jury, and the world was watching.

With that, some jurors shook their heads—a few in disgust, others out of frustration—and reluctantly went back to deliberating.

Back at Rees's office, we all engaged in the self-destructive analysis of what had just happened.

Were they deadlocked on all three?

On Charlie Robertson only?

What about Greg Neff?

Who on the jury were the holdouts?

Who was the foreman? What about the young juror, the corrections officer? What about the school teacher next to him? What about the woman in the back row, who had lived near Henry Schaad when she was a little girl? What about the woman in the front row; she looked mad? What about? What about? What about?

What about the fact that we were going fucking nuts?

I promised myself, and I meant it this time, that I was never going to put myself through this again—never, as in for as long as I live.

I didn't know why I took this case in the first place. I didn't know why I went to law school. I didn't know why I ever became a defense lawyer. I fucking hated it.

4:00 p.m.

The phone rang in Rees's office.

They had a verdict!

4:15 p.m.

We were all stressed out, but did the walk to the courthouse, and said nothing to the gathering media.

Once seated in the courtroom—no one was at Messersmith's table, or Neff's, and the prosecutors weren't there—a subdued tipstaff came out to tell us to come back at 6:00 p.m. We were reminded that security and the media needed time to get in.

What was there to say?

Or do?

We walked back to Rees's office to wait, a wait I will never forget.

Charlie Robertson asked Rich Oare to follow him home. He didn't want his car left on the street, "just in case." Robertson also called his brother from the house, telling him that the bills to be paid were on the kitchen table, that the checkbook was in the top drawer, and that he should turn the utilities off and sell the house, "just in case."

6:30 p.m.

Everybody was there this time. The courtroom was packed and the media were waiting outside with a phalanx of microphones at a podium, cameras poised.

I kept my head down as the jury filed into the jury box. I could not look at them, but I could hear their footsteps, and I could hear them stop and take their seats. Charlie Robertson was seated to my immediate right, and he was trembling. With his hands propped beneath his chin, Charlie kept his eyes on the papers being handed to Judge Uhler.

I could hear Judge Uhler unfold the verdict slips on the bench, knowing the judge reviews the slips before the verdict is announced.

The seconds this took seemed like hours, and I wanted to throw up.

"Would the jury please rise?" the tipstaff formally requested.

And the jury rose to announce their verdicts.

"In the case of Commonwealth versus Charles Robertson—charge, murder in the first degree—how do you find the defendant?" the tipstaff asked.

"Not guilty," the foreman answered.

I was still scared to death because the big one, the most threatening one, was next.

"In the case of Commonwealth versus Charles Robertson—charge, murder in the second degree—how do you find the defendant?" the tipstaff asked.

"Not guilty," the foreman answered.

There was an explosion in my heart. Charlie immediately broke down crying, and I took his trembling hand. I still couldn't look up, but could feel the relief and euphoria rushing in.

"In the case of Commonwealth versus Robert Messersmith— charge, murder in the first degree—how do you find the defendant?" the tipstaff asked.

"Guilty of murder in the second degree," the foreman answered.

Immediately, there was an outburst of tears and cries from the back of the courtroom. It was from the family and friends of Bob Messersmith, and it was horrible. I felt bad for Messersmith, worse for Pete Solymos. Tom Sponaugle wasn't in the courtroom.

"In the case of Commonwealth versus Gregory Neff—charge, murder in the first degree—how do you find the defendant?" the tipstaff asked.

"Guilty of murder in the second degree," the foreman answered.

Again, there was an outburst of pain and anguish from the back of the courtroom, this time from the Neff family.

I felt terrible for Harry Ness, for it is an awful moment under any circumstances. I honestly believed that Greg had a shot at an acquittal, with a good shot at voluntary manslaughter. I was wrong again.

"Sheriffs," Judge Uhler said after Pete and Harry pled for bail pending the ordered pre-sentence investigation, "please remove defendants Messersmith and Neff from the courtroom, and transport them directly to the York County Prison . . . to be returned here for sentencing on December 18, 2002."

With that directive, uniformed sheriffs entered the well of the courtroom. Messersmith and Neff were handcuffed, and the loud, metallic click of the cuffs seemed to reverberate throughout the room. The sheriffs walked them out of a courtroom that was now in hysteria. It began with mournful wailing and turned to anger.

Robertson continued to stare straight ahead. He could hear screaming, yelling, and cursing behind him.

It was difficult to distinguish the voices, but Charlie thought it came primarily from Messersmith's family.

As Bob Messersmith was led away, he turned to his wife Deborah and said, "Love you, baby."

The chaos continued with a confrontation later ensuing between the Messersmith and Allen families in the hallway outside the courtroom. It was a verbal exchange. As Deborah sat in the hallway, cradling her head with her hands, someone from the Allen family objected to being told to move, saying, "You don't need to treat me like a dog."

At one point, Deborah Messersmith was overheard saying to someone in the Allen group, "I hope you burn in hell."

Outside, the media was waiting for York's former mayor.

Charlie Robertson stood at the podium, as he had done many times in his career.

It was dark outside, and the cameras were flashing from all angles. The lighting from the film crews was intense and blinding. The microphones were piled on top of each other.

Teary-eyed and emotional, trying to hold it back, Charlie faced his community one more time — this time with restored pride.

"I'd like to thank all the people who prayed for me," Charlie said. "You people don't know what it's like to be 68 years old and oppressed . . . . I just want to go home now . . . I'm very tired . . . . Thank you."

And that was it.

The camera crews followed Charlie up the street, but he had nothing more to say, and I watched him disappear into the darkness.

22

SOCRATES

A long time ago (469–399 B.C.), dressed in linen robes, he sat with his disciples and discussed the same subjects that I have thought about for years. Roaming the hillsides of Athens, he engaged in dialogue with his philosophic friends and knew then what I know now: "justice" transcends the ways of man, for it is divine, godlike.

He was my forefather, Socrates.

"Nothing is to be preferred before justice," he wrote.

I don't know what he would have said about the prosecutions in York. He certainly would have applauded the jury's verdict for Charlie Robertson, and denounced his arrest by the authorities in that community. My guess is he would have been troubled by the spectacle of a trial 32 years after the fact, and would have questioned the bogus reasoning of the district attorney's office.

I do know the verdict is not in, not yet it isn't, on whether the criminal justice system was abused by young prosecutors out to make a name for themselves. I do know the verdict is not in, not yet it isn't, on whether the bad—arresting an innocent man on baseless testimony—outweighs the good—possible justice for the family of Lillie Belle Allen. I don't think this case is going to go down in history as anything the criminal justice system should be proud about.

The prosecution of Charlie Robertson in York was bullshit.

He was a scapegoat.

"There was no evidence that Charlie did anything," York City Councilman William Smallwood, one of the former mayor's critics, said after the verdict.

His acquittal went a long way to restoring my belief in a fragile system, a system that often dumps the resolution of high-profile cases, with enormous social consequences, on 12 innocent people who must go back into their communities after their verdict. The Charlie Robertson jury, the same jury as for Messersmith and Neff, did not ask for that assignment.

Those jurors—six men and six women—were denied their loved ones, their jobs, their chosen way of life for almost a month. From early morning until dusk, they sat patiently listening to 63 prosecution witnesses, dozens of defense witnesses, nine lawyers arguing, and a two-hour jury charge. They never complained, but they did suffer, and their suffering would peak during the deliberation process.

For three days they argued.

They fought.

They compromised; some were unwilling, others intimidated.

"Besides the death of my parents, this was one of the most difficult things I've ever done in my life," juror Charles Law, a man from northern York County who works for the state, told reporters after the verdict.

Ed Blankenstein, a middle-school history teacher, became jury foreman. He told Rich Oare afterward that "the stress was unbelievable . . . some jurors were crying . . . we thought we were hung." Ed could not get over what they had to do—the seriousness of it all, the consequences—and will forever remember the experience. He certainly became a bigger person, a better teacher, because of it.

Juror Beverly Frederick, 41, was overwhelmed by the experience. The intensity made her cry a lot, but she did her duty.

The other jurors withheld comment, as is their absolute right, when the media rushed them after the verdict. They too did their civic duty, with courage, before returning to their communities to hear from their families, friends, detractors, and, oh yes, the media.

The local York papers, instead of applauding the jury's efforts, ran the headlines, "Acquittal disappoints many" . . . "Miscarriage of justice."

Like angry jackals that had lost their prey.

§

"Congratulations, son," my father said, "good job, good job."

"I'm glad you're home," my mother added, for she and my father had been watching the endless stream of news on television.

And I was glad to be home, glad I didn't have to go back to York to visit Charlie Robertson in prison, glad I didn't have to go back for sentencing, glad to be spared endless appeals that would have spanned years.

There was a sense of euphoria.

Waking up the next morning to headlines of acquittal was a rush.

Most of all, there was relief. I was free of the stress wrapped around my chest like a great band of steel.

And I had my life back. The following Monday evening I drove to Elliottsburg to watch the West Perry Mustangs play field hockey. The team and coach Jody Heberlig were glad to see me, and I was sure glad to see them. Callista, who played mid-field center, had a great game, scoring a goal from the top of the circle on a corner shot.

Life was good.

But it can shift so abruptly. Two weeks after the acquittal in York — a zenith of my career — my beloved father passed away in his sleep. My mother was by his side, as she had been for 66 years of marriage, and it was a difficult hour.

For all of us.

I know he was 94, and that's a long life.

I know that I was blessed to be 58 and still have even one parent.

I know all that, and it's true, but when I got that expected call at 5:00 a.m. on November 4, 2002, from my brother Tom — it hurt. He was still my father, and my friend, and I will always remember him behind the counter serving hot dogs at the Texas Restaurant, his second home, in Carlisle, Pennsylvania. Less than six years before, he had shot a seven-point buck on the first day of deer season, and the local Carlisle paper did a front-page story; his picture, with one arm around Callista and the other holding his long rifle, portrayed him as the George Foreman of Pennsylvania's buck hunters.

That's how I would remember him, not ill at home, with my mother and Tom caring for him.

Hundreds of people came to the funeral to pay their respects. Many traveled from New York, old villagers from Greece, the last of his generation. Their love and condolences truly helped us get through the sadness. My brother Paul did the service, with assistance from three Orthodox priests — one being Nick Ressetar's father — in two languages.

All of Costos's children were there, and his grandchildren, and great-grandchildren.

When the final church bell rang throughout the Holy Trinity Greek Orthodox Church, the six children—Jim, John, Paul, Ginny, Tom, and I—carried the heavy bronze casket to the waiting hearse. It was a tearful walk for five sons and a daughter, trailed by our grieving mother, but we were honored at that difficult hour to let him go home. Our father always believed, and taught us to believe, there was life after death.

§

The verdict in York prompted controversy, for there was unfinished business in that beleaguered community.

The sentencing of those who pled guilty was fast approaching, scheduled for November 13, 2002.

Ezra Slick, 52, was the sole remaining defendant charged with murder in Allen's slaying. He was not tried with the others, because his arrest came too late. Slick admitted that he fired four shots at the car, and a plea bargain was in the works; his leverage was significant, for the prosecution was not going to try this case again.

Bob Messersmith and Greg Neff were to be sentenced on December 18, 2002. Until then, they were in lockdown at the York County Prison, in isolation because they were convicted of murder in the second degree.

The trial of Leon "Smickle" Wright, 54, and Stephen Donald Freeland, 50—the African Americans alleged to have killed Officer Henry Schaad—was scheduled for early 2003. In the meantime, the same pretrial issues raised in the earlier cases were being battled out in Courtroom 1 at the York County Courthouse. First Assistant District Attorney Bill Graff, veteran prosecutor and Stan Rebert's top gun, was marching toward his victory, his definition of justice: guilty verdicts for murder.

"What about the fact you had an 'all-white jury' in the Robertson case?" I was asked by every media caller who got through to my office.

My answer was always the same.

First, the defense had no role in the jury pool. The selection process for jury panels has been in place in York for as long as I can remember. We interviewed over 100 prospective jurors to get a jury of 12; only two African Americans were candidates, as three others were excused for cause. The prosecution, for the first time ever that I could recall, was offended by the jury selection process and the resulting pool.

Maybe the district attorney's office of York should do something about that.

Second, that same "all-white jury" convicted Bob Messersmith and Greg Neff of murder. They were young men 33 years ago, in a situation that gave rise to a perception of self-defense, or defense of others. At a minimum, the jury could have found they had an unreasonable belief that they were in harm's way and delivered a verdict of voluntary manslaughter. That "all-white jury" found those two young whites guilty of murder and, I believe, went out of their way to give the Allen family, and the York community, reverse racial justice.

Maybe the callers just overlooked the Messersmith and Neff verdicts by the "all-white jury."

I know it will forever be remembered by Bob Messersmith and Greg Neff, and, I hope, by Lillie Belle Allen's family.

"Do you believe that Judge Uhler should have recused himself as the trial judge?" I'm asked.

No, I don't.

I know that he was the District Attorney of York from 1978 to 1982. I also know that he was the presiding judge of the grand jury that investigated the '69 riots. Those two roles did not give him a personal interest in the outcome of the case. Those two roles developed no friendships or associations with anyone that would give rise to a perception of partiality.

The defense lawyers agreed not to seek his recusal because we believed that he would call things the way he saw them, and handle this case from the bench evenhandedly.

In my opinion, as I look back, Uhler was an excellent trial judge. He had his hands full with all of us; we were arguing much of the time—in his chambers every morning, at side bar, and in the well of the courtroom. He made rulings I disagreed with; nothing new there. He made rulings the prosecution disagreed with; nothing new there.

Whether Messersmith and Neff get a new trial on appeal is for the appellate courts to decide. It won't be on the grounds that Judge Uhler should have recused himself, nor should it be. I would hate to have his job, but especially in a case like this.

"What do you have to say to the Lillie Belle Allen family?" I'm asked.

That I'm truly sorry they lost a loved one; her death was horrific.

However, the acquittal of Charlie Robertson should not give rise to animosity. He should not have been charged with her murder in the first place, and the acquittal of an innocent man by a jury is no reflection on the goodness of Lillie Belle Allen.

What I would not tell them, for her children don't deserve to hear this, especially from me, is that the riots of '69 were an uncertain time in history and a long time ago. The violence experienced in York was not limited to York; it was nationwide. I believe that that social movement—brought about in part by the words and actions of the Reverend Martin Luther King, who was assassinated in April 1968—resulted in positive social change, a much-needed step toward social equality. Such change, a never-ending process, must continue.

I would not say that I don't know why the Allen Cadillac made its way onto Newberry Street. There's no question in my mind that those barricades were up. But it's very possible that the entry of the Allens onto Newberry Street was innocent.

Some still believe otherwise.

I believe the '69 investigations were thorough and complete. The Pennsylvania State Police did a good job. The United States Attorney's Office followed up. The hearings before Judge Nealon aired racial grievances against the York City Police in detail. District Attorney John Rauhauser had his hands full in '69, and made judgment calls, decisions rendered in a historic context—honest and informed, not corrupt.

The law enforcement boys in '69 could have made arrests for the death of Lillie Belle Allen. They knew who the shooters were, as evidenced by Sergeant Creavey's 33-page report. The empaneling of a grand jury back then would have provided Rauhauser with details to prosecute a case, assuming he needed more details. In fact, Detective Tom Chapman of the York City Police suggested that investigative tool.

But District Attorney Rauhauser said no.

The law enforcement boys in '69 could have made arrests for the death of Officer Schaad. They knew who the shooters were, including Leon "Smickle" Wright and Stephen Donald Freeland. A grand jury would have flushed out the necessary information to prosecute the killing of an innocent police officer. Rauhauser had the plea-bargaining weaponry. And the boys in blue could have gotten confessions their own way, with gun barrels in the mouths of suspects, for a beloved comrade had fallen.

But District Attorney Rauhauser said no.

His reason for twice saying no in 1969?

Though the Pennsylvania National Guard and the Pennsylvania State Police had restored order in York, the city was still a flashpoint, and racial violence could have erupted again at any moment and brought about more deaths, injuries, and destructive fires.

A prosecution in York in '69 for the killing of a white police officer, based on the evidence, would have resulted in a public hanging.

A prosecution in York in '69 for the killing of a black woman, based on the evidence, would have resulted in an acquittal. And in '69, especially in '69, that's all York needed. District Attorney Rauhauser did not want to go there. That was his decision.

Not Charlie Robertson's.

"Everyone knew who was involved. But everyone thought it was even. One black had been killed, one white—even."

That was Charlie Robertson's much-publicized quote in *Time* magazine. He was referring to Rauhauser's decision, certainly not his own. Charlie was a police officer at the time, not the mayor, and certainly not the district attorney of York County. The jackals made a full meal out of that one quote.

They had no frigging idea what it really meant.

"What's Charlie Robertson going to do from here?" I'm asked.

That's a tough one, for him.

I can tell you this ordeal has been difficult for Charlie, very difficult.

At 68 years old, he was damaged by a prosecution that was senseless and ruthless. It was so unfair, for though he may have been a racist 33 years ago, he didn't murder anybody. He walked the streets of York as a police officer, and more than once put his life on the line. He became the city's mayor, and that's what he always wanted. His vision included a baseball team and stadium, and throwing the first pitch.

That was all taken from him in the early winter of his life.

Charlie didn't deserve that.

And though he will try to forgive his oppressors, he cannot forget.

"I think about selling my home," Charlie has said, "and moving to Florida where I have some family."

"I still love York, though, and hate to leave," he has admitted, "but it is so difficult."

We had gone to a girls basketball game together, in Dillsburg, to watch the Northern Polar Bears play the West Perry Mustangs. Jayme Emig coached the Northern junior-varsity team, and Charlie cheered her on from the heart. Scott Moyer, a friend of Charlie's, coached the West Perry varsity team, and he cheered him on the same way. That night, Callista and her team controlled the game, but Charlie made it a point to root for all the girls out there.

"I really love kids, and sports." Charlie said. "I sure do miss it."

§

What am I going to do from here? I ask myself that question all the time, especially at this point in my life. I'm Socrates, remember.

The real Socrates was charged with impiety and condemned by the Athenian authorities to die by drinking hemlock, which he did.

I don't want to go there; I don't like hemlock and would have fought the authorities all the way.

Maybe, instead of engaging in impiety, with wanton and reckless disregard of the consequences, I'll just pack up my dog Lacy and head for Blaine. It's pretty quiet up there, in the vast uplands, away from it all. Working a good lab in the early morning, especially with frost on the ground, is not a bad way to wrap things up.

Maybe I'll work younger horses, faster horses with a lot of buck in them, just to push the envelope.

Maybe I'll mount that old Harley-Davidson dresser, fire up that 1300 cc engine, and head for Callista's college of choice. That way, I'll be able to watch more field hockey and basketball, maybe even softball, for four more years. I'll just have to make sure that Callista doesn't see me; otherwise, I'd be better off with the hemlock.

I know Kara and Khristina want me out of their way, except maybe on holidays.

Jill, of course, has much to say about my unpredictable thoughts and moods and visions. She is my beloved wife, has stuck with me through thick and thin, but doesn't feel like hunting birds for the rest of her life, or getting bucked off a horse, or hanging out with our grown daughters forever.

Jill—without any Greek philosopher genes—reminds me often that it's time to turn the page, to gently let go of a career that has served me well. "You've done it long enough," she says.

"You started your career in York, defending your cousin, 30 years ago. You were 28 years old then, with an attitude," she reminds me.

"To defend Charlie, you went back to York . . . to the same courthouse," she notes.

With an attitude, I thought.

"But 30 years, Bill, have come and gone, and you've done it," she says, and adds with concern in her voice, "Otherwise, I can see you 30 years from now, going back to York . . . you'll be 88."

That's true, and I know it, but my dad was 94.

21

LAMBS

I will bring them down like lambs
to the slaughter,
like rams and he-goats.

—Jeremiah, Chapter 51

All six defendants who were originally charged with first- and second-degree murder entered guilty pleas before the trial. The plea agreements for each of them were entered in open court, and the prosecutors invited the approval of Lillie Belle Allen's family. The family accepted that open invitation, and appeared with counsel when the pleas were entered, assuring Judge Uhler that they were in agreement with the terms.

Yes, they said on the record, they were in agreement with Chauncey Gladfelter's plea to an ungraded misdemeanor, knowing his maximum exposure. Their lawyer told Judge Uhler, "the family understands the nature of the plea agreement and does not in any way object and agrees with the district attorney's recommendation."

Yes, they said on the record, they were in agreement with Rick Knouse's plea to an ungraded misdemeanor, knowing his maximum exposure. Assistant District Attorney Tom Kelley told Judge Uhler, "the family members and the representatives of the family today agree with the disposition of this defendant . . . . We've advised them and their counsel at length of the agreement, and they support it entirely."

Hattie Dickson personally assured Judge Uhler that she was in agreement and added, "I trust you and the DA to do whatever, you know. I believe in the DA and I trust them."

Yes, the family said, they were in agreement with Clarence Lutzinger's plea to an ungraded misdemeanor, knowing his maximum exposure. Judge Uhler stated on the record that the family was in "support of the proposed agreement relative to Mr. Lutzinger."

Yes, they said, they were in agreement with William Ritter's plea to an ungraded misdemeanor, knowing his maximum exposure. Judge Uhler incorporated by reference the earlier representations made by the family members.

Yes, they said, they were in agreement with Thomas Smith's plea to an ungraded misdemeanor, knowing his maximum exposure. Tom Kelley assured Judge Uhler that "the family members and the representatives of the family today agree with the disposition of this Defendant . . . they and their counsel support it entirely."

Yes, they said, they were in agreement with Art Messersmith's plea to an ungraded misdemeanor and felony, knowing his maximum exposure. Hattie Dickson personally made it known to Judge Uhler that she was in agreement.

§

November 13, 2002
York County Courthouse
York, Pennsylvania

The six defendants appeared in court with their counsel for sentencing. The pre-sentence investigations of the probation officer were complete, the defendants had kept their end of the bargain, and the defense lawyers were hoping for leniency.

They were also hoping to be out of there before noon.

But it would not be so easy.

Little did the defendants and their lawyers know the venom that was about to be unleashed by Debra Taylor, the daughter of Lillie Belle Allen, starting with the sentencing of Chauncey Gladfelter.

Matt Gover made a compelling argument for Gladfelter's probation. His client had fired no weapon, intended to kill no one, and had been a productive member of society for the past 33 years.

Gladfelter apologized again to the relatives of Lillie Belle Allen who were in the courtroom; they included a brother, a daughter, and two sisters.

That's when Debra Taylor went off on him, questioning the sincerity of his apology and chastising him for not volunteering information earlier, for not providing investigators with more names and identities of suspects, and for not seeking the family out and apologizing before.

"Some people in this courtroom said I should die and go to hell for the guilty verdicts," she said. "We were just passing through."

Chauncey Gladfelter and Matt Gover just stood there, somewhat taken aback.

They weren't ready for that, nor were the other defendants waiting in the back of the courtroom with their lawyers. This was the day of reckoning, and victims have a right to be heard, but suddenly they feared a bloodletting was coming.

Judge Uhler remained patient and calm, having been through this before. The unleashing of pent-up emotions is common on the courtroom floor.

When it was all said and done, Judge Uhler imposed sentence. Chauncy Gladfelter, 50, received 3 to 23 $\frac{1}{2}$ months with a December 10 reporting date, a $500 fine, 200 hours of community service, and a share of court costs.

Rick Knouse, 50, was sentenced to 9 to 23 months with a reporting date of January 1. He was to perform 200 hours of community service and pay his share of the costs of prosecution.

John Moran was really disappointed, for he truly thought Knouse might get probation. His client was instrumental in getting Charlie Robertson arrested, and tried. His client was the first rollover to the others, and that deserved something more. Moran had impressed upon the court that Knouse had a longtime drug problem, ongoing emotional problems, and a list of physical ailments. He characterized Knouse as an abused child and a follower who was easily influenced by "older kids" and "authority figures."

Debra Taylor went off on him, too, demanding that he take responsibility for his misdeeds.

"If you do the crime, you do the time," she told Knouse to his face.

Knouse hung his head in shame.

Moran vowed that he would petition Judge Uhler within a week to reconsider the sentence.

Clarence "Sonny" Lutzinger was next.

He was still in a wheelchair, recovering from a heart attack and recent hip surgery. A former heroin addict with a long record of petty crimes, Lutzinger cried when a local police chaplain and a longtime friend spoke on his behalf.

"I was part of something real wrong. For some reason, at the time, I thought I was doing the right thing. But this isn't about me. It's about an innocent lady who died," he said.

Debra Taylor was unmoved.

"If you do the crime, you do the time," she repeated to Lutzinger.

Clarence "Sonny" Lutzinger, 50, was sentenced to 9 to 23 $\frac{1}{2}$ months with a reporting date of January 1.

Art Messersmith, 49, received the lengthiest sentence: 1 $\frac{1}{2}$ to 3 years in state prison for felony attempt with intent to kill and a concurrent one to two years for misdemeanor criminal conspiracy to commit an unlawful act of first-degree murder. He was placed in handcuffs immediately after sentencing and remanded to the county prison to await transfer to a state correctional institution.

Frank Arcuri had argued that Art Messersmith should not be punished for being a Messersmith.

"This is a particular case of the sins of the father being visited on the son," he said.

Art Messersmith turned around and told Allen's family, "I truly have a repentative heart. I apologize to all of you folks."

That wasn't good enough for Debra Taylor, who was still reeling.

"It would have meant so much to us if you said 'It was a terrible thing. I am sorry.' It would have meant more than doing life."

"Today, I don't believe you," she said. "You say you're sorry but it seems to me you've got your butt stuck in a crack and you will do anything to get out of it."

Walt Trayer, a paralegal for Frank Arcuri, was disgusted. He thought Art Messersmith got fucked, and Debra Taylor was enjoying her moment. He walked out of the courtroom and did not look back.

William Ritter got the same sentence as Knouse. He received 9 to 23 $\frac{1}{2}$ months with a reporting date of December 13, a $500 fine, 200 hours of community service, and his share of court costs.

Debra Taylor continued to show her outrage.

"This community still has this attitude of 'Let's get it over with,'" she said. "This slave mentality has got to end. A mother, a daughter, a sister died and you're still trying to sweep it under the rug."

Ritter wasn't trying to sweep anything under the rug, but said nothing. He always maintained that bullets came at him . . . he ran home, retrieved a gun, and fired back in the direction of the bullets.

Al Barnes also said nothing, but was upset. He had been upset at everything from day one. He resented the arrest of Ritter, and never believed for one second that his client conspired to murder anybody. He resented having to plead guilty to avoid a trial. He's not convinced to his day that there wasn't a gun brandished.

Over the lunch hour, Joe Metz told Tom Smith that it didn't look good for the probation.

"I didn't even fire a shot, or intend to," Tom said.

"I know," Joe answered apologetically.

And Joe was right, there would be no probation for Tom Smith, but they had to plead when they did, for a jury trial on a charge of murder was too risky. Joe Metz never believed that Tom Smith conspired to murder anybody.

Debra Taylor continued her public scolding in open court.

Thomas P. Smith, 51, was sentenced to 3 to 23 $\frac{1}{2}$ months with a reporting date of December 13, a $500 fine, 200 hours of community service, and a share of court costs.

The Allen family kept up their venting on the courthouse steps.

"Under the circumstances, it was the best we could get because they had plea bargains," Jennie Settles, one of Allen's sisters, told a horde of reporters.

"That's right," said Debra Taylor.

Maybe the reporters weren't present when the family had agreed to the plea bargains in Judge Uhler's courtroom.

§

December 18, 2002
York County Courthouse
York, Pennsylvania

Outside, the entry to the courthouse was adorned with a towering, festive Christmas tree. Market Street and George Street were decorated with wreaths and red bows on the light poles. A man on the corner was ringing a bell for Salvation Army contributions. The gray sky was ready to bless York with a white Christmas.

Inside the courthouse, in Courtroom 1, there would be no Christmas.

Bob Messersmith and Greg Neff were to be sentenced, and unlike the others, they exercised their right to a trial by jury. Their jury, after three days of deliberation, found them both guilty of murder in the second degree, a felony with a maximum exposure of 10 to 20 years in a state correctional institution. Their bail had been revoked by Judge Uhler the night of the verdict, October 23, 2002.

Messersmith and Neff were brought to the courthouse in handcuffs and shackles, standard procedure when transporting prisoners to the courthouse from the York County Jail. They had been there almost two months, and the pallor was already showing on their faces. Being held in lockdown is a difficult stint.

Bob Messersmith was first up, with Tom Sponaugle and Pete Solymos at his side.

The family of Lillie Belle Allen was back, and Debra Taylor was ready to express her feelings again.

The emotions this time, from both sides, would reach another level.

It started when Messersmith made it perfectly clear that he had no intention of going down alone. He told Judge Uhler in the packed courtroom that Donnie Altland, who had recently committed suicide, was the one who killed Lillie Belle Allen. Messersmith told Uhler that Altland confessed to him three times that "he felt the responsibility of her death and he was deeply remorseful."

It was true Donnie Altland had committed suicide; he had killed himself a day after detectives met with him to discuss the death of Lillie Belle Allen.

It was also true that Donnie Altland had left a tape recording, a dying declaration.

It was not true that Altland admitted to killing Lillie Belle Allen, either to the detectives or on the tape; in fact, his only admission was that he shot at the car like everyone else.

Bob Messersmith said that Charlie Robertson and Dennis McMaster gave Altland a rifle, and that they were incited by Jim VanGreen, York County Sheriff Bill Hose, Jim Brown, Mike Brown, Newt Brown, Willard Dinges, and other police officers.

Donnie Altland had certainly never told the police that, or it would have appeared in a police report.

We had listened to Altland's tape, and there was nothing there about that.

The Altland family was interviewed, and they never heard that.

The police referred to by Messersmith were irate, calling him a fucking liar.

As did the district attorney's office.

In the midst of Messersmith's scattergun assault, Debra Taylor went ballistic from the back of the courtroom.

"Why didn't you tell this before?" she screamed at him. "You sorry son of a bitch. Why didn't you tell before? You are just as guilty. You are a bastard . . . How can you stand there and say you are sorry? You lying son of a bitch. You act sorry. You are not sorry."

At that point, Judge Uhler had to take control of the courtroom. It's one thing to allow venting, but this proceeding had crossed the line. Debra Taylor was immediately escorted out of the courtroom, and a recess was called.

Tom Sponaugle tried his best to cut Messersmith's losses, but it was too late, way too late. His clean criminal record for the past 30 years, his mild mental retardation, his urological and spinal problems, his overcoming of drug and alcohol addiction, his abusive father, and his expression of remorse to Allen's family were all brought to the attention of Judge Uhler, who just shook his head.

Judge John C. Uhler handed down his sentence of 9 to 19 years in the state penitentiary, banged his gavel, and Bob Messersmith was promptly removed from the emotionally charged courtroom.

That left Greg Neff, the last of the eight to be sentenced.

Harry Ness argued the philosophy of the Honorable Stephen McEwen. He beseeched the court to impose sentence on Neff, based on evidence and not on the fact that he elected to go to a trial by jury. He argued to the court that Neff's culpability was no different from that of Rick Knouse, Clarence Lutzinger, Art Messersmith, or William Ritter.

Greg Neff turned and faced the Allen family. "I am not responsible for the death of Lillie Belle Allen but I am responsible for my actions that day. For my actions, I sincerely apologize," he said.

To this day, Greg Neff believes he saw a gun brandished by Lillie Belle Allen; he gave up a deal for probation, but not his principles or beliefs.

Harry then called a number of friends and family members to ask for leniency, but to no avail.

Judge Uhler sentenced Greg Neff to $4\frac{1}{2}$ to 10 years, thus bringing closure to this notorious case.

EPILOGUE

No one knows how these trials
will come out ... Only when they
are resolved, one way or another,
no one can predict, can this past
be put fully and permanently
behind this city.

> —Judge Edward G. Biester Jr.
> Prejudicial-delay hearing
> December 18, 2001

January 11, 2003,
around 6:30 p.m.

Charlie Robertson parked his car on the corner of King and West Streets. He walked briskly in the cold night to his favorite restaurant, Norma's, a small family place in downtown York, blocks from City Hall. It was not a fancy spot to eat, with only three tables and a small counter that seated eight, but the food was great and the service friendly. For 15 years, every morning, Charlie would have two eggs sunnyside up, homefries, ham or bacon, toast and coffee.

Not any more.

His days as a police officer, and as the elected mayor of York, were over. He had done a lot of good for the city of York, or at least he had tried to. There were new economic ventures, housing projects, and urban development programs underway in the city he loved. Charlie gave the best part of his life to the youth of his community, coaching and refereeing, and would do it again if he were younger.

196

Since the trial, he preferred not going out. He wasn't much of a cook, though he could manage a simple meal. He would frequently get food to go, often from Norma's, where they were still friendly to him. He'd take it home. It wasn't so bad eating alone, especially if there was a good football or basketball game on television.

"I'll have a cheeseburger sub to go," Charlie said politely to the waitress behind the counter.

"You going to watch the (NFL) playoffs?" the waitress asked, smiling, knowing the answer.

"You bet," Charlie answered, laughing.

On his way back to the car that cold winter night, seven or eight African American males and females were waiting for him.

"So you want to kill us all, huh, motherfucker," one said, taunting.

"So you want to have us all killed, is that what you want?" another said threateningly.

"Not guilty, huh?" a female said sarcastically.

"Not guilty, my ass, motherfucker," her male friend added.

"You want to try killing us tonight, big man?" another chimed in.

Charlie Robertson hesitated, his heart racing, but said nothing. Maybe he would have answered them years ago, but not tonight.

Instead, showing no fear, he walked between them to his car and left, without a confrontation or further incident. He went home alone with his cheeseburger sub.

Wednesday, January 29, 2003
York, Pennsylvania

The lawyer for the family of Lillie Belle Allen stood on the courthouse steps, surrounded by Lillie Belle's sisters, son and daughter, and other supporters. He had called another press conference to announce that they had filed a federal civil rights lawsuit against the city of York, Ray Markle, Dennis McMaster, Charles Robertson, James VanGreen, and Ronald Zeager.

None of the shooters was named in the lawsuit, only the police and the city.

He said that the suit was being brought "to vindicate racially motivated acts of cowardice perpetrated by the individual defendants."

The lawyer then proceeded to hand out to reporters copies of his 20-page complaint, which was requesting "compensatory damages" from the city and the named police officers, to be awarded to Debra Taylor, Michael Allen, Hattie Dickson, and Jennie Settles. The allegations to support their quest for money tracked the prosecution's case that had just been tried.

The lawsuit that they had been promising during the trial, at every opportunity with the media, was filed in the United States District Court for the Middle District of Pennsylvania in Harrisburg.

This was the same forum, the same courthouse, where the '69 civil rights action had been heard by Judge William Nealon.

Judge Nealon concluded back then, after eight days of testimony repeated in York, that "in society's day-to-day efforts to protect its citizens from the suffering, fear, and property loss produced by crime and the threat of crime, the policeman occupies the front line. It is he who directly confronts criminal situations, and it is to him that the public looks for personal safety. The freedom of Americans to walk their streets and be secure in their homes—in fact, to do what they want when they want—depends to a great extent on their policemen."

Thereafter, Judge Nealon dismissed the claim, but not before writing a well-reasoned 22-page opinion with 129 findings of fact.

Maybe Judge Nealon, who is still living, will hear it again.

The young prosecutors, after 32 years, had gone to Aiken, South Carolina, to exhume the body of Lillie Belle Allen. This was an important, high-profile case, and a second autopsy was their purpose. Their reason for bringing this prosecution was not publicity, they said, but to expose the wrongs of York's sordid past, and thereby bring closure.

What they found was an abandoned gravesite, grown over with weeds and brush, with not even a marker to memorialize her life.

But closure was their cause, they said, not only for Lillie Belle Allen, but for the family and the community of York.

That's right, the York papers proclaimed, closure for Lillie Belle Allen, the family, and York.

Closure?

Closure, my ass.

ATTRIBUTIONS

My personal involvement in the case is evident in the opinions and tone throughout the book. However, most of the material was taken from the trial transcripts, court records, police reports, correspondence, and interviews with hundreds of witnesses and personnel.

Endless interviews with Mayor Charlie Robertson, some brutal, provided invaluable insights into his past and the racially sensitive times covered in this account. His emotional turmoil and anguish following his arrest for murder had to be dealt with in the courtroom and in the writing of this book.

We owe special thanks to Dr. Mike Young, a retired Penn State political science professor, who was instrumental in the writing of the Prologue. Many quotes attributed to people beyond the well of the courtroom—comments of lawyers to the media, litigants, witnesses, police officers, and jurors—were taken from newspaper accounts and television sound bites. Sincere credit is hereby given to the *York Daily Record*, the *York Dispatch*, the *York Sunday News*, the *Patriot-News* of Harrisburg, *Central Pennsylvania Magazine*, the *Baltimore Sun*, the *New York Times*, *Time* magazine, the *New York Times Sunday Magazine*, *Newsweek*, *U.S. News & World Report*, the *Washington Post*, the *Philadelphia Inquirer*, the *Pittsburgh Tribune-Review*, the Associated Press, United Press International, ABC, NBC, CBS, Fox, CNN, and their local affiliates.

Reports from local radio broadcasts were also noted, which included but were not limited to, WHP with Lynne Richarde, WITF, WINK 104, WSBA, The River 97.3, Kool 99.3 and KYW.

CAST OF
CHARACTERS

Lillie Belle Allen: A 27-year-old preacher's daughter and mother of two from Aiken, South Carolina, who was visiting her family in York, Pennsylvania, when she was fatally wounded in a predominantly white neighborhood on North Newberry Street on July 21, 1969, while getting out of a car.

Frank C. Arcuri: Attorney who was court-appointed to represent Art Messersmith.

Timothy J. Barker : York County district attorney who was a prosecutor in the Allen trial.

Albert G. Barnes Jr.: Attorney who represented William "Sam" Ritter.

Edward G. Biester Jr.: Judge appointed by the Supreme Court of Pennsylvania to preside over the prejudicial-delay hearing in the Allen case.

James Brown: Former York police officer who testified for Charles Robertson's defense about the conditions during the York riots.

Emanuel A. Cassimatis: Judge appointed to preside over the preliminary hearing in the Allen case.

Leo Cooper: President of the York chapter of the NAACP. He made a public statement asking that Charles Robertson and Herbert Grofcsik resign as mayor and police commissioner, respectively.

Francis T. Chardo, III: Chief deputy district attorney of Dauphin County, who assisted the York County prosecution during the Allen case.

Thomas V. Chatman, Jr.: York County detective who investigated the Lillie Belle Allen and Henry Schaad cases in 1969.

J. Robert Chuk: Court administrator of York County.

Sgt. John Creavey: Homicide investigator with the Pennsylvania State Police, who was assigned to handle the Allen case. He filed a 33-page report of every interview that was conducted, including the names of the shooters on Newberry Street in 1969.

Herbert Grofcsik: York County police commissioner and personal friend of Charles Robertson.

Hattie Dickson: Lillie Belle Allen's sister who lived in York, Pennsylvania, during the riots. Dickson was driving the car on the night that Allen was shot.

Murrey Dickson: Hattie Dickson's husband, who was in the car on the night that Lillie Belle Allen was shot.

Jayme M. Emig: Assisted William Costopoulos in document and trial preparation.

Fred Flickinger: Former member of the Newberry Street Boys who testified for the Commonwealth that Officer Charles Robertson had shouted "white power" during a rally at Farquhar Park and on another occasion had told him that "if I weren't a cop, I'd be leading commando raids against the niggers in black neighborhoods."

Rodney George: York County detective who reinvestigated the Lillie Belle Allen and Schaad cases.

Gregory E. Gettle: Attorney who represented Gregory Neff through his plea arrangements, which were ultimately vacated by the court.

Chauncey Gladfelter: Charged with conspiracy to commit murder, pled guilty to conspiracy to commit an unlawful act in return for cooperation with the prosecution, and was sentenced to 3 to 23 $\frac{1}{2}$ months in county jail.

Matthew R. Gover: Attorney who represented Chauncey Gladfelter.

William H. Graff, Jr.: Assistant district attorney of York County, who was the lead prosecutor in the Henry Schaad homicide case.

Rees Griffiths: Local co-counsel for Charles Robertson.

Harold N. Fitzkee Jr.: Former District Attorney of York County, who represented William "Sam" Ritter at the preliminary hearing in the Allen case.

Thomas H. Kelley: First assistant district attorney of York County, who was the main prosecutor in the Allen trial. He also was in charge of the grand jury investigation; after the trial, he would win election as a York County Common Pleas Court judge.

Rick L. Knouse: Former member of the Girarders gang, who was charged in the 1969 death of Lillie Belle Allen. He pled guilty to conspiracy to commit an unlawful act in exchange for his cooperation. He testified that Charles Robertson provided him with ammunition that he used to fire upon the vehicle of Lillie Belle Allen, and was sentenced to 9 to 23 months in county jail.

Clarence Lutzinger: Charged with conspiracy to commit murder, pled guilty to conspiracy to commit an unlawful act in return for cooperation with the prosecution, and was sentenced to 9 to 23 $\frac{1}{2}$ months in county jail.

Ray I. Markle: Former York police officer, who was assigned to "Big Al" on the night Lillie Belle Allen was killed. He testified for Robertson's defense that he was not on Newberry Street until after Allen was killed.

Dennis McMaster: Former York police officer, who was an occupant of "Big Al" on the night Allen was killed. He also indicated that it was not illegal to give out ammunition. During Robertson's trial, McMaster was chief of police of East Pennsboro Township in Cumberland County.

Arthur N. Messersmith: Charged with conspiracy to commit murder, pled guilty to conspiracy to commit an unlawful act in return for cooperation with the prosecution, and was sentenced to 1 $\frac{1}{2}$ to 3 years in county jail.

Robert N. Messersmith: Charged with the actual killing of Lillie Belle Allen, went to trial, was found guilty of second degree murder, and was sentenced to 9 to 19 years in a state correctional institution.

Joseph U. Metz: Dauphin County attorney who represented Thomas Smith.

Beatrice P. Mosley: Lillie Belle Allen's mother, who was in the car on the night Lillie Belle Allen was fatally wounded.

Rev. James Mosley: Lillie Belle Allen's father, who was in the car on the night Lillie Belle Allen was fatally wounded. He was also minister of the Cedar Grove Baptist Church in Aiken, South Carolina.

John J. Moran II: Attorney who represented the Commonwealth's lead witness, Rick Knouse.

William J. Nealon: Federal judge in the U.S. Middle District Court of Pennsylvania, who issued his ruling in a suit (*Rhoda Barton and Lewis Johnson v. Eli Eichelberger, Mayor of York, et al.*) alleging excesses by the York police. He dismissed the case against the 94-man force in 1970.

Gregory H. Neff: A former member of the Girarders gang; 21 years old at the time of the Allen shooting. Charged with criminal homicide in York County for the death of Lillie Belle Allen, went to trial, was convicted of second-degree murder, and was sentenced to $4 \frac{1}{2}$ to 10 years in a state correctional institution.

Harry M. Ness: Attorney who represented Gregory Neff.

J. Richard Oare: Attorney and personal friend of Charles Robertson; asked William C. Costopoulos to assist in representing Robertson in his criminal case.

Edward A. Paskey: York County district attorney who was the lead prosecutor at the preliminary hearing before Judge Cassimatis and at the prejudicial-delay hearing before Judge Biester. Paskey left the district attorney's office in November 2001.

H. Stanley Rebert: York County district attorney, who asked for the Lillie Belle Allen and Henry Schaad murders to be investigated.

Nicholas Ressetar: Chief law clerk to William C. Costopoulos, defense attorney for Charles Robertson. Did all legal research and writing; Columbia graduate, who has been with Costopoulos since 1985.

Major Robert Rice: Former Pennsylvania State Police official who wrote the final 42-page report on the York riots in 1969. Testified for Robertson's defense on the condition of the community during the riots; called in by Governor Raymond Shafer on July 22, 1969, to take charge of the situation.

William C. Ritter: Charged with conspiracy to commit murder, pled guilty to conspiracy to commit an unlawful act in return for cooperation with the prosecution, and was sentenced to 9 to $23 \frac{1}{2}$ months in county jail.

Charles Robertson: A 29-year police veteran and mayor of York from 1994 to 2002, who was charged in York County with the murder of Lillie Belle Allen in 1969.

Ezra Slick: Charged with criminal homicide in 2002 for firing shots from a handgun in the direction of the car occupied by Lillie Belle Allen; pled guilty to a lesser charge and was sentenced to 2 to 5 years in a state correctional institution.

Thomas P. Smith: Charged in the death of Lillie Belle Allen; testified that he was on Newberry Street at the time of the shooting and that he had a rifle. Smith pled guilty to conspiracy to commit an unlawful act in exchange for his cooperation with the prosecution, and was sentenced to 3 to 23 $\frac{1}{2}$ months in county jail.

Peter D. Solymos: Attorney who represented Robert N. Messersmith.

Thomas B. Sponaugle: Attorney who represented Robert N. Messersmith.

Debra Marie Taylor: Lillie Belle Allen's daughter, who was 11 when her mother was killed.

Walter Trayer: Paralegal to Attorney Frank Arcuri.

John C. Uhler: York County judge, who presided over the trial of Charles Robertson. He also authorized and impaneled the grand jury investigation into the Lillie Belle Allen and Henry Schaad murders.

James VanGreen: Former York police officer, who was in "Big Al" on the night that Lillie Belle Allen was murdered. He testified for the defense that there was no wrongdoing by Charles Robertson.

Ellen Wagner: Legal assistant to attorney J. Richard Oare.

Ronald Zeager: Former York police officer, who testified at trial that the barricades were up at Newberry Street to prevent passage by African Americans because of the racial tension. He testified that he moved the barricades for the white Cadillac occupied by the Allen family at the request of the driver.